CHRIS SLOANE

Marketing For Paving Companies

The Complete Guide To Growth

HEAVISIDE

First published by Heaviside Group 2025

Third edition

ISBN (print): 978-1-7353136-5-8
ISBN (digital): 978-1-7353136-6-5

This book was professionally typeset on Reedsy.
Find out more at reedsy.com

Contents

Preface

This book would not be possible without our paving company customers, who I greatly appreciate. I'd like to share some of their feedback with you, before you begin this book.

These quotes are all from our customers.

"I have been getting really good leads. My leads have improved, there are more of them, and I'm quite happy.

"We are so happy with Paving Marketers. We have so many leads. I wouldn't change a thing with what they are doing!

We were really hesitant to change marketing companies but Paving Marketers has exceeded our expectations. We have been more busy than we've been in years, the calls are much better quality than we used to get, and they have been hard to keep up with!"

"We have been burned many, many times. All we ever got was smoke and mirrors and bs and we were very hesitant to try again. The difference has been remarkable. We know now what every lead is actually costing us and are able to calculate a true return on our investment with these guys. Last month was over 15 to 1. Absolutely recommend!"

"We're real pleased with Paving Marketers' work. They took care of our Google Ads and that SEO stuff, and made our website look fantastic. We've been getting a bunch more phone calls from good customers, and it's not costing us an arm

and a leg. It's been great for our business."

"Paving Marketers has been great. They delivered what they said they would. Support has been fast and responsive. We're getting the leads we were looking for cheaper than we expected - could not be happier."

"The folks at Paving Marketers are so helpful and on the ball! We are getting excellent results. THANK YOU!"

"We are starting our third season with them and its so helpful to know that our phone will be ringing every day. It has definitely been worth it."

"Paving Marketers has been great to work with. Everything promised has been delivered. Highly recommended!"

"Quality of leads has been steadily improving. We have more paving jobs this month than anytime in our past. I understand why paying more for a better company counts. It's the customer service. The communication is way better with you guys than other companies. We don't have to call constantly. You are always communicating with us."

"We want to rate Paving Marketers five stars because of the communication."

"Working with Paving Marketers has been great for our business. Ever since we teamed up with them, our website has never looked better and we've noticed a significant increase in phone calls. The quality of leads we receive has greatly improved. We're beyond satisfied with the impact they have had on our business!"

"They did an amazing job on our website. I am very picky and they were patient with my requests and made it exactly how I wanted. We're seeing more leads already and I can pick up the phone and reach my account manager promptly. Very happy."

"Pavement Marketers have been handling our PPC and SEO for a little over a year and have been great to work with. Customer service is by far the best we have ever dealt with in many years of dealing with companies that promise the world but a very short on delivery. The team at Pavement Marketers are top notch caring people we would highly recommend their services."

"I appreciate the communication and professionalism!"

"It has been nice to work with people who get the business and know what to do to get more leads. We are busier than ever and couldn't be happier."

"We are so happy with Paving Marketers. We have so many leads. I wouldn't change a thing with what they are doing!"

"I am very happy with my leads. We have been receiving web forms and calls."

"You guys have been great. I even recommended you to a cousin. I have had more leads this year and I am very happy with the results."

Introduction

Thanks for reading our new and revised book, Marketing For Paving Companies! This is now the third edition — and we've changed the title to reflect the expanded scope of what we're going to talk about here. While the main focus is still with online and digital marketing, we're also going to talk about offline marketing.

In this guide we will walk you through the important things you need to do to establish an effective online presence and explain:

- How the search engines work and what you need to do to handle each part of them for maximum visibility and return.
- How the map listings work and how to get your paving company listed on the map.
- Our search engine optimization strategy for paving companies.
- Our social media strategy specifically for paving companies.
- Our paid search strategy designed to be effective for paving companies.
- Traditional marketing approaches that still work for paving contractors.
- How to measure and track the success of all your marketing efforts.

I am excited to be sharing this information with you. There are tons of information sources out there from lots of so-called experts, but it can be very hard to tell what is good information and what is not. What I'm going to talk about in this book is based on our work with dozens of paving companies just like yours over the past few years. We know what works because we've done it, and I'm going to show you exactly what to do.

"We were really hesitant to change marketing companies but Paving Marketers has exceeded our expectations. We have been more busy than we've been in years, the calls are much better quality than we used to get, and they have been hard to keep up with!" — Joni Seyko, JR Paving & Construction Co

Who Are These Guys?

Before getting too deep here I would like to introduce myself.

My name is Chris Sloane. I am the founder of Paving Marketers. I have been working in SEO, web development, and digital marketing for over 10 years. In 2011 I founded Heaviside Group, which grew over time to one of the top marketing agencies in the Midwest, formerly in Waukesha, WI and now in Cincinnati, OH, with over six hundred five-star reviews. Heaviside has worked with over 1,000 clients all around the world, spanning all six inhabited continents. If I could sell SEO to penguins it would be all seven.

My background prior to that was in physics — and while it may seem unrelated, the process of breaking something down to find out why and how it works is very relevant to this profession. Unlike physics, the rules are constantly changing as the search engine algorithms evolve. What worked well a year ago is often not quite the same today. I have worked with international enterprises to SaaS companies to small retail storefronts. While I cannot say we have seen it all, I can say we have seen enough! Everything I will be talking about here has been learned "in the trenches" on real projects that helped grow leads and sales for businesses of all types.

What We Do

Spoiler alert: our company does this stuff. My team has built websites, attracted search engine traffic, driven profitable paid visitors, increased conversion rates with retargeting, and on and on. We have a proven process designed to triple your sales by getting your internet marketing right. That process is what this book is based on.

We would love the opportunity to work with you and do this for your business. But that is not what this book is — it is not going to be a hidden sales presentation that is going to require you to buy services from us to really make things work. I want to give you the best information out there on how to do this stuff for your own business. If you take this information and implement the process, it is going to work for you, and you are going to succeed.

Thanks again for checking out our book!

Chris Sloane

Founder, Paving Marketers

About Paving Marketers

Based in Cincinnati, Ohio with clients throughout the United States, Paving Marketers was founded by Chris Sloane. Our mission is to help 300 paving companies dominate their market and triple their sales. We strive for excellence in everything we do; from the websites we design and engineer, to the results we deliver, to the customer service our clients receive. Our proven solutions are built on 10+ years of marketing experience. With Paving Marketers, you get paving industry expertise, proven strategies, market exclusivity, complete transparency, and unmatched support. Proud member of the National Asphalt Paving Association.

About You

What do we know about you? Obviously we don't know who you are, but we know who is interested in what we do. We've learned a lot from talking to paving/concrete companies. Each one is different, but the people we talk to generally have this in common:

- They know marketing on the internet is important, and they want to get more (or LOTS more) inbound leads for commercial jobs. Quality residential jobs too!
- They have been burned before and want to work with someone who knows the industry and can deliver results.

If the first one applies to you, you're going to love this book. If the second one applies to you, you're also going to love this book. Then, once you are done reading it you're going to want to go to https://pavingmarketers.com/apply-now and set up a call to talk to us about how we can do this for you.

Overview of the Paving Industry Marketing Landscape

The marketing landscape for paving companies has dramatically shifted over the past decade. While word-of-mouth and traditional advertising were once the primary drivers of business, the digital revolution has transformed how potential customers find and choose paving contractors.

We focus on helping our clients get leads from people searching online for paving companies. At the end of June in 2022, I looked at all of the 1342 leads that came in for our paving clients and broke down where they came from:

- 33.6% from Google Ads
- 36.9% from Google Maps
- 20.1% from Google Organic
- 9.4% from Other
- Mostly direct, could be any of the other three
- Yahoo and Bing almost nothing

These numbers have remained consistent each year since within a few percent.

Keep this in mind as you read this book, so that you can understand where you should prioritize your efforts. Today's paving contractors need to maintain a presence across multiple channels, both online and offline, to maximize their visibility and lead generation capabilities. Successful paving companies leverage a mix of search engine optimization, paid advertising, social media marketing, and targeted offline strategies to create a comprehensive marketing approach.

Key Industry Statistics

Understanding the data behind how customers find paving services is crucial to developing an effective marketing strategy. Recent research has revealed some eye-opening statistics:

- 85-98% of people search online when looking for local contractors. This massive shift to digital search means your online presence is no longer optional—it's essential.
- 92% of consumers trust recommendations from friends and family over any form of advertising. This highlights why reputation management and encouraging satisfied customers to spread the word remain vital components of any marketing strategy.
- For every $1 spent on Google Ads, businesses earn an average of $2 in revenue. When properly managed, paid advertising can deliver a strong return on investment.
- 94% of users click on organic search results rather than paid ads, emphasizing the importance of a solid SEO strategy alongside paid campaigns.
- 70% of web traffic now happens on mobile devices, making mobile optimization absolutely critical for paving companies.

- 40% of mobile users search for local businesses and often include the phrase "near me", highlighting the importance of local SEO strategies.

These statistics paint a clear picture: paving companies must build a strong online presence while still nurturing the word-of-mouth recommendations that have traditionally driven the industry.

Client Success Stories

Before we get started, let me show you some client results. Some are spending a lot on ad spend, some are not. Some are getting huge results from maps and some are still in progress. I want to show you a range of possible outcomes here — but mostly that the results from the things we talk about are real.

Here are some examples. These are the raw lead totals, unfiltered. Some are going to be not quotable, some are duplicates, a few would be repeat customers from before. But all of these clients are seeing enough activity from online searches to create estimates and book jobs for their crew(s) to produce.

[redacted]
Dashboard
Leads
Reports
Tracking
192 Leads
Day
Week
Month
Unique
Repeat
Quotable
Pending
Not Quotable
Not Set
20
10
0
Jun 01
Jun 04
Jun 07
Jun 10
Jun 13
Jun 16
Jun 19
Jun 22
Jun 25
Jun 28
Leads by Type
Calls 163
Forms 29
Chats 0
Transactic 0
Events 0
Emails 0

[redacted]
Dashboard
Leads
Reports
Tracking
138 Leads
Day
Week
Month
Unique
Repeat
Quotable
Pending
Not Quotable
Not Set
20
10
0
Jun 01
Jun 04
Jun 07
Jun 10
Jun 13
Jun 16
Jun 19
Jun 22
Jun 25
Jun 28
Leads by Type
Calls 98
Forms 21
Chats 0
Transactic 0
Events 19
Emails 0

These results demonstrate the real-world impact of implementing the strategies we'll discuss throughout this book. While every company's situation is unique, these case studies show what's possible when you apply these proven marketing approaches to your paving business.

Purpose of This Book

The purpose of this book is straightforward: to give you a complete roadmap for marketing your paving company effectively in today's digital-first world, while still leveraging the traditional marketing methods that continue to deliver results. We'll cover everything from building your website and optimizing for search engines to creating effective social media campaigns and implementing targeted offline marketing tactics. We'll explain not just what to do, but why it works and how to measure your results.

Whether you're a small residential paving contractor or a larger commercial operation, the strategies in this book can be scaled to fit your needs and budget. By the end, you'll have a comprehensive understanding of how to:

- Build a high-converting website that attracts and engages potential customers
- Rank higher in Google's local and organic search results
- Create effective paid advertising campaigns on Google and social media
- Implement offline marketing tactics that complement your digital efforts
- Track and measure your marketing performance
- Generate a steady stream of qualified leads for your paving business

Throughout the book, we'll provide practical, actionable advice based on our extensive experience working with paving companies across the country. You'll get access to the same strategies and tactics that have helped our clients achieve remarkable growth. As we move forward, remember that effective marketing is not about following trends or using the newest technologies for their own sake. It's about understanding your customers, communicating your value proposition clearly, and being visible where your potential customers are looking. Let's dive in and discover how to make that happen for your paving company.

I

Part One

This part covers the foundations of marketing, and basic digital marketing practices that every paving company should be doing.

1

Start With The Fundamentals

Before we delve into Internet Marketing, SEO, and Social Media Marketing, I want to be sure we have built a strong marketing foundation. After talking with owners and leaders at various paving companies across the United States, I have come to the realization the vast majority of you tend to skip straight past the basic fundamentals of your marketing strategy and dive headfirst into tactics (Pay-Per-Click advertising, SEO, Social Media, etc.).

The 3 M's: Message, Market, Media

So, what do I mean when I say "Fundamentals"? All marketing has 3 core components:

- **Message** (what)
- **Market** (who)
- **Media** (how)

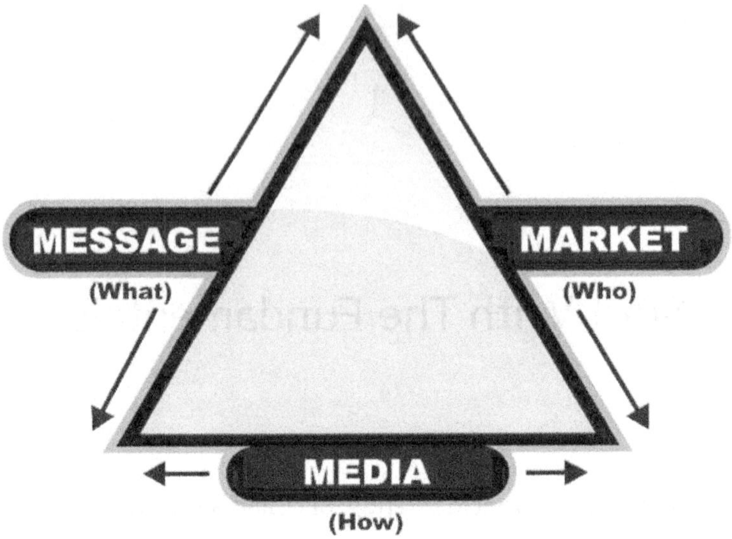

You have to have a unique "Message" (who you are, what you do, what makes you unique, and why someone should hire you rather than another business offering the same service), a specifically defined "Market" (who you sell to and who your best customers are), and then look at "Media" (where you can reach those best customers). The tactics (Pay-Per-Click, SEO, Social Media, Direct Mail, etc.) fall into the "Media" category. If you focus solely on the Media or Tactics, you will likely fail regardless of how well-selected that Media is.

With that being said, you need to scale back to the fundamentals. Invest the time and energy in fleshing out your "Message" and figuring out who your "Market" is. By doing so, ALL of your Media choices will be vastly more effective. How can you do that? Spend a few minutes and THINK. Take out a scratch pad and answer these questions:

Message

What do I do which is unique and different from my competitors?

- Do you offer a guaranteed time frame for your appointments?
- Do you offer written estimates prior to starting work, promising to stand by that estimate?
- Maybe you offer a guarantee for all of your work and will look after any issues within a one-year period of time after the project is complete.
- Perhaps you offer a free consultation to showcase the services you have to offer to potential customers.

If you think about the psychology of a customer, what concerns or apprehensions do you think they have about hiring the services of a new business organization?

- "They won't be able to finish the job on schedule, so I will probably have to waste a lot of time waiting around for them,"
- or "They are going to be a crude mess and leave me with more work in the end,"
- or "They are going to give me one price over the phone, tell me another when they start with the job and then charge me something VASTLY different once all is said and done."

How can you address your customers' common concerns in a unique way? Answer these questions, and you will be able to define your message.

Let me use Paving Marketers as an example — we are one of a very small number of marketing agencies that focus exclusively on paving companies, and we have a more comprehensive and thorough solution than anyone else. We have proven services tested over a decade and thousands of projects. We're the #1 choice for paving companies.

Developing Your Unique Value Proposition

Your unique value proposition (UVP) is a clear statement that describes the benefit of your offer, how you solve your customer's needs, and what distinguishes you from the competition. For paving companies, a strong UVP might focus on:

- **Quality materials**: "We use premium-grade asphalt with polymer additives that extends pavement life by 40%"
- **Expert craftsmanship**: "Our crews average 15+ years of experience, ensuring flawless finishes every time"
- **Reliability**: "On-time, on-budget completion guaranteed or we pay you $500"
- **Customer service**: "24/7 project manager access throughout your paving project"
- **Specialized expertise**: "The only contractor in the region certified in permeable paving systems"

To develop your UVP, consider:

- What specific problems do you solve for your customers?
- What tangible benefits do customers receive?
- Why should customers choose you over competitors?
- Can you quantify your advantages (years of experience, number of

projects completed, etc.)?
- How can you prove your claims (certifications, guarantees, warranties)?

Your UVP should be prominently featured on your website, business cards, estimates, and other marketing materials. It should be clear, specific, and focused on customer benefits rather than just listing features.

Market

Who is my ideal customer?

Please realize not everyone resides in your city nor within a 25-mile radius of your office. You need to be clear about the audience that you are looking to attract. Look at your last 25 customers and evaluate who spent the most money, who had the highest profit margins, and who was genuinely pleased with your service. What are the unique characteristics of those good customers? Do they live in a particular area of town? Do they have a higher income level? How did they hear about your service offerings?

It could be that you want to focus on commercial work. You may subcontract out much of your paving work and want to focus on the more profitable (for you) sealcoating and asphalt maintenance jobs. Start to define who your ideal customer is so you can put a marketing plan in place to attract similar customers. This is also very important to keep in mind when crafting your message. You are talking to your future customers — make sure they know you are talking to them.

Most of our clients are looking for more commercial jobs. If that's you — think about the commercial clients you've had. What were they looking for when they hired someone and why did they choose you? Make sure potential customers can find that information.

At Paving Marketers, our market is paving companies. While the mix of services may be different, all would consider paving to be the core of their business. Some will do paving and concrete, some will do a lot of construction or sitework. Some will focus more on sealcoating and maintenance. Some only do pavers and hardscapes. But all consider themselves to be working in the paving industry. We work with sole proprietors who run the machines themselves, to small businesses with one or two crews, to more established companies with multiple locations and territories.

Identifying Ideal Customer Profiles

Creating detailed customer profiles helps you target your marketing efforts more effectively. For paving companies, the typical division is between residential and commercial clients, but you can get much more specific:

Residential Profiles:

- **Luxury Homeowners**: High-end properties, custom driveways, decorative options
- **New Homeowners**: Recently purchased homes with aging driveways
- **HOA Communities**: Neighborhoods with shared roads and parking areas
- **Rural Property Owners**: Long driveways, often unpaved, needing solutions

Commercial Profiles:

- **Property Managers**: Managing multiple commercial properties with

parking lots
- **Retail Businesses**: Customer-facing businesses concerned about appearance and safety
- **Industrial Facilities**: Heavy-use areas requiring durable solutions
- **Municipal Clients**: Government contracts for roads and public facilities
- **Educational Institutions**: Schools and universities with large campus parking
- **Healthcare Facilities**: Hospitals and medical centers needing ADA-compliant surfaces

For each profile, document:

- Their typical paving needs and concerns
- Budget range and decision-making factors
- How they typically find contractors
- Their communication preferences
- Common objections you need to overcome

Understanding these profiles allows you to craft targeted messages and choose the right marketing channels to reach each segment effectively.

Media

Where do I find my ideal customer online (and offline)?

Once you have fleshed out your Message and your Market, then you can start to think about Media. To determine what media will be most effective for you, you need to think about where you can reach your IDEAL customer. Clearly, the Internet is a great "media" for connecting with your ideal customer who is proactively in the market for your services. Throughout the remainder of this book, we will be explaining the various Internet marketing channels and how you can use them to connect with your ideal customer.

Remember, you need to start with the FUNDAMENTALS (Message, Market and Media) before running headstrong into any marketing. Don't forget about offline channels — postcards, newspapers, radio, TV, networking groups, etc. Take advantage of every channel available to you to get your Message out to your Market. We're focused on the Internet here, but it all matters to grow your business.

Paving Marketers has a website that is the hub of our online operations, and we do SEO to help paving companies find us. We have a content strategy to consistently grow our internet presence for search terms. We run Google Ads and Facebook Ads, and do monthly webinars and a podcast. We have a (free!) private Facebook Group to share tips and take questions from members. We will participate in the National Pavement Expo and the World of Asphalt conferences by hosting a booth and applying for speaking/training spots. We send out lots of emails and also have salespeople calling out to potential customers.

Setting Marketing Goals and Budgets

Effective marketing requires clear goals and appropriate budgets.

When setting your marketing goals, follow the SMART framework:

- **S**pecific: "Generate 50 new residential driveway leads per month" (not just "get more leads")
- **M**easurable: Use concrete metrics like lead count, conversion rate, cost per acquisition

- **A**chievable: Base goals on your company's capacity and market conditions
- **R**elevant: Align with your business objectives (growth, entering new markets, etc.)
- **T**ime-bound: Set deadlines and review periods

When it comes to budgets, there are several approaches:

- **Percentage of Revenue**: The industry standard for paving companies is typically 5-10% of gross revenue for established businesses and 10-15% for newer companies trying to gain market share.
- **Competitive Analysis**: Research what competitors are spending and allocate similar amounts to stay competitive.
- **Cost Per Acquisition**: Calculate how much you can profitably spend to acquire a new customer based on your average job value and profit margins.
- **Task-Based Budgeting**: Determine what marketing initiatives you need and build a budget around those specific tasks.

For example, a paving company with $1 million in annual revenue might allocate $50,000-$100,000 to marketing. This might break down as:

- Website development/maintenance: $5,000-$10,000/year
- SEO: $12,000-$24,000/year ($1,000-$2,000/month)
- Google Ads: $18,000-$36,000/year ($1,500-$3,000/month)
- Social media: $6,000-$12,000/year ($500-$1,000/month)
- Offline marketing: $9,000-$18,000/year

Your specific allocation should reflect your company's goals, target market, and competitive landscape.

Building an Integrated Online/Offline Strategy

The most effective marketing approach combines online and offline channels in a coordinated strategy. Each channel should complement and reinforce the others, creating multiple touchpoints with potential customers.

Integration Best Practices:

- **Consistent Messaging**: Ensure your branding, messaging, and offers are consistent across all channels.
- **Cross-Promotion**: Have your offline materials point to your online assets (website, social media) and vice versa.
- **Coordinated Timing**: Align your campaigns across channels, such as launching a direct mail campaign just before a Google Ads push.
- **Unified Data Collection**: Track leads from all sources in a single CRM system.
- **Channel-Specific Content**: Adapt your content to each channel's strengths while maintaining consistent themes.

Example Integrated Campaign:

- **Direct Mail**: Send targeted postcards to neighborhoods with aging driveways
- **Google Ads**: Run search campaigns targeting the same neighborhoods
- **Social Media**: Share before/after photos of completed projects in those areas

- **Yard Signs**: Place signs at active job sites in target neighborhoods
- **Email**: Send follow-up emails to direct mail recipients who haven't responded
- **Local Newspaper**: Run small ads featuring the same offer as your direct mail
- **Website**: Create a dedicated landing page for the campaign offer

This approach ensures potential customers encounter your message multiple times through different channels, significantly increasing the likelihood of conversion.

Tracking Marketing ROI Across Channels

To optimize your marketing efforts, you need to track performance and calculate return on investment (ROI) for each channel.

Essential Tracking Methods:

- **Unique Phone Numbers**: Use different tracking numbers for different marketing channels to attribute calls correctly.
- **UTM Parameters**: Add these to your digital campaign URLs to track website traffic sources accurately.
- **Landing Pages**: Create dedicated landing pages for specific campaigns to measure conversion rates.
- **Conversion Tracking**: Set up Google Analytics goals to track form submissions, call clicks, and other conversions.
- **CRM Integration**: Ensure all leads feed into your CRM system with proper source attribution.
- **Customer Surveys**: Ask new customers how they heard about you to verify your tracking.

Calculating ROI:

The basic formula for marketing ROI is:

ROI = (Revenue from Marketing - Cost of Marketing) / Cost of Marketing

For example, if you spent $5,000 on Google Ads that generated $25,000 in project revenue: ROI = ($25,000 - $5,000) / $5,000 = 4 (or 400%) This means you earned $4 for every $1 spent on that marketing channel.

For paving companies, consider these additional metrics:

- **Cost Per Lead (CPL)**: Total marketing spend divided by number of leads generated
- **Cost Per Acquisition (CPA)**: Total marketing spend divided by number of new customers
- **Customer Lifetime Value (CLV)**: The total revenue a customer will generate over time
- **Lead-to-Sale Conversion Rate**: Percentage of leads that become customers

By regularly reviewing these metrics for each marketing channel, you can make data-driven decisions about where to increase or decrease your marketing investments. Remember, marketing fundamentals provide the foundation for all your tactical efforts. By clearly defining your message, understanding your market, and strategically selecting your media channels, you'll maximize the effectiveness of every marketing dollar you spend.

In the next chapters, we'll dive deeper into specific marketing channels and tactics, but always keep these fundamentals in mind as we proceed.

2

Your Digital Home Base: Website Development

Before diving into specific marketing channels, we need to establish your digital home base - your website. This is the foundation of all your online marketing efforts and often the first impression potential customers will have of your business.

Website Platforms and CMS Options

Let's talk about the formats and different options available for building your paving company website.

HTML Sites

Traditional HTML sites consist of basic HTML pages and/or individual pages linked together into a website. This is how most websites were built several years ago - multiple pages hyperlinked together.

Pros:

- Extremely fast loading speeds

- Highly secure
- Complete customization potential
- No reliance on third-party plugins that might break

Cons:

- Requires coding knowledge or a web developer to build and update
- More expensive to develop initially
- Less flexible for frequent content updates
- Typically requires developer intervention for changes

Template-Based Site Builders

Services like GoDaddy, Wix, Squarespace, and similar platforms offer turnkey solutions where you buy your domain and set up your website through their drag-and-drop interfaces.

Pros:

- Quick to set up
- No coding knowledge required
- Lower initial cost
- Managed hosting and security

Cons:

- Limited flexibility
- Often less optimized for search engines
- Recurring subscription costs
- Can be difficult to migrate away from
- Sometimes slower loading speeds
- Less customization options

Content Management Systems (CMS)

Content Management Systems like WordPress, Joomla, and Drupal are powerful platforms that give you both customization and ease of use.

Pros:

- Highly scalable
- Easy to update content without technical knowledge
- Excellent for SEO
- Thousands of plugins and themes available
- Large developer communities
- Can be as simple or complex as needed

Cons:

- Requires some learning curve
- Security depends on keeping software and plugins updated
- Performance can vary based on hosting and setup

Recommendation: WordPress

Based on my experience with websites for paving companies and contractors in general, WordPress is the ideal CMS platform. Here's why:

- **Scalability**: You can easily add pages for new services, locations, or content.
- **SEO-friendly**: WordPress has excellent built-in SEO features and plugins like Yoast SEO or Rank Math.
- **User-friendly**: You can update content, add photos of recent jobs, and make changes without a developer.
- **Plugin ecosystem**: You can add contact forms, photo galleries, testimonial sections, and other features without custom coding.

- **Cost-effective**: While initial setup might cost a bit, ongoing maintenance is much more affordable than HTML sites.
- **Industry standard**: WordPress powers over 40% of all websites on the internet, including many successful paving companies.

Most importantly, WordPress allows you to create a website structure that supports your SEO goals - with dedicated pages for each service and location, proper heading structures, and easy content updates.

Essential Website Elements for Paving Companies

Now, let's discuss what pages and elements your paving company website should include. The structure below represents the fundamentals that have proven effective for paving contractors:

Core Website Pages

1. **Home Page** Your homepage should clearly communicate:

- Who you are and what services you provide
- Your service area
- Your unique value proposition (why choose you?)
- A prominent call-to-action (phone number, contact form)
- Trust indicators (certifications, years in business, etc.)
- Featured work with high-quality photos

2. **About Us** This section helps build trust and connection:

- Company history and founding story
- Meet the team (with photos)
- Your values and approach
- Equipment and capabilities
- Certifications and affiliations

- Why Choose Us (differentiators)

Many visitors will check this page before calling, so ensure it portrays your company as professional, established, and trustworthy.

3. **Services Pages** Create individual pages for each core service:

- Driveway Paving/Resurfacing
- Parking Lot Paving
- Asphalt Repair
- Sealcoating
- Concrete Services (if applicable)
- Commercial Paving
- Residential Paving
- Other specialized services you offer

Each service page should include:

- Detailed description of the service
- Benefits to the customer
- Your process (step-by-step)
- Photos of completed projects
- FAQs specific to that service
- Relevant testimonials
- Clear call-to-action

4. **Service Area Pages** Create location-specific pages for each major area you serve:

- "[Service] in [City]" (e.g., "Driveway Paving in Dallas")
- Include local information and references
- Mention nearby landmarks or neighborhoods
- Showcase projects completed in that area

- Local testimonials when possible

This geotargeting strategy is crucial for local SEO. Ensure each location page has unique content - don't just replace the city name.

5. **Portfolio/Project Showcase** Evidence of your work quality is extremely important:

- High-quality before/after photos
- Project descriptions
- Organized by service type or location
- Video testimonials if available
- Details about challenges overcome

6. **Testimonials and Reviews** Social proof is vital for contractors:

- Featured reviews from Google, Facebook, etc.
- Testimonial videos if available
- Written testimonials with names and locations
- Before/after photos with customer quotes

7. **Blog** Regular content helps with SEO and positions you as an expert:

- Educational posts about asphalt maintenance
- Seasonal content (e.g., "Preparing your driveway for winter")
- Project spotlights
- Industry news relevant to property owners
- FAQs and guides

8. **Contact Us** Make it easy for prospects to reach you:

- Contact form
- Phone number

- Email address
- Office location and hours
- Service area map
- Emergency contact information if applicable

Essential Website Elements

Beyond these core pages, your website should include these critical components:

1. Clear Contact Information

- Phone number in the header (visible on every page)
- Mobile-tap-enabled for smartphone users
- Email and contact form easily accessible
- NAP (Name, Address, Phone) consistent with Google Business Profile

2. Prominent Call-to-Action (CTA)

- "Request a Free Quote" button
- "Call Now" button
- These should be visible without scrolling on most pages

3. Mobile-Friendly Design

- Responsive layout that works on all devices
- Click-to-call functionality
- Streamlined navigation for mobile users
- Fast loading on mobile networks

4. Trust Indicators

- License information

- Insurance details
- Professional association memberships
- Awards and recognitions
- Years in business
- BBB accreditation if applicable

5. Authentic Imagery

- Real photos of your crew, equipment, and completed jobs
- Avoid generic stock photos that visitors recognize as inauthentic
- Before/after photos that demonstrate your quality
- Videos of your work process if possible

6. Easy Navigation

- Intuitive menu structure
- Clear service categories
- Location-based navigation if you serve multiple regions
- Search functionality for larger sites

7. Fast Loading Speed

- Optimized images
- Minimal unnecessary scripts
- Caching enabled
- Mobile optimization

8. Social Proof Elements

- Google review rating
- Testimonial snippets
- Customer logos (especially for commercial work)
- "Featured in" logos if you've been in local media

9. Social Media Integration

- Links to your social profiles
- Social sharing buttons on portfolio items and blog posts
- Feed of recent social posts if you're active on platforms

Mobile Optimization

Mobile optimization is no longer optional - it's essential. Consider these statistics:

- Up to 70% of web traffic now happens on mobile devices (CIODive, 2018)
- 80% of users used a mobile device to search the internet in 2019 (Google)
- 40% of mobile users search for local businesses and often include the phrase "near me" (Aumcore, 2019)
- 61% of users will have a more positive opinion about your business if you have a good responsive website (Smart Insights, 2019)
- 57% of users say they wouldn't recommend a company if their mobile website design is bad (Google)

Mobile Optimization Best Practices

- **Responsive Design**: Ensure your website automatically adjusts to any screen size, from desktop computers to smartphones.
- **Touch-Friendly Elements**: Make buttons and links large enough to tap easily with a finger. Avoid tiny links that are difficult to press.
- **Click-to-Call Functionality**: Allow users to tap your phone number to call you directly. This removes friction from the contact process.
- **Simplified Navigation**: Mobile menus should be streamlined, with drop-downs that are easy to tap and navigate.
- **Prioritized Content**: On mobile, show the most important information

first. Mobile users often need quick access to:

- Your phone number
- Service areas
- Basic services offered
- Request a quote form
- Directions/location
- **Fast Loading**: Mobile users often have slower connections. Optimize images, minimize code, and use caching to ensure fast loading.
- **Legible Text Without Zooming**: All text should be readable without the user needing to pinch and zoom.
- **Avoid Pop-ups**: Pop-ups can be particularly frustrating on mobile devices and may harm your search rankings.
- **Local Search Optimization**: Ensure your site includes local keywords and information, as mobile searches are frequently location-based.
- **Test on Multiple Devices**: Test your site on various devices and screen sizes to ensure consistent functionality.

Mobile-First Strategy

Google has moved to mobile-first indexing, meaning they predominantly use the mobile version of your site for ranking and indexing. This makes mobile optimization critical for SEO success. When developing your paving website, consider a "mobile-first" approach - design for mobile users first, then expand the design for desktop users. This ensures the most critical information is prioritized across all devices.

Conversion Optimization Strategies

Getting traffic to your website is only half the battle. Converting visitors into leads and customers is where you see ROI. Here are proven conversion strategies for paving websites:

1. Clear, Compelling Above-the-Fold Content The "above the fold" area (visible without scrolling) should include:

- Your company name and logo
- Phone number
- Primary service offering
- Service area
- A strong value proposition
- A prominent call-to-action button

This example shows excellent above-the-fold organization:

[LOGO] [PHONE NUMBER: 555-555-5555] [Navigation Menu]

PROFESSIONAL ASPHALT PAVING & REPAIR *Serving Dallas County for Over 25 Years*

[GET A FREE ESTIMATE TODAY] [CALL 555-555-5555]

[Image of beautifully paved driveway or parking lot]

2. Multiple Contact Options Different prospects prefer different contact methods:

- Phone number (prominently displayed)
- Contact form (simple, 3-5 fields maximum)
- Email address
- Chat functionality (if staffed)
- Social media links

For forms, ask only for essential information - name, phone, email, and project details. Every additional field reduces conversion rates.

3. Trust-Building Elements Place trust indicators strategically throughout your site:

- Customer testimonials (with photos when possible)
- Google Reviews widget showing your star rating
- Industry certifications and memberships
- Insurance and licensing information
- Years in business
- Guarantees or warranties
- Photos of your team and equipment

4. Before/After Project Showcases Visual proof of your work quality is incredibly persuasive:

- High-quality photos showing dramatic improvements
- Brief project descriptions
- Location information
- Specific challenges overcome
- Customer comments when available

Before/after sliders are particularly effective, allowing visitors to see the transformation directly.

5. Social Proof Integration Leverage the power of social validation:

- Feature recent Google reviews on your homepage
- Include testimonial snippets near call-to-action buttons
- Show the number of projects completed
- Display logos of notable commercial clients
- Include "as seen in" media mentions if applicable

6. Clear Service Differentiators Tell visitors why they should choose you:

- Proprietary techniques or materials

- Free estimates
- Extended warranties
- Price matching (if offered)
- Financing options
- Same-day service (if available)
- Insurance claim assistance

7. Effective Call-to-Action (CTA) Buttons CTAs should be:

- Visually distinct (contrasting colors)
- Action-oriented ("Get Your Free Quote Now")
- Placed strategically throughout the page
- Sized appropriately for easy clicking
- Mobile-friendly for tapping

Test different CTA placements and wording to see what drives the most conversions.

8. Simplified Quote Request Process Make it easy for prospects to request an estimate:

- Minimize form fields (name, contact info, project type)
- Clearly state what happens next
- Provide estimated response time
- Consider offering online scheduling options
- Include privacy assurance

9. Educational Content Help visitors make informed decisions:

- FAQ sections addressing common concerns
- Blog posts about paving materials and techniques
- Cost guides and calculators
- Maintenance tips

- Seasonal recommendations

Educational content builds trust and positions you as an expert rather than just a service provider.

10. Optimized Load Times Speed matters for conversions:

- 47% of users expect a page to load in under 2 seconds
- Conversion rates drop by about 7% for each second of delay
- Mobile users are even more sensitive to slow loading

Optimize images, leverage browser caching, minimize code, and consider AMP (Accelerated Mobile Pages) for critical landing pages.

11. Geographically Targeted Content Include content specific to your service areas:

- Mention local landmarks and neighborhoods
- Address area-specific challenges (e.g., local soil or weather conditions)
- Feature projects completed in the visitor's area
- Include testimonials from nearby customers

12. Exit-Intent Offers Consider adding exit-intent popups offering:

- Special seasonal discounts
- Free inspection
- Educational guides
- Limited-time promotions

Use these sparingly and ensure they don't appear on mobile devices where they harm user experience.

Authenticity in Website Design

For paving contractors, authenticity builds trust. Visitors can quickly spot generic websites with stock photos. Incorporate these elements for authenticity:

Real Photography Use actual photos of:

- Your crew at work
- Your equipment and trucks
- Completed projects (before/after)
- Your office or headquarters
- The business owner and key team members

If you're just starting out and don't have many project photos, invest in professional photography of your next few jobs to build a portfolio.

Team Introductions Put faces to your company name:

- Brief bios of key personnel
- Experience and qualifications
- Photos of team members
- Personal quotes about their commitment to quality

This humanizes your business and helps customers feel comfortable with who will be working on their property.

Branded Graphics and Vehicles Show your branded vehicles and equipment:

- Trucks with your logo and contact information
- Equipment in action on job sites
- Uniformed crew members

- Branded materials and signage

These elements reinforce that you're an established, professional operation.

Integration with Revenue Commander

While the original document doesn't mention Revenue Commander specifically, modern paving websites benefit from integration with marketing automation and lead management systems. Here's how to ensure your website works smoothly with such systems:

1. **Form Integration** Configure contact forms to feed directly into your CRM or lead management system. This ensures:

- Immediate lead capture
- Automated follow-up sequences
- Lead source tracking
- Conversion attribution

2. **Call Tracking** Implement call tracking to measure phone leads from your website:

- Dynamic number insertion based on traffic source
- Call recording for quality assurance
- Integration with CRM for lead tracking
- Conversion reporting

3. **Analytics Setup** Ensure proper analytics integration:

- Goal tracking for form submissions and calls
- Event tracking for important interactions
- User flow analysis

- Traffic source reporting

4. Chat Integration If using live chat, ensure it connects with your lead management system:

- Chat transcripts stored with lead records
- Chat-to-call functionality
- Automated follow-up for after-hours inquiries

5. Landing Page Capability Your CMS should support creation of targeted landing pages:

- Service-specific pages
- Location-targeted content
- Promotion-specific pages
- Seasonal offerings

6. A/B Testing Framework Implement testing capabilities to optimize conversions:

- Button and form placement testing
- Headline variations
- CTA wording tests
- Layout optimization

Website Conversion Factor Analysis

When analyzing how effectively your website converts visitors to leads, focus on these key areas:

1. Homepage Banner Optimization The "Above the Fold" section is critical for engagement. This space should contain:

- Attention-grabbing headline that speaks to customer pain points
- Subheading with your unique value proposition
- Strong call-to-action button
- High-quality background image (ideally showing your work)
- Phone number and contact information

For example:

TRANSFORM YOUR CRACKED DRIVEWAY *Professional Asphalt Paving with a 5-Year Guarantee*

[GET A FREE ESTIMATE TODAY] [CALL 555-555-5555]

Family-owned and serving Dallas County since 1995

2. User Engagement Elements Incorporate features that actively engage visitors:

- Quick quote calculator
- Before/after image sliders
- Video testimonials
- Interactive service area map
- Downloadable resources (in exchange for contact information)

3. Company Profile Section The homepage should balance company information with service focus (approximately 60% company focus, 40% service focus). Include:

- Brief company history
- Core values and mission
- Key differentiators (bullet points)
- Certifications and accreditations
- Team introduction

4. **Latest News/Project Updates** A section showcasing recent activity builds credibility:

- Recent project completions
- Awards or recognitions
- Community involvement
- Seasonal specials
- Industry news relevant to customers

5. **Blog Section** Maintain an active blog highlighting:

- Recent projects with photos
- Maintenance tips
- Industry insights
- Seasonal advice
- DIY information (that ultimately shows why professionals are needed)

6. **Testimonials Display** Prominently feature customer feedback:

- Rotating testimonial carousel
- Star ratings
- Before/after photos with customer quotes
- Video testimonials when possible
- "Read More" links to detailed case studies

Summary & Implementation Checklist

As you build or redesign your paving company website, use this checklist to ensure you're covering all the essentials:

Platform Selection

- Choose WordPress or another flexible CMS

- Select a responsive, mobile-friendly theme
- Ensure fast, reliable hosting
- Set up proper security measures

Core Pages

- Home page with clear value proposition and CTAs
- About Us page with company story and team
- Individual service pages for each offering
- Service area pages for each location you target
- Portfolio/Project showcase with quality photos
- Testimonials and reviews page
- Blog for ongoing content updates
- Contact page with multiple contact options

Conversion Elements

- Above-the-fold optimization
- Multiple, prominent CTAs
- Easy quote request process
- Trust indicators
- Mobile optimization
- Fast loading times
- Authentic imagery and content

Technical Setup

- SEO plugin installed (Yoast, Rank Math, etc.)
- Mobile responsiveness tested
- Analytics integration
- Lead tracking system
- Form integrations with CRM/lead management
- Secure HTTPS implementation

- XML sitemap creation

Your website serves as both your digital storefront and your most important marketing tool. By building it with both user experience and conversion in mind, you'll create a solid foundation for all your digital marketing efforts.

In the next chapters, we'll explore how to optimize this foundation for search engines and other marketing channels to ensure potential customers can find you online.

3

Search Engine Optimization (SEO)

Search Engine Optimization (SEO) is the process of improving your website to increase its visibility when people search for paving services in your area. Without effective SEO, even the best website will remain hidden from potential customers.

Local SEO Fundamentals for Paving Companies

For paving contractors, local SEO is particularly critical since you serve specific geographic areas. Understanding how search engines determine local relevance is the first step to optimizing your online presence.

Why SEO Matters for Paving Companies

The importance of search engine visibility cannot be overstated:

- 85-98% of people now search online when looking for local contractors
- Yellow Pages and traditional advertising continue to decline in effectiveness
- A recent survey of 2,000 consumers found that 86% used the internet to find a local business

- 74% of respondents said they use a search engine when looking for a local service business

If you're not appearing on page one of Google, Yahoo, and Bing for paving-related keywords in your area, you're missing significant opportunities.

Understanding Search Engine Results Pages (SERPs)

Modern search results typically display three key elements:

- **Paid Ads**: These appear at the top of search results with an "Ad" designation and are based on pay-per-click advertising.

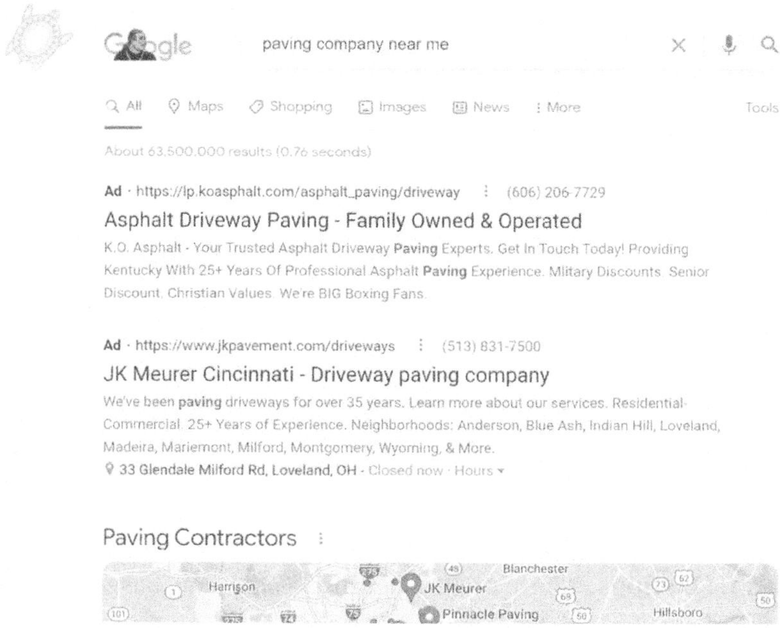

- **Map Listings**: Also called the "Local Pack" or "Map Pack," this shows 3 businesses on a map, generally below ads and above organic results.

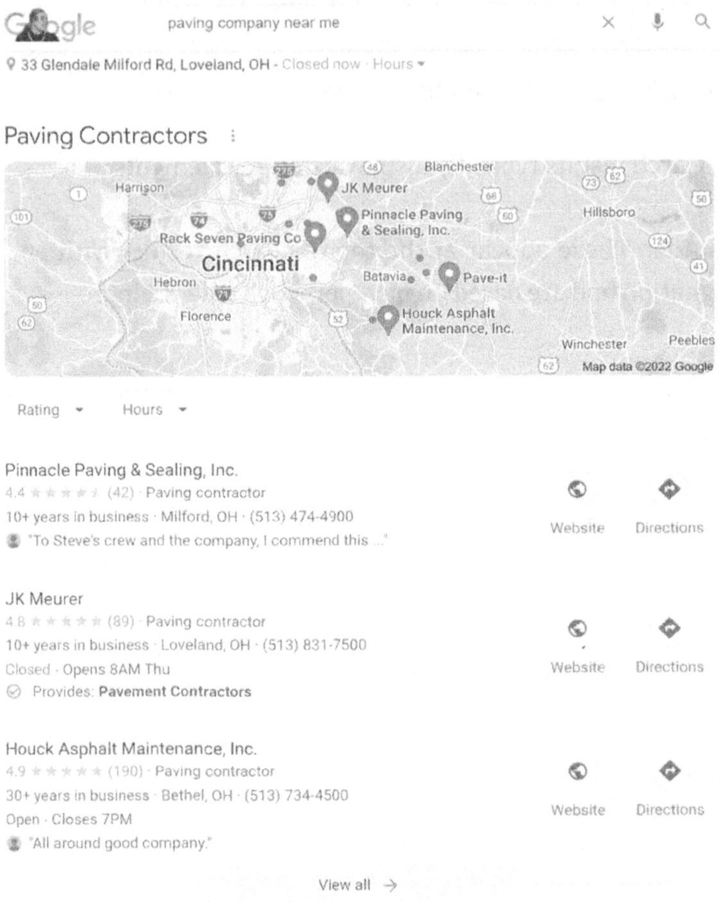

- **Organic Listings**: These are the "earned" positions based on relevance, authority, and other ranking factors.

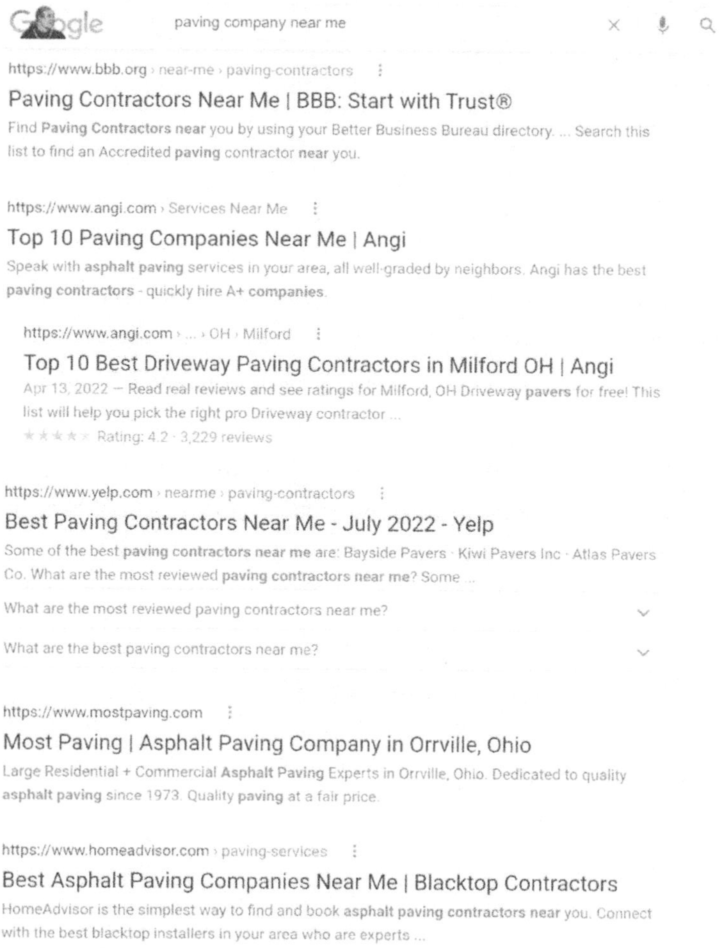

For paving companies, you ideally want visibility in all three sections, but organic and map results carry special importance because:

- 78% of searchers click on organic or map results rather than paid ads
- These positions convey more trust and credibility to searchers
- There's no per-click cost, making them highly cost-effective over time

Research Findings: SEO's Superior ROI

Recent industry data confirms that SEO provides exceptional value for paving contractors:

- SEO tends to produce the lowest cost per lead of any channel when done properly
- One industry source notes that SEO is the most profitable lead generation channel for paving contractors in 2025
- 94% of users click on organic search results instead of paid ads

Unlike paid advertising, which stops generating leads when you stop paying, SEO creates compounding returns. As your site builds authority and rankings improve, you continue to receive traffic without ongoing per-click costs.

SEO vs. Other Lead Generation Methods

Let's compare the cost-effectiveness of different marketing channels for paving contractors:

Channel	Typical Cost Per Lead	Pros	Cons
Organic SEO	$15-35 (over time)	- Builds lasting value - High trust factor - No per-click costs	- Takes time (3-6+ months) - Requires consistent effort
Google Ads	$45-80	- Immediate visibility	- Stops when you stop paying

Channel	Typical Cost Per Lead	Pros	Cons
		- Precise targeting	- Increasing competition/costs
Social Media Ads	$40-75	- Visual format - Demographic targeting	- Lower intent than search - Requires creative content
Lead Services	$50-100+	- Immediate leads - No setup needed	- Shared with competitors - Variable quality - No brand building

While the initial investment in SEO might seem high, its long-term value becomes clear when you consider the ongoing lead generation without per-click fees.

The Three Components of Effective SEO

For paving contractors, a comprehensive SEO strategy must address three key areas:

On-Page SEO: Optimizing your website content and structure.

- Service pages with targeted keywords
- Location pages for each area you serve
- Technical elements like title tags and headers
- Content that answers common questions
- Mobile-friendly design

Local SEO: Optimizing for location-based searches.

- Google Business Profile optimization
- Local citation building
- Local link acquisition
- Review management
- Location-specific content

Off-Page SEO: Building your website's authority and reputation.

- Backlink building from reputable sources
- Brand mentions across the web
- Social signals
- Online directories and associations

Keyword Research for Paving Services

Keyword research is the foundation of SEO – you need to know what terms potential customers are using to find services like yours.

Top Keywords for Paving Companies

Based on search volume data, here are the most searched paving-related terms nationwide:

Keyword	**Monthly Search Volume**
asphalt	75,000
asphalt paving	20,000
paving companies near me	19,000
asphalt driveway	15,000
asphalt calculator	12,000
asphalt paving near me	12,000

Keyword	Monthly Search Volume
asphalt companies near me	11,000
driveway paving near me	10,000
paving contractor	7,500
asphalt mixing plant	6,400
driveway paving	6,300
asphalt plant near me	6,100
asphalt plant	5,800
asphalt sealer	5,300
asphalt company near me	5,200
asphalt driveway cost	5,200
asphalt contractor	5,100
paving companies	5,100
asphalt repair	4,900
asphalt contractors	3,100

However, these national figures need to be localized for your service area. The most relevant keywords combine your services with location terms:

- "asphalt paving Dallas"
- "driveway paving contractors San Antonio"
- "commercial parking lot paving Austin"
- "asphalt repair Fort Worth"
- "sealcoating company Houston"

Conducting Your Own Keyword Research

To develop a comprehensive keyword strategy:

Start with services you offer:

- Driveway paving/resurfacing
- Parking lot paving
- Asphalt repair
- Sealcoating
- Crack filling
- Concrete work (if applicable)

Add location modifiers:

- Your city
- Surrounding suburbs and towns
- County names
- Neighborhoods for larger cities

Use keyword research tools:

- Google Keyword Planner
- Ahrefs
- SEMrush
- Ubersuggest (free option)

Analyze search intent:

- Informational queries ("how much does asphalt paving cost")
- Commercial intent ("paving contractors near me")
- Research queries ("asphalt vs concrete driveway")

Examine competitor rankings:

- See what terms your successful competitors rank for
- Identify gaps they're not targeting

Understanding Keyword Types

Different keywords serve different purposes in your SEO strategy:

- **Primary keywords**: Core services + location (e.g., "asphalt paving Dallas")
- **Long-tail keywords**: More specific, lower competition (e.g., "commercial parking lot striping McKinney TX")
- **Question keywords**: Address specific concerns (e.g., "how long does a new asphalt driveway last")
- **Problem-solution keywords**: Target pain points (e.g., "fix cracked asphalt driveway Richardson")

A strong SEO strategy incorporates all these keyword types across your website content.

Website Structure for SEO Success

Search engines rank individual pages, not entire websites. Each page on your site can really only be successfully optimized for one main keyword or a small group of closely related terms.

Expanding Your Website for Keyword Coverage

Most basic business websites have only 5-6 pages (Home, About, Services, Contact, etc.), which severely limits SEO potential. For effective paving SEO, you need to build out a more comprehensive structure:

Service Pages Create individual pages for each service you offer:

- Residential driveway paving
- Commercial parking lot paving
- Asphalt repair
- Sealcoating
- Crack filling
- Line striping
- Concrete services (if applicable)
- Excavation (if applicable)

Each service page should focus on a specific service and related keywords.

Location Pages Create location-specific pages combining services and geographic areas:

- "Driveway Paving in [City]"
- "Commercial Paving in [City]"
- "Asphalt Repair Services in [County]"

This strategy allows you to target location-based searches more effectively.

Example of Effective Site Structure:

- **Top Navigation:**
- HOME | ABOUT | SERVICES▼ | AREAS SERVED▼ | PORTFOLIO | TESTIMONIALS | BLOG | CONTACT
- **Services Dropdown:**
- Residential Driveway Paving
- Commercial Parking Lot Paving
- Asphalt Repair & Patching
- Sealcoating

- Concrete Services
- Line Striping
- **Areas Served Dropdown:**
- Dallas
- Fort Worth
- Arlington
- Plano
- Frisco
- [Other service areas]

In the website footer, you might include an expanded "Areas Served" section with links to all your location pages.

This structure creates dozens of optimizable pages, vastly expanding your keyword coverage and local search potential.

> ***IMPORTANT NOTE*** *– this strategy can only work if these pages are* useful *to end users, well-built, and significantly different from each other one.*

On-Page Optimization for Paving Websites

Once your structure is in place, each page needs proper on-page optimization to send the right signals to search engines.

Title Tags

The title tag is one of the most important on-page SEO elements:

- Should contain your primary keyword for the page
- Keep under 60 characters to avoid truncation in search results
- Include your company name
- Follow a consistent format

Recommended format: "Keyword Phrase | Your Company Name" **Examples:**

- "Asphalt Driveway Paving Dallas TX | ABC Paving"
- "Commercial Parking Lot Repair Arlington | ABC Paving"
- "Residential Sealcoating Services Fort Worth | ABC Paving"

Header Tags

Header tags (H1, H2, H3, etc.) create a hierarchical structure on your page:

- Each page should have **exactly one H1 tag** containing the primary keyword
- Use H2 tags for major sections
- Use H3 tags for subsections within H2 sections

Example H1: "Professional Asphalt Driveway Paving in Dallas" **Example H2s:**

- "Our Driveway Paving Process"
- "Benefits of Asphalt Driveways"
- "Driveway Paving Options and Materials"
- "Driveway Paving FAQs"

Meta Descriptions

Though not a direct ranking factor, meta descriptions affect click-through rates:

- Include your primary keyword
- Keep between 120-160 characters
- Include a call-to-action
- Highlight unique selling points

Example: "Transform your Dallas home with a new asphalt driveway from ABC Paving. Professional installation, 5-year warranty, and free estimates. Call today!"

URL Structure

Use clean, descriptive URLs that include your target keyword:

- Keep URLs short and simple
- Include the main keyword
- Use hyphens to separate words
- Avoid unnecessary parameters or numbers

Examples:

- example.com/services/driveway-paving
- example.com/locations/dallas-asphalt-repair
- example.com/blog/asphalt-vs-concrete-driveways

Image Optimization

Images are important for paving websites but need proper optimization:

- Use descriptive filenames (e.g., "asphalt-driveway-installation-dallas.jpg")
- Add alt text with relevant keywords
- Compress images for faster loading
- Consider adding schema markup for before/after photos

Content Quality and Length

Content for service pages should be:

- Comprehensive (at least 500-750 words for main service pages)
- Unique (no duplicate content across locations)
- Structured with proper headers
- Useful to potential customers
- Naturally incorporating keywords (avoid "keyword stuffing")

For location pages, focus content on area-specific information while maintaining uniqueness across pages. Mention local landmarks, neighborhoods, and unique challenges in that area.

Schema Markup

Schema markup helps search engines understand your content better:

- **LocalBusiness** schema for your company information
- **Service** schema for your offerings
- **Review** schema for testimonials
- **FAQ** schema for frequently asked questions

This structured data can help you earn rich snippets in search results, increasing visibility and click-through rates.

Location-Based Pages Strategy

For local service businesses like paving contractors, location pages are crucial for capturing city-specific searches.

Creating Effective Location Pages

Each location page should:

- Target a specific geographic area you serve
- Focus on one primary service + that location
- Include unique, location-specific content
- Address local concerns or regulations
- Feature projects completed in that area

Important: Google penalizes duplicate content. Don't simply copy and paste content across location pages with only the city name changed.

Differentiating Location Content

To avoid duplication issues while creating multiple location pages:

- **Research local specifics**: Each area may have different soil conditions, climate considerations, or common problems.
- **Mention local projects**: "Recently, we completed a major parking lot renovation for the Trinity Shopping Center in Arlington..."
- **Discuss area-specific regulations**: Local permitting requirements, HOA restrictions, etc.
- **Include area testimonials**: Feature reviews from customers in that location.

- **Add local landmarks**: "We serve all of Plano, including Legacy West, Downtown Plano, and Willow Bend."

Geographic Targeting Hierarchy

Consider organizing your location strategy in tiers:

- **Tier 1**: Main city/service area pages
- "Asphalt Paving Dallas, TX"
- "Commercial Paving Fort Worth, TX"
- **Tier 2**: Suburb and surrounding community pages
- "Driveway Paving Plano, TX"
- "Parking Lot Paving Arlington, TX"
- **Tier 3**: Neighborhood or district pages (for larger cities)
- "Asphalt Repair North Dallas"
- "Commercial Paving Downtown Fort Worth"

Prioritize development based on population, competition, and business potential in each area.

Link Building Strategies for Paving Companies

Links from other websites to yours serve as "votes of confidence" in search algorithms. Building quality backlinks is essential for competitive SEO.

Why Links Matter

Links remain one of the strongest ranking signals Google uses to assess website quality. They help establish:

- **Authority** in your industry
- **Relevance** to specific topics
- **Trustworthiness** of your business

Types of Valuable Links for Paving Contractors

Local Business Associations

- Chamber of Commerce memberships
- Better Business Bureau profiles
- Local business organizations
- Construction industry associations

Industry Directories

- Asphalt and paving industry listings
- Construction directories
- Supplier partnerships and dealer locators

Local Media

- Coverage of significant projects
- Community involvement stories
- Press releases about company news
- Sponsorship announcements

Citation Sources

- Google Business Profile
- Yelp
- Yellow Pages
- Angi
- HomeAdvisor
- Local directories

Educational Content

- Guest posts on home improvement blogs
- Contributions to property management resources
- HOA newsletters
- Real estate websites

Citation Building for Local SEO

Citations are mentions of your business name, address, and phone number (NAP) across the web. They're particularly important for local SEO and map rankings.

Key citation sources for paving companies:

- Google Business Profile (most important)
- Yelp
- Facebook Business Page
- Apple Maps
- Bing Places
- Yellowpages.com
- Better Business Bureau
- Angi
- HomeAdvisor
- Thumbtack
- Local chambers of commerce
- Industry associations

Citation consistency is crucial:

- Use identical NAP information everywhere
- If your address includes Suite #300, use that exact format consistently
- Choose either "Street" or "St." and stick with it
- Maintain consistent business name formatting

Competitor Link Analysis

One effective link building strategy is to analyze your competitors' back-links:

- Identify top-ranking competitors in your market
- Use tools like Ahrefs, SEMrush, or Moz to analyze their backlinks
- Look for opportunities you can replicate
- Prioritize links that are most relevant to your business

Common competitor link sources might include:

- Local business organizations they belong to
- Media coverage of their projects
- Sponsorships they've undertaken
- Industry associations they've joined

Leveraging Partnerships

Build links through your business relationships:

- **Suppliers**: Get listed on their dealer/contractor pages
- **Complementary businesses**: Cross-promotions with related services (landscapers, concrete contractors, builders)
- **Commercial clients**: Case studies on your website with links from their testimonials
- **Community organizations**: Sponsorship acknowledgments

Link Building Tools and Services

If you have a budget for link building, consider:

- BrightLocal for citation building

- Moz Local for citation management
- Professional link building services
- Digital PR for larger companies

A modest monthly investment of $300-500 in quality link building can significantly enhance your authority over time.

Content Marketing for Sustainable SEO Growth

Content marketing helps you maintain relevance and attract organic traffic through valuable information.

Why Fresh Content Matters

Google rewards sites that consistently add valuable content:

- Signals that your site is active and maintained
- Creates opportunities to rank for additional keywords
- Provides reasons for visitors to return
- Builds authority in your industry

Types of Content for Paving Companies

Educational Blog Posts

- "How to Know When Your Driveway Needs Replacing"
- "Asphalt vs. Concrete: Which is Right for Your Property?"
- "5 Warning Signs Your Parking Lot Needs Repairs"
- "How to Extend the Life of Your Asphalt Driveway"

Seasonal Content

- "Preparing Your Asphalt for Winter Weather"

- "Spring Maintenance Tips for Commercial Parking Lots"
- "Summer Heat and Your Asphalt: What Property Owners Should Know"

Cost and Planning Guides

- "Understanding Asphalt Paving Costs: A Homeowner's Guide"
- "Planning Your Commercial Paving Project: Timeline and Considerations"
- "Budgeting for Asphalt Maintenance: What Property Managers Need to Know"

Project Spotlights

- Before/after case studies
- Challenging projects and solutions
- Different property types (residential vs. commercial)

FAQ and How-To Content

- Answers to common customer questions
- DIY maintenance tips
- How to choose a reputable paving contractor

Content Creation Approaches

You don't need to be a professional writer to create valuable content:

1. Written Content Options:

- Write it yourself (you're the expert in your field)
- Hire a freelance writer with construction industry experience
- Use team members' knowledge to draft content

- Repurpose existing materials (estimates, customer communications)

2. Visual and Video Content:

- Before/after project photos
- Time-lapse videos of paving projects
- Equipment demonstrations
- Maintenance tip videos
- Customer testimonial videos

3. Repurposing Strategies:

- Turn a video into a blog post via transcription
- Create infographics from written guides
- Extract FAQs from customer questions
- Convert presentations into blog content

Content Calendar for Paving Companies

Organize your content creation with a simple calendar:

- **Winter (Dec-Feb):** Snow/ice damage prevention, planning spring projects, indoor concrete options, commercial budget planning.
- **Spring (Mar-May):** Post-winter damage assessment, spring driveway maintenance, commercial curb appeal, HOA planning.
- **Summer (Jun-Aug):** Heat-related asphalt concerns, parking lot maintenance, residential driveway projects, sports courts.
- **Fall (Sep-Nov):** Pre-winter sealcoating, fall maintenance checklists, end-of-season promotions, commercial budget planning.

Content Distribution

Creating content is only half the battle – you also need to distribute it:

- Share on social media platforms
- Include in email newsletters
- Mention in customer communications
- Feature on your Google Business Profile
- Promote to past customers who might find it useful

Technical SEO Considerations

While content and links are the most visible parts of SEO, technical aspects ensure search engines can properly crawl and index your site.

Mobile Optimization

As mentioned in the previous chapter, mobile optimization is essential:

- Google primarily uses mobile versions of pages for indexing
- Page speed is a ranking factor, particularly on mobile
- Mobile-unfriendly sites experience higher bounce rates

Page Speed Optimization

Slow loading sites lose visitors and rankings:

- Compress images properly
- Minimize CSS and JavaScript
- Use browser caching
- Consider a content delivery network (CDN)
- Enable GZIP compression

Use Google's PageSpeed Insights to identify specific improvements for your site.

XML Sitemaps

An XML sitemap helps search engines find and index all your pages:

- Install an SEO plugin like Yoast SEO or Rank Math to generate a sitemap
- Submit the sitemap to Google Search Console
- Update the sitemap when adding new content
- Ensure all important pages are included

Secure Website (HTTPS)

Google considers security in rankings:

- Install an SSL certificate (many hosting companies offer free certificates)
- Ensure all content loads securely
- Fix mixed content warnings

Crawl Budget Optimization

Ensure search engines focus on your important pages:

- Use robots.txt to block unimportant pages
- Implement proper canonical tags for similar content
- Minimize duplicate content
- Create a logical internal linking structure

Tracking SEO Performance

Measuring your SEO results helps refine your strategy and demonstrate ROI.

Key Metrics to Track

Rankings

- Position for target keywords
- Map Pack inclusion
- Featured snippet appearances

Traffic

- Organic search visitors
- Geographical source of traffic
- Pages receiving the most traffic
- Mobile vs. desktop traffic

Engagement

- Time on site
- Pages per session
- Bounce rate
- Scroll depth

Conversions

- Contact form submissions
- Phone calls from organic search
- Quote requests
- Conversion rate by page

SEO Tools for Tracking

Several tools can help monitor your SEO performance:

- **Google Search Console**: Free tool showing how Google sees your site, including impressions, clicks, and technical issues
- **Google Analytics**: Tracks user behavior on your site
- **BrightLocal**: Monitors local rankings and citations
- **Ahrefs/SEMrush**: Comprehensive SEO platforms for keyword and competitor analysis
- **Rank Math or Yoast SEO**: WordPress plugins that help optimize content and track basic metrics

Regular SEO Audit Process

Implement a quarterly SEO audit process:

- Review rankings for target keywords
- Check for technical issues in Search Console
- Analyze top-performing and underperforming pages
- Evaluate backlink profile growth
- Assess competitor changes
- Update content as needed
- Identify new keyword opportunities

Implementation Timeline and Expectations

SEO is a long-term strategy. Here's a typical timeline for a paving company:

Months 1-3: Foundation

- Website structure & on-page optimization
- GBP setup & optimization

- Initial citation building
- Basic content creation
- Technical SEO corrections
- *Expected results:* Minor ranking improvements, increased indexing, correction of technical issues

Months 3-6: Building

- Expanded content creation
- Active link building
- Location page development
- Review acquisition
- Regular blog posts
- *Expected results:* Noticeable ranking improvements, some Map Pack appearances, increasing traffic

Months 6-12: Growth

- Continued content expansion
- Advanced link building
- Conversion optimization
- Expansion to secondary keywords
- Advanced schema implementation
- *Expected results:* Strong rankings for primary keywords, regular Map Pack inclusion, significant traffic growth, steady lead generation

Beyond Year 1: Maintenance and Expansion

- Content refreshes and updates
- Ongoing link acquisition
- New location targeting
- Competitive strategy adjustments
- Advanced technical optimizations

- *Expected results:* Market leadership for target keywords, dominant local presence, consistent lead flow, expanding geographic reach

Summary: SEO Success Framework for Paving Companies

To implement a successful SEO strategy for your paving business:

- **Research and Planning**: Identify keywords, map to pages, analyze competitors, set goals.
- **Technical Foundation**: Ensure mobile-friendliness, page speed, site structure, analytics.
- **On-Page Optimization**: Optimize titles, headers, content, schema.
- **Local SEO**: Optimize GBP, build citations, location pages, local schema.
- **Content Development**: Create service, location, blog, and resource content.
- **Link Building**: Secure industry, local, citation, and partnership links.
- **Monitoring and Optimization**: Track rankings, traffic, competitors, and refine strategy based on data.

By implementing this comprehensive SEO framework, your paving company can build a sustainable source of high-quality leads with the lowest long-term cost per acquisition. SEO is not a quick fix, but for paving companies willing to invest in a proper strategy, it delivers exceptional long-term value. When done correctly, it becomes your most cost-effective lead generation channel and builds a digital asset that continues to deliver returns for years to come.

4

Google Maps and Local Search

For paving companies, appearing in Google Maps and local search results is absolutely essential. The "Map Pack" (the local business listings that appear with a map) is prime real estate for local contractors, often appearing above organic search results and capturing a significant share of clicks.

The Importance of Google Maps for Paving Companies

The Google Map result is what shows up when someone searches for "[your city] + [your services]" in Google. For example, when a potential customer searches "Dallas paving contractor" or "asphalt repair near me," they'll typically see a map with three local businesses highlighted.

These map listings are incredibly valuable because:

- They appear prominently at the top of search results (after ads)
- They include visual indicators like star ratings and reviews
- They show location proximity, which is important for service businesses
- They offer quick access to directions, phone numbers, and website links

Most importantly, they generate a significant portion of leads for local businesses. Our data analysis of leads for paving companies shows the breakdown of where online leads come from:

- 33.6% from Google Ads
- **36.9% from Google Maps** (the largest single source!)
- 20.1% from Google Organic
- 9.4% from Other sources (direct traffic, other search engines, etc.)

This means Google Maps alone accounts for over a third of all online leads for paving companies – making it your most important visibility platform.

Google Business Profile Optimization

The cornerstone of your Maps visibility is your Google Business Profile (GBP), formerly known as Google My Business. Setting up and optimizing this profile is your first priority.

Claiming and Verifying Your Profile

If you haven't already claimed your GBP listing, go to https://www.google.com/business/ to begin. First, check if your listing already exists by searching for your business on Google Maps. If it appears but shows "Claim this business," click that option to start the process.

Verification Steps:

- Google will typically verify your business by mailing a postcard with a verification code to your business address
- When you receive the card (usually within 5-14 days), enter the code in your GBP dashboard
- Verification is required to make changes to your listing and access insights

Important: If you already have a listing, be extremely careful not to create a duplicate. Duplicate listings create confusion for Google and can harm your visibility. If you have trouble accessing an existing listing, use Google's recovery options rather than creating a new one.

Optimizing Your Business Information

Complete every section of your GBP profile with accurate, comprehensive information:

Business Name: Use your exact legal business name – not a keyword-stuffed version.

- ✅ "Smith's Paving"
- ✕ "Smith's Paving - #1 Dallas Asphalt & Concrete Contractor" Adding keywords to your business name violates Google's terms of service and can result in penalties or removal of your listing.

Business Categories: Categories tell Google what kind of business you are and what searches to show you for. For paving contractors, use:

- **Primary category**: "Paving contractor"
- **Secondary categories**: "Asphalt contractor," "Concrete contractor," etc. Choose categories that accurately reflect your services, but don't select categories for services you don't actually provide.

Address: Enter your complete, exact physical address. Use the exact same format consistently across all your online profiles.

Service Area: Define the geographic regions you serve. Be realistic and specific – don't claim to serve areas that are too far from your location.

Hours of Operation: List accurate business hours. Update these during holidays or seasonal changes.

Phone Number: Use your main business line, preferably a local number rather than a toll-free number.

Website: Link to your homepage or, ideally, a location-specific landing page if you serve multiple areas.

Business Description: Write a compelling 750-character description that includes:

- Brief company history
- Primary services
- Geographic areas served
- Unique selling propositions
- A call-to-action

Services: Add all your specific services in the appropriate section, such as:

- Asphalt driveway installation
- Parking lot paving
- Asphalt repairs
- Sealcoating
- Concrete services
- Line striping

Photos and Visual Content

Visual content significantly impacts engagement with your listing. Upload multiple high-quality photos:

Must-have photos:

- Logo (this appears as your icon in search results)
- Cover photo (exterior of your business)
- Team photos (showing your crew and leadership)
- Work vehicles and equipment
- Before/after project photos
- Action shots of work in progress

Aim for at least 10-15 photos initially, and add new project photos regularly.

Photo best practices:

- Use high-resolution images (at least 720px wide)
- Ensure proper lighting and clear focus
- Avoid heavy filters or excessive editing
- Include your actual work, not stock photos
- Update seasonally to keep content fresh

Google Posts

Google Posts allow you to share updates, offers, events, and news directly on your Business Profile. These appear in your knowledge panel when customers find your business.

Effective post types for paving contractors:

- **What's New**: Showcase recently completed projects with before/after photos
- **Offers**: Promote seasonal discounts or special pricing
- **Events**: Announce participation in home shows or community events
- **COVID-19 Updates**: Share any changes to your operations or safety protocols

Post best practices:

- Include eye-catching images
- Keep text concise and action-oriented
- Include a clear call-to-action button
- Post at least 2-4 times per month
- Monitor engagement and click-through rates

Products and Services

Add your core services to the Products section of your GBP. For each service:

- Include an image
- Write a detailed description
- Add the price range or starting price if appropriate
- Link to the relevant service page on your website

This helps customers quickly understand what you offer and can improve your visibility for those specific services.

Managing Reviews and Ratings

Reviews are perhaps the most influential aspect of your Google Business Profile. They impact both your ranking and your click-through rate from searchers.

The Impact of Reviews on Maps Ranking

Reviews influence your Maps visibility in multiple ways:

- **Review quantity**: More reviews signal popularity to Google

- **Review quality**: Higher star ratings indicate quality
- **Review recency**: Fresh reviews show current relevance
- **Review diversity**: A range of customers reviewing different aspects of your service
- **Review engagement**: How you respond to reviews

Our analysis of top-ranking paving contractors shows that businesses appearing in the top 3 Map Pack positions typically have:

- At least 15-20 Google reviews (often many more)
- An average rating of 4.2 stars or higher
- At least 1-2 new reviews each month
- Owner responses to most or all reviews

Building a Review Generation Strategy

Implement a systematic approach to gathering reviews:

1. When to ask:

- After project completion and customer satisfaction is confirmed
- During follow-up calls or emails
- At final inspection when work quality is visible
- When customers express satisfaction

2. How to ask:

- In person while on-site (highest success rate)
- Via text message with a direct link
- Through follow-up emails
- With leave-behind cards containing QR codes to your review page

3. Making it easy:

- Create a short URL for your review page (e.g., bit.ly/reviewABCpaving)
- Generate QR codes that link directly to your review page
- Send direct links via text or email
- Provide simple step-by-step instructions

4. What to say when asking:

"We're a small business that relies on reviews to help other homeowners find us. Would you mind taking a minute to share your experience on Google? It would really help us out."

Review Management Software

Consider using review management software to streamline the process:

- BrightLocal
- GatherUp
- Birdeye
- NiceJob
- Podium

These tools help you:

- Send automated review requests
- Track review acquisition
- Monitor reviews across platforms
- Generate reports on review performance
- Identify potential issues from negative reviews

Responding to Reviews

Every review, positive or negative, deserves a response:

For positive reviews:

- Thank the customer by name
- Reference specific aspects of their project
- Reinforce your commitment to quality
- Invite them to contact you for future needs

Example: "Thank you, John! We really appreciate your kind words about your driveway project. Our team takes pride in our craftsmanship, and we're thrilled you're happy with the results. Please don't hesitate to reach out if you need any maintenance or have questions in the future."

For negative reviews:

- Respond professionally and courteously
- Acknowledge their concerns
- Take the conversation offline
- Provide contact information for resolution
- Avoid making excuses or being defensive

Example: "Thank you for your feedback, Sarah. We're sorry to hear about your experience with your parking lot project. Customer satisfaction is our top priority, and we'd like to learn more about how we can address your concerns. Please contact our office at (555) 123-4567 and ask for Mike, our customer service manager, who will work with you to resolve this situation."

Handling Fake Reviews

Occasionally, you may receive fake or malicious reviews. In such cases:

- Respond professionally, noting you have no record of serving this customer
- Flag the review through your GBP dashboard for Google's review
- Ask Google to remove it if it violates their policies
- If it persists, focus on generating more positive reviews to dilute its impact

Remember that one negative review among dozens of positive ones won't significantly harm your overall rating.

Building Citations for Local SEO

Citations are mentions of your business name, address, and phone number (NAP) across the web. They play a crucial role in establishing local relevance and authority.

What Makes a Good Citation

A complete citation includes:

- Business name (exactly as it appears on your GBP)
- Address (complete and formatted consistently)
- Phone number (preferably your main local number)
- Website URL
- Business categories or description
- Hours of operation
- Photos (when the platform allows)

Primary Citation Sources

Focus first on these major citation platforms:

- Google Business Profile (most important)
- Yelp
- Facebook Business Page
- Apple Maps
- Bing Places
- Yellowpages.com
- Better Business Bureau
- Angi
- HomeAdvisor
- Thumbtack

Industry-Specific Citations

Then target industry-relevant directories:

- National Asphalt Pavement Association
- Paving.org
- Local contractors' associations
- Regional construction directories
- Chamber of Commerce listings
- Local business organizations

Data Aggregators

Consider using data aggregators to distribute your information broadly:

- Foursquare
- Data Axle (formerly Infogroup)
- Neustar Localeze

- Factual (now part of Foursquare)

These services feed data to hundreds of smaller directories and apps.

Citation Consistency

NAP consistency is critical. Inconsistencies can confuse search engines and dilute your local search authority. Common consistency issues to avoid:

- "Road" vs. "Rd."
- "Suite" vs. "#"
- Phone number formatting differences
- Business name variations
- Outdated addresses from previous locations

Citation Building Tools

Several tools can simplify the citation building process:

- BrightLocal
- Moz Local
- Yext
- Whitespark
- Semrush Listing Management

These platforms verify your existing citations, fix inconsistencies, and help you build new ones.

Local Ranking Factors for Service Businesses

Google's local algorithm considers many factors when determining Map Pack rankings. For service-area businesses like paving contractors, these factors are particularly important:

Proximity

Proximity to the searcher is a major factor in local rankings. Google tends to show businesses that are physically close to the searcher's location.

How to optimize for proximity:

- Ensure your physical location is in or near your service area
- If you serve multiple regions, consider having satellite offices
- Create location-specific content for areas farther from your physical location
- Build strong local citations in specific neighborhoods you target
- Generate reviews from customers across your service area

Relevance

Relevance measures how well your business matches what someone is searching for.

How to optimize for relevance:

- Choose the most accurate GBP categories
- Include detailed service information in your GBP
- Create service-specific pages on your website
- Use consistent business descriptions across platforms
- Include relevant keywords in your business description (naturally, not stuffed)

- Build citations on industry-relevant platforms

Prominence

Prominence refers to how well-known or established your business is.

How to optimize for prominence:

- Generate more Google reviews
- Build a robust profile of diverse citations
- Earn links from local and industry-relevant websites
- Generate local press coverage
- Maintain active social media profiles
- Sponsor local events or organizations

Website Signals

Your website plays a crucial role in local rankings.

Important website signals:

- Mobile-friendliness
- Page loading speed
- Local keyword optimization
- Location pages
- Embedded Google Map
- NAP information matching your GBP
- Location schema markup
- Quality of on-site content
- Internal linking structure

Research Findings on Map Pack Prominence and Conversion

Our analysis of high-performing paving companies reveals some important insights about Map Pack visibility and lead generation:

Map Pack Visibility Patterns

When a paving company first sets up their GBP listing without additional optimization, they typically show up with visibility heavily concentrated around the physical office location. The company appears in the Map Pack only for searches conducted very close to their location.

However, after comprehensive optimization including citation building, review generation, and website alignment, the visibility pattern expands significantly.

This optimized profile shows up in the Map Pack consistently across the entire service area, not just near the office. This expanded visibility dramatically increases lead potential.

Map Pack Click-Through Rates

Research on user behavior shows:

- The top position in the Map Pack receives approximately **44%** of all clicks
- The second position receives about **29%** of clicks
- The third position receives roughly **18%** of clicks
- Only **9%** of users click "More places" to see additional listings

This means **91% of all Map Pack clicks go to just the top 3 positions**, highlighting the importance of ranking in those spots.

Converting Map Pack Visibility to Leads

Our client data shows that Map Pack visibility converts to leads better than organic results for several reasons:

- The visual map creates location context immediately relevant to service needs
- Star ratings provide instant social proof
- One-click calling removes conversion friction
- Photos showcase work quality
- Business hours and basic info are visible without clicking through

On average, a well-optimized GBP listing converts visitors to leads at rates of **7-12%** (meaning 7-12 out of 100 people who view your detailed listing will contact you).

Monitoring and Improving Local Presence

Ongoing management of your local presence is essential for maintaining and improving your Map Pack performance.

Local Search Rank Tracking

Use specialized tools to track your Map Pack rankings:

- BrightLocal
- Whitespark Local Rank Tracker
- Local Viking
- Local Falcon
- Semrush Local

What to track:

- Rankings for core service keywords + city combinations
- Rankings for "near me" searches from multiple points in your service area
- Position changes over time
- Competitor position changes
- Correlation between ranking changes and GBP updates

Google Business Profile Insights

Your GBP dashboard provides valuable performance data:

Key metrics to monitor:

- **How customers search for your business**: Direct (your business name), Discovery (category or service searches), or Branded (branded terms)
- **Actions**: Website clicks, direction requests, phone calls
- **Photo views**: How your photos perform compared to competitors
- **Query insights**: What search terms trigger your listing (available in Google Search Console)

Use these insights to identify strengths and weaknesses in your local presence.

Continuous Improvement Strategies

Based on your monitoring, implement these ongoing improvement tactics:

1. Content Updates:

- Add new photos monthly
- Create Google Posts weekly
- Update services as your offerings evolve

- Refresh your description seasonally

2. Review Acquisition:

- Set monthly review targets (e.g., 5 new reviews)
- Respond to all new reviews within 24-48 hours
- Address any negative feedback promptly
- Implement a systematic review request process

3. Citation Management:

- Audit citations quarterly
- Fix any inconsistencies
- Add new citations on relevant platforms
- Update citations when any information changes

4. Competitor Analysis:

- Monitor top competitors' GBP activity
- Note new features they implement
- Identify gaps in your profile compared to theirs
- Adopt successful strategies they employ

5. Local Content Development:

- Create neighborhood guides on your website
- Publish case studies of local projects
- Develop content about local asphalt/paving regulations
- Address specific paving challenges in your service area

Advanced Local SEO Strategies

Once you've implemented the fundamentals, consider these advanced strategies to further enhance your local presence:

Local Link Building

Build links from locally relevant websites:

- Local news sites
- Community organizations
- Neighborhood associations
- Local business partners
- Event sponsorships
- Local business blogs

These local links send geographic relevance signals to Google.

Local Schema Markup

Implement structured data on your website to provide clear signals to search engines:

- LocalBusiness schema
- Service schema
- GeoCoordinates schema
- Rating schema for testimonials
- FAQ schema for common questions

Use Google's Structured Data Testing Tool or Schema.org to validate your implementation.

Google Posts Strategy

Develop a comprehensive Google Posts calendar:

- Monday: Educational content (maintenance tips, etc.)
- Wednesday: Project highlight with before/after photos
- Friday: Special offer or promotion

Maintain this posting schedule consistently for optimal visibility.

Featured Image Optimization

Since visual content heavily influences Map Pack engagement:

- Test different cover images to see which generates more clicks
- Analyze which project photos receive the most views
- Ensure each photo has proper metadata including your business name and relevant keywords
- Add new photos that showcase different aspects of your services

Local Search Ads

Consider using Google's Local Search Ads to enhance your Map Pack visibility:

- These ads appear within the Map Pack with a small "Ad" designation
- They can boost visibility even if your organic Map Pack ranking isn't top 3
- You can target specific service + location combinations
- Performance can be measured through Google Ads reporting

Implementation Checklist for Google Maps Optimization

Use this comprehensive checklist to ensure you've covered all aspects of Google Maps optimization:

Initial Setup

- Claim and verify Google Business Profile
- Complete all profile information
- Select appropriate primary and secondary categories
- Define accurate service area
- Add comprehensive business description
- Upload 10+ high-quality photos
- Add all services with descriptions
- Set correct business hours

Review Management

- Implement systematic review request process
- Respond to all existing reviews
- Create review generation materials (cards, emails, etc.)
- Set up review monitoring alerts
- Train staff on proper review request timing
- Establish review response templates
- Set monthly review acquisition goals

Citation Building

- Audit existing citations for consistency
- Build profiles on top 10 citation sources
- Add listings to industry-specific directories
- Create consistent NAP information document
- Implement regular citation audit schedule

- Consider using citation management software

Ongoing Management

- Post on Google Posts weekly
- Add new photos monthly
- Monitor insights and performance data
- Track Map Pack rankings
- Update information as needed
- Respond to Q&A section promptly
- Check for Google updates to GBP features

Case Study: Paving Company Map Pack Optimization

To illustrate the impact of comprehensive Maps optimization, consider this case study from one of our paving clients:

Initial Situation:

- Recently established paving company (2 years in business)
- Basic GBP listing with minimal information
- 6 reviews (4.2-star average)
- Inconsistent citations across web
- Map Pack visibility limited to 1-mile radius around office
- Receiving approximately 8-10 leads per month from Maps

Optimization Strategy:

- Completely filled out GBP profile with detailed service descriptions
- Added 20+ project photos with proper descriptions
- Implemented review generation system targeting 5+ new reviews monthly
- Built 50+ consistent citations across key platforms

- Created weekly Google Posts highlighting recent projects
- Added service-specific content to website aligned with GBP services
- Ensured NAP consistency across all platforms

Results After 90 Days:

- Map Pack visibility expanded to entire service area (15-mile radius)
- Reviews increased to 27 (4.7-star average)
- Appeared in top 3 Map Pack positions for 15+ keyword combinations
- Map Pack leads increased to 35-40 per month
- Conversion rate from listing views to leads improved from 5.2% to 9.1%

This represents a **300+% increase in lead generation** from Maps listings within three months of optimization.

Summary: The Map Pack Advantage

Google Maps optimization should be a top priority for any paving company's marketing strategy. The data clearly shows:

- Map Pack listings generate the largest single portion of online leads (36.9%)
- Users trust Map Pack results due to their visual nature and review integration
- Map visibility can be significantly expanded beyond your immediate physical location
- A systematic approach to optimization can yield dramatic improvements in lead generation
- Ongoing management is required to maintain and improve performance

By implementing the strategies outlined in this chapter, you'll position your paving company to capture the maximum share of this critical lead source. Remember that visibility in both Maps and organic results creates a powerful "double exposure" effect – when potential customers see your business in multiple places on the search results page, your perceived credibility and likelihood of contact substantially increase.

In the next chapter, we'll explore paid search marketing strategies to complement your organic and Maps presence, creating a comprehensive search engine visibility strategy.

5

Paid Search Marketing

Paid search marketing, often called Pay-Per-Click (PPC) advertising, is one of the most effective ways to generate immediate leads for your paving business. Unlike SEO which builds over time, PPC can deliver qualified prospects to your website the same day you launch your campaign.

Understanding Paid Search Marketing for Paving Companies

When most people think of internet marketing for paving companies, they immediately think of SEO. However, pay-per-click advertising can be an equally powerful tool when implemented correctly. The primary difference is that PPC delivers immediate results while SEO builds long-term, sustainable visibility.

For paving contractors, paid search offers several distinct advantages:

Immediate visibility: Your business appears at the top of search results the day you start your campaign

- **Targeted reach**: You only pay when someone interested in your services clicks your ad
- **Geographic precision**: Target only the areas you service, down to

specific neighborhoods
- **Budget control**: Set your daily or monthly spend limits with no minimum requirements
- **Measurable results**: Track exactly which ads generate calls and leads

These benefits make paid search marketing an essential component of a comprehensive digital strategy, particularly for paving companies looking to grow quickly or fill scheduling gaps.

The Paid Search Landscape

The paid search ecosystem has evolved significantly in recent years. While Google Ads remains dominant, there are now multiple platforms where paving companies can effectively advertise:

- Google Ads (Search, Display, Local Services Ads)
- Microsoft Advertising (formerly Bing Ads)
- Yelp Ads
- NextDoor Ads
- LinkedIn Ads (for commercial/B2B paving services)
- Facebook/Instagram Ads (technically social, but with paid search elements)

Each platform has unique strengths and audience characteristics, which we'll explore throughout this chapter.

Google Ads & Microsoft Ads Setup

There are really two main players in the Pay-Per-Click space — Google, and Microsoft (Bing). Google has the vast majority of the market share, while Microsoft Ads also serves ads on Yahoo and AOL Search.

For most paving companies, we recommend focusing on Google Ads first.

Once your Google campaigns are performing well, you can easily import them into Microsoft Ads to capture additional search volume. Microsoft's platform makes this process simple with their import tool.

Some people include Facebook in the PPC category because it also uses a pay-per-click pricing model. However, it's more accurately categorized as "Social Media Marketing" rather than "Search Engine Marketing" (SEM). Search ads target users actively looking for your services, while social media ads interrupt users while they're engaging with content.

Types of Google Ads Campaigns

Google offers several campaign types, each with specific benefits for paving contractors:

1. **Search Ads** Text-based ads that appear at the top and bottom of Google search results when someone searches for relevant keywords like "driveway paving" or "asphalt contractor near me." For paving companies, search ads typically yield the highest quality leads because they target users actively searching for your services. These users have high commercial intent—they're looking to hire a paving contractor right now or in the near future.

2. **Display Ads** Visual banner ads that appear on websites across the Google Display Network. These come in two main campaign types:

- **Standard display campaigns** that target specific websites or users with certain interests
- **Remarketing campaigns** that show ads to people who have previously visited your website

Display ads work well for building brand awareness and staying top-of-mind with potential customers who visited your site but didn't convert. For paving companies, we recommend using display primarily for remarketing rather than cold audience targeting.

3. Local Services Ads These "Google Guaranteed" ads appear at the very top of search results for local service businesses. Unlike traditional PPC, you pay per lead rather than per click. Local Services Ads include the Google Guaranteed badge, which signals trust to potential customers. Google verifies your business credentials and insurance, then stands behind your work with a limited guarantee that covers claims up to $2,000. This significantly increases trust and click-through rates.

For paving companies, Local Services Ads often deliver the highest quality leads because:

- Your business is verified by Google
- The leads come pre-qualified (location and service match)
- Customers can call or message directly from the ad
- The trust badge enhances credibility

BUT – they are only available for certain landscaping-related services.

4. Performance Max Campaigns Performance Max is Google's newest AI-driven campaign type that runs across all Google properties (Search, Display, YouTube, Gmail, Maps, etc.). It uses machine learning to find potential customers wherever they are online.

For paving companies, Performance Max can be effective for:

- Finding customers who might not explicitly search for "paving" but show interest in home improvement or property enhancement
- Automatically adjusting your budget toward the channels that drive the most leads
- Utilizing Google's data to identify potential customers you might miss

with traditional targeting

To set up an effective Performance Max campaign for a paving business:

- Provide high-quality images of your projects (before/after shots work best)
- Create short video content if possible (even simple slideshows of your work)
- Include clear text assets highlighting your key selling points
- Set specific location targeting to your service area
- Connect your Google Merchant Center if you sell products (sealants, concrete mixes, etc.)

Performance Max works best for paving companies that have:

- A solid conversion tracking setup
- At least 3-6 months of conversion data
- High-quality visuals of their work
- Multiple service offerings

Research Findings on Paving PPC Costs

Our extensive research monitoring the top 200 markets in the US has given us valuable insights into paid search for paving companies:

- The average cost-per-click (CPC) for paving-related keywords ranges from **$4-$8** depending on location and competition
- In more competitive markets, clicks can cost over $10 each
- A well-run campaign might yield leads at around **$40-$80** each

In one case study we analyzed, a paving company's Google Ads campaign generated:

- 271 clicks at an average CPC of **$8.66**
- 47 conversions (leads) at a cost per lead of **$49.92**
- A conversion rate of 17.3%

This performance is excellent compared to industry standards. While conversion rates vary widely based on landing page quality and targeting, 5-15% is typical for well-optimized campaigns.

Benchmarking Your PPC Performance

To evaluate if your PPC campaigns are performing well, compare your metrics against these industry benchmarks for paving and construction services:

Metric	Poor Performance	Average Performance	Excellent Performance
Click-Through Rate (CTR)	Below 2%	2-4%	Above 4%
Conversion Rate	Below 3%	3-8%	Above 8%
Cost Per Click (CPC)	Above $12	$5-12	Below $5
Cost Per Lead (CPL)	Above $100	$50-100	Below $50

Metric	Poor Performance	Average Performance	Excellent Performance
Quality Score	Below 5	5-7	Above 7

Remember that these benchmarks can vary by location, seasonality, and competition. In major metropolitan areas, expect higher CPCs but potentially better conversion rates due to higher population density.

Keyword Selection for Paving Businesses

Keyword selection is critical to PPC success. You want to target terms potential customers use when searching for your services. Here are the highest-volume keywords nationwide for paving companies:

Keyword	Monthly Search Volume
asphalt paving	20,000
paving companies near me	19,000
asphalt driveway	15,000
asphalt paving near me	12,000
asphalt companies near me	11,000
driveway paving near me	10,000
paving contractor	7,500
driveway paving	6,300
asphalt company near me	5,200
asphalt contractor	5,100

Keyword	Monthly Search Volume
paving companies	5,100
paving contractors near me	4,100
paving company near me	3,800

When setting up your campaign, be sure to include:

- **Service-specific terms** — "asphalt paving," "driveway paving," "parking lot resurfacing"
- **Location-modified terms** — "paving companies in [city]," "asphalt contractor near me"
- **Commercial intent terms** — "paving estimate," "hire asphalt contractor"
- **Problem-based terms** — "fix cracked driveway," "repair pothole"

Be selective about broad terms like "asphalt" or "paving" without qualifiers, as these can bring irrelevant clicks and waste your budget.

Keyword Organization Strategy

Effective PPC campaigns require thoughtful keyword organization. We recommend structuring your paving company's campaigns by service type with dedicated ad groups for each variation:

Campaign 1: Residential Paving

- Ad Group 1: Driveway Paving
- Ad Group 2: Driveway Resurfacing
- Ad Group 3: Driveway Repair
- Ad Group 4: Driveway Sealcoating

Campaign 2: Commercial Paving

- Ad Group 1: Parking Lot Paving
- Ad Group 2: Parking Lot Repair
- Ad Group 3: Parking Lot Resurfacing
- Ad Group 4: Parking Lot Striping

Campaign 3: Specialized Services

- Ad Group 1: Asphalt Patching
- Ad Group 2: Crack Filling
- Ad Group 3: Concrete Services (if offered)
- Ad Group 4: Sports Courts/Recreational Paving

This structure allows you to:

- Write highly relevant ad copy for each service type
- Create specific landing pages for each service
- Adjust bids based on the profitability of each service
- Allocate budget according to seasonal demand
- Analyze performance by service type

Using Google's Keyword Planner

Google Ads provides a free Keyword Planner tool to research relevant keywords and estimate costs for your specific area. Here's how to use it:

1. Set up a Google Ads account if you haven't already
2. Navigate to Tools > Keyword Planner
3. Enter your primary service categories (like "paving contractors")
4. Review the suggested keywords and their estimated bid ranges
5. Add your city modifier to see more localized results
6. Download these keyword lists to guide your campaign setup

The Keyword Planner will show you estimated bid ranges, search volumes, and competition levels. Use this data to prioritize keywords with the best potential ROI.

Negative Keywords: Protecting Your Budget

Just as important as the keywords you target are the ones you exclude. Negative keywords prevent your ads from showing for irrelevant searches. Common negative keywords for paving companies include:

- **DIY terms**: "how to pave driveway yourself", "DIY asphalt repair"
- **Job searches**: "paving jobs", "asphalt worker", "paving careers"
- **Material-only searches**: "buy asphalt", "asphalt for sale", "paving stones"
- **Unrelated terms**: "paving the way", "road paving schedule" (government projects)
- **Low-intent modifiers**: "pictures", "images", "videos", "free"

Start with these categories and regularly review your Search Terms report to identify additional negative keywords. Adding just a few effective negative keywords can significantly improve campaign performance by eliminating wasted clicks.

Creating Effective Ad Copy

Your ad copy needs to capture attention and motivate clicks from qualified prospects. Here are principles for creating effective paving ads:

- **Include your main keyword in the headline** — If someone searches "asphalt driveway repair," your headline should contain those words
- **Highlight your unique selling proposition** — What makes your paving company better than competitors? Experience? Warranties? Fast service?
- **Add a clear call-to-action** — "Get a Free Estimate," "Call Today," etc.
- **Mention your service area** — Include city names when possible
- **Use ad extensions** — These provide extra information like phone

numbers, location, and callout features

Example of effective paving ad copy:

Headline 1: Professional Asphalt Driveway Paving | [City Name] **Headline 2:** 25+ Years Experience & 5-Year Warranty **Headline 3:** Free Estimates Within 24 Hours

Description: Family-owned paving contractors serving [City] area home-owners and businesses. Commercial and residential asphalt specialists. Call now for your free, no-obligation quote!

Call Extension: 555-123-4567 **Location:** Your business address **Callouts:** Same-Day Quotes • Licensed & Insured • Financing Available

Always create multiple ad variations to test different messages, and let Google optimize toward the best performers.

Ad Extensions That Drive Conversions

Ad extensions provide additional information and give your ads more real estate on the search results page. For paving companies, these extensions are most effective:

- **Call Extensions**: Display your phone number directly in the ad for one-click calling on mobile devices.
- **Location Extensions**: Show your business address and a map marker, especially useful for customers wanting to verify you service their area.
- **Callout Extensions**: Highlight key selling points like "Family-Owned Since 1995" or "Free Estimates" or "5-Year Warranty."
- **Structured Snippets**: List your services such as "Services: Driveways, Parking Lots, Patios, Walkways."

- **Price Extensions**: Show pricing for different services like "Driveway Sealcoating - Starting at $X per sq ft."
- **Sitelink Extensions**: Add links to specific pages like "Residential Services," "Commercial Projects," "About Our Process," and "View Our Work."
- **Image Extensions**: Show photos of your completed projects directly in the search results.

Here's how a fully-extended ad might appear for a paving company:

Professional Asphalt Paving | Dallas's Top-Rated Contractor | Free Estimates www.examplepaving.com Family-owned paving contractors serving Dallas area homeowners and businesses. Commercial and residential asphalt specialists. Call now for your free quote!

Call: 555-123-4567 123 Main St, Dallas, TX

Sitelinks: Residential Paving | Commercial Services | Our Process | Photo Gallery

Callouts: 25+ Years Experience | 5-Year Warranty | Financing Available | Licensed & Insured

Structured Snippets: Services: Driveways, Parking Lots, Patios, Walkways, Repairs

[Image of completed driveway project]

Ad extensions typically improve click-through rates by 10-15% and don't cost extra, making them essential for maximizing PPC performance.

Landing Page Optimization

Where you send your PPC traffic matters tremendously. A common mistake is directing paid clicks to your homepage. Instead, create **dedicated landing pages** for each service you advertise. For example, if someone clicks an ad about "asphalt driveway installation," they should land on a page specifically about driveways — not your general services page.

Effective landing pages for paving companies include:

- Clear, specific headline **matching the ad they clicked**
- Compelling **before/after photos** of your paving work
- Concise explanation of your **service and process**
- **Social proof** — reviews, testimonials, project examples
- Multiple **contact options** — prominent phone number, contact form, chat
- **Trust indicators** — licenses, certifications, guarantees
- **Mobile optimization** — most searches happen on phones

The alignment between your keywords, ad copy, and landing page content affects both conversion rates and your Google Quality Score, which can lower your cost per click.

The "Message Match" Principle

One of the most important aspects of landing page optimization is ensuring a strong "message match" between your ad and the landing page. This means the headline, images, and offer on your landing page should directly reflect what was promised in the ad.

Example:

- **Ad Headline**: "Driveway Paving in Dallas | 15% Off This Month"
- **Landing Page Headline**: "Professional Driveway Paving in Dallas | Limited Time: 15% Off All Installations"

This tight alignment reassures visitors they've come to the right place and significantly increases conversion rates. Studies show that strong message matching can improve conversion rates by 25% or more.

Mobile-First Landing Page Design

Since over 60% of searches now happen on mobile devices, your landing pages must be designed with mobile users in mind. For paving company landing pages, consider these mobile optimization principles:

- Prominent **click-to-call buttons** at the top and bottom of the page
- Large, easy-to-tap **form fields** for quote requests
- **Quick-loading images** optimized for mobile connections
- **Short paragraphs and bullet points** for scannable content
- **Minimal form fields** (name, phone, email, project type)
- **Sticky header** with contact information that remains visible as users scroll
- **Location information** that integrates with mobile map apps

Remember that mobile users often have different intent than desktop users – they're frequently looking for immediate contact options rather than detailed information. Make it effortless for them to call or request a quote with a single tap.

Budget Management and Bid Strategies

Managing your budget effectively ensures you don't overspend while maximizing results.

How Much Should You Budget?

For a small to mid-sized paving company just starting with PPC:

- Begin with at least **$1,000-2,000 per month** for Google Ads
- This typically generates **5-15 quality leads** (varies by market)
- Start with **one core service** (like residential driveways)
- Expand to additional services after proving ROI

A good rule of thumb for established paving companies is to allocate **7-12%** of your target revenue from advertising to your Google Ads budget. For example, if you want to generate $20,000 in new business from Google Ads monthly, budget approximately $1,400-$2,400 per month.

Geographic Targeting

One of the most important settings is your geographic targeting. Only show ads to people in areas you service. You can:

- Target specific cities or zip codes
- Create a radius around your business location
- Exclude areas you don't serve
- Use different bid adjustments for prime service areas

For paving companies, we recommend a tiered approach to geographic targeting:

- **Tier 1**: Primary service area (0-10 miles from your location) - **100% bid adjustment**
- **Tier 2**: Secondary service area (10-20 miles) - **0% adjustment** (baseline bids)
- **Tier 3**: Extended service area (20-30 miles) - **-20% bid adjustment** (lower bids)

This structure allows you to bid more aggressively for nearby jobs while still capturing opportunities in outlying areas at a lower cost. You can also exclude areas with geographic barriers (like across a body of water) that make service impractical.

Bid Strategies

Google offers several automated bidding strategies, but we recommend these approaches for paving companies:

- **Maximize Clicks** — Good when starting out to gather data
- **Target CPA (Cost Per Acquisition)** — Once you know your lead costs, set a target amount per lead
- **Enhanced CPC** — Allows manual control with some Google automation for better results

Most importantly, track your return on ad spend (ROAS). If you spend $2,000 on ads and generate $20,000 in new business, that's a 10x ROAS — excellent performance.

Seasonal Bidding Adjustments

Paving is a seasonal business in many regions, and your PPC strategy should reflect this reality. Consider implementing these seasonal adjustments:

- **Spring (March-May)**: Increase budgets as demand rises after winter. Focus on keywords like "driveway repair after winter" and "pothole repair." Highlight early-season discounts in ad copy. Target commercial properties preparing for summer season.
- **Summer (June-August)**: Peak season in most areas. Maximum budget allocation. Target both residential and commercial keywords equally. Emphasize your scheduling availability in ad copy. Consider conquest

campaigns targeting competitors who may be booked solid.
- **Fall (September-November)**: Moderate demand. Focus on "before winter" messaging. Target commercial properties preparing for winter. Highlight sealcoating and preventative maintenance.
- **Winter (December-February)**: Low season in cold-weather areas. Reduce budgets in snow-prone regions. Focus on planning/consult ation for spring projects. Target commercial planning departments with next-year budgets. Consider running display campaigns to stay visible during off-season.

In warm-weather regions without significant seasonality, maintain consistent budgets with adjustments based on rainfall patterns instead.

Microsoft Advertising (Formerly Bing Ads)

While Google dominates search traffic, Microsoft Advertising (which powers Bing, Yahoo, and AOL search results) shouldn't be overlooked. Microsoft's search network reaches 51 million users that Google doesn't, and these users tend to be:

- Older (45-65 age range)
- Higher-income professionals
- More likely to have commercial intent

For paving companies, these demographics align well with property owners and business decision-makers—exactly the customers you want to reach.

Benefits of Microsoft Advertising for Paving Companies

- **Lower CPCs**: Keywords on Microsoft typically cost 20-30% less than Google
- **Less competition**: Fewer advertisers means better ad positions

- **Higher conversion rates**: Often 10-15% better than Google due to user demographics
- **Easy implementation**: Import campaigns directly from Google Ads
- **Incremental reach**: Access users not found on Google

Implementation Strategy

We recommend a phased approach to Microsoft Advertising:

1. First, build and optimize your Google Ads campaigns
2. Once stable and profitable, import them to Microsoft Advertising
3. Adjust bids downward by 20-30% initially
4. Monitor performance and optimize separately
5. Allocate approximately 15-25% of your PPC budget to Microsoft

A typical allocation for a $3,000 monthly PPC budget might be:

- Google Search: $1,800 (60%)
- Google Local Services Ads: $600 (20%)
- Microsoft Advertising: $600 (20%)

This approach ensures you're capturing high-intent traffic across all major search engines without spreading your budget too thin on any platform.

Other Paid Advertising Platforms for Paving Companies

While Google and Microsoft search ads often deliver the highest ROI, several other platforms can effectively generate leads for paving companies. Each offers unique advantages and audience characteristics.

Yelp Ads

Yelp is a powerful platform for service businesses like paving contractors because users often have high purchase intent. When someone searches Yelp for "paving companies," they're actively looking to hire, not just researching.

Benefits for paving companies:

- Highly qualified leads with immediate intent
- Enhanced profile features with Yelp Ads
- Ads appear above organic listings for relevant searches
- Phone calls and website clicks are trackable
- Competitor ad blocking on your business page

Typical costs:

- Most paving companies spend $300-600/month on Yelp Ads
- Cost per click ranges from $2-5 in most markets
- Lead costs generally fall between $40-90 each

Implementation tips:

- Ensure your Yelp profile is complete with quality photos before advertising
- Respond to all reviews, especially negative ones
- Focus on service categories with the highest profit margins
- Use a dedicated phone tracking number to measure ROI
- Consider Yelp's "Call to Action" button for quote requests

For most paving companies, Yelp works best as a supplementary lead source rather than a primary channel. Allocate approximately 10-15% of your digital marketing budget to test its effectiveness in your specific market.

NextDoor Ads

NextDoor is a neighborhood-focused social platform that can be particularly effective for residential paving services. Its hyperlocal nature makes it ideal for targeting homeowners in specific neighborhoods.

Benefits for paving companies:

- Extremely precise neighborhood targeting
- Recommendations and social proof from neighbors
- Trust-based community environment
- Less competition than Google or Facebook
- Strong performance for home service contractors

Typical costs:

- CPM (cost per 1,000 impressions) ranges from $25-40
- Minimum budgets start around $300/month
- Lead costs average $60-100 but can vary widely

Implementation tips:

- Use "neighbor offer" ad formats for best performance
- Feature photos of work done in the targeted neighborhoods
- Highlight your local business status and community connections
- Include special offers exclusive to NextDoor members
- Respond quickly to all inquiries (response time affects performance)

NextDoor works particularly well for establishing your company as the neighborhood's preferred paving contractor. It's especially effective for companies focusing on residential driveways and smaller projects rather than large commercial work.

LinkedIn Ads

While not typically a primary channel for residential paving, LinkedIn can be extremely effective for B2B paving companies targeting commercial clients, property managers, and facility directors.

Benefits for commercial paving contractors:

- Direct targeting of decision-makers by job title
- Reach property managers, facility directors, and commercial real estate professionals
- Target specific industries (retail, healthcare, education) that need parking lot services
- Professional context enhances your company's credibility

Typical costs:

- Higher than other platforms - $6-12 per click is common
- CPM ranges from $30-60
- Lead costs typically $100-200 each
- Minimum suggested budget: $500-1,000/month

Implementation tips:

- Use specific job title targeting (Facility Manager, Property Manager, etc.)
- Create content focused on commercial paving challenges and solutions
- Emphasize credentials, experience with similar properties, and commercial specialization
- Use Lead Gen forms for easiest conversion
- Include case studies of successful commercial projects

LinkedIn makes sense primarily for paving companies with a strong commercial focus. If more than 50% of your business comes from commercial clients, consider allocating 15-20% of your digital marketing budget to LinkedIn campaigns.

Facebook & Instagram Ads

While Facebook and Instagram are social platforms rather than search engines, they offer excellent targeting capabilities for paving companies, particularly for awareness and consideration-stage marketing.

Benefits for paving contractors:

- Extensive demographic and behavioral targeting options
- Powerful remarketing to website visitors
- Visual format showcases your work quality
- Lower cost per click than search platforms ($1-3 typical)
- Multi-platform presence (Facebook, Instagram, Messenger)

Typical costs:

- CPM: $10-25 for targeted local audiences
- CPC: $1-3 in most markets
- Lead costs: $30-60 on average
- Recommended minimum budget: $500/month

Most effective strategies for paving companies:

- **Before/After Campaigns**: Show dramatic transformations of driveways and parking lots
- **Neighborhood Targeting**: Focus on neighborhoods with homes of similar age and value
- **Life Event Targeting**: Target people who recently moved or purchased

homes

- **Video Demonstrations**: Show your equipment and crew in action
- **Lead Generation Campaigns**: Use Facebook's native lead forms for quote requests

Facebook works best as part of an integrated strategy rather than a standalone channel. Many paving companies find success using Facebook for upper-funnel awareness while capturing bottom-funnel intent with Google Ads.

Revenue Commander Integration for Tracking

To truly measure PPC performance, you need proper tracking. Our Revenue Commander platform offers comprehensive PPC tracking capabilities:

- **Call tracking** — Unique phone numbers for each campaign show exactly which ads generated calls
- **Form submission tracking** — Track which ads lead to quote requests
- **Lead attribution** — See every touchpoint in the customer journey
- **ROI calculation** — Connect ad spend directly to revenue generated
- **Automated reporting** — Get daily, weekly or monthly performance summaries

Revenue Commander also integrates with Google Analytics and Google Ads, allowing cross-platform data sharing for deeper insights.

Setting Up Conversion Tracking

Proper conversion tracking is essential. Make sure you have:

- Google Ads conversion tracking codes on your website
- Phone call tracking for all campaigns
- Form submission tracking for contact forms

- Revenue Commander tracking pixels installed

Without conversion tracking, you're flying blind and likely wasting ad budget on clicks that don't generate leads.

Lead Source Attribution

Understanding which marketing channels drive leads is critical for optimizing your budget allocation. Revenue Commander provides comprehensive attribution reporting that shows:

- **First-touch attribution** (which channel initially brought the visitor to your site)
- **Last-touch attribution** (which channel directly generated the lead)
- **Multi-touch attribution** (all channels that influenced the customer journey)
- **Assisted conversions** (channels that contributed but didn't directly convert)

This data allows you to understand the true value of each marketing channel. For example, you might discover that while Google Ads directly generates most leads, Facebook advertising significantly assists those conversions by creating awareness earlier in the customer journey.

Closed-Loop Reporting

The ultimate measure of marketing effectiveness is not leads, but revenue. Revenue Commander's closed-loop reporting connects marketing activities to actual sales:

- Track each lead from initial marketing touchpoint through the sales process
- Record actual revenue from closed deals back to the original marketing

source

- Calculate true ROI by channel, campaign, ad group, and even keyword level
- Identify which types of leads have the highest close rates and job values

This closed-loop system reveals insights like:

- Google Ads might generate leads at $60 each, but they close at 40% with an average job value of $4,500
- Facebook leads might cost only $40 each, but close at 25% with an average job value of $3,200

Without this level of tracking, you can't optimize for profitability—only for lead generation.

Advanced PPC Strategies for Paving Companies

Once you've mastered the basics, consider these advanced strategies:

Single Keyword Ad Groups (SKAGs)

Create highly targeted ad groups with just one keyword variation. This allows extremely relevant ad copy and higher quality scores. For example, instead of having one ad group for "driveway paving" with multiple keyword variations, create separate ad groups for:

- "driveway paving"
- "driveway paving company"
- "asphalt driveway paving"
- "concrete driveway paving"

Each SKAG would have its own tailored ad copy that precisely matches the keyword, significantly improving quality scores and reducing CPCs.

Dayparting

Show your ads only during business hours when someone can answer the phone, or adjust bids by time of day based on when leads convert best. For example, you might discover that:

- 8am–10am generates leads at the lowest cost
- 12pm–2pm sees the highest call volume but lower quality leads
- 4pm–7pm produces the highest-quality leads with the best close rates

With this data, you could adjust bidding by time of day:

- Increase bids by 20% from 4pm–7pm
- Maintain standard bids from 8am–4pm
- Decrease bids by 30% or pause ads entirely outside business hours

Weather-Based Bidding

Increase bids during good weather when paving projects are more likely to be considered, and reduce during rainy periods. This can be implemented using:

- **Script automation**: Custom scripts that adjust bids based on local weather data
- **Manual adjustments**: Regular bid changes based on weather forecasts
- **Third-party tools**: Services that connect weather data to Google Ads

For example, you might:

- Increase bids by 30% during dry periods after heavy rain (when pothole awareness is high)
- Decrease bids by 50% during active rainfall when paving work can't be done

- Increase bids during the first warm weekend of spring when property owners are assessing winter damage

Competitor Targeting

Bid on competitor business names (where legally permitted) to capture customers comparing options. Create dedicated ad groups targeting your main competitors with messaging that highlights your advantages:

- "Comparing ABC Paving? See Why Customers Choose Us"
- "Better Alternative to XYZ Asphalt | Higher Quality, Same Price"
- "Local Alternative to National Paving Chains | Personal Service"

This strategy works particularly well when bidding on:

- Competitors with poor online reviews
- National chains with less personalized service
- Companies known for higher pricing

Seasonal Adjustments

Increase budgets during peak paving seasons (typically spring and early summer) and reduce during off-seasons. A typical seasonal budget allocation might look like:

- March-May: 120% of baseline budget
- June-August: 150% of baseline budget
- September-November: 100% of baseline budget
- December-February: 50-70% of baseline budget (depending on climate)

During slower seasons, shift messaging toward planning and early booking discounts for the upcoming season.

RLSA (Remarketing Lists for Search Ads)

Target past website visitors when they search for paving-related terms. These prospects have already shown interest in your services and are more likely to convert. Set up RLSA campaigns to:

- Bid more aggressively on previous website visitors
- Show different ad copy to past visitors
- Target broader keywords for people who've already visited your site
- Extend remarketing windows during your off-season (e.g., 180 days instead of standard 30 days)

This strategy can increase conversion rates by 2-3x compared to standard search campaigns.

Conclusion

Paid search marketing provides immediate visibility and leads for paving companies. While it requires ongoing investment, a well-managed campaign can deliver consistent, high-quality leads at a predictable cost.

By focusing on relevant keywords, creating compelling ads, optimizing landing pages, and properly tracking results through Revenue Commander, you can build a PPC campaign that delivers reliable growth for your paving business.

Remember these key takeaways:

- Start with Google Ads search campaigns targeting your core services
- Expand to Microsoft Advertising once your Google campaigns are profitable
- Consider specialized platforms like Yelp, NextDoor, and LinkedIn based on your specific business focus

- Implement comprehensive tracking to measure true ROI
- Continuously optimize based on performance data
- Adjust strategies seasonally to match demand patterns

Paid search should be viewed as a powerful tool in your overall marketing strategy. When combined with SEO, social media, and traditional advertising, the results can be amazing.

6

Social Media Marketing

Social media has transformed from a simple networking platform to a powerful marketing channel for businesses of all types, including paving contractors. While you might think social media isn't relevant for a paving company, the data shows otherwise. When executed properly, social media can significantly boost your brand awareness, generate quality leads, and strengthen customer relationships.

The Evolution of Social Media for Businesses

There is a lot of BUZZ around Social Media (Facebook, Instagram, LinkedIn, YouTube, etc.), but how can it be leveraged by a paving company? How can you use social media to grow your business?

As I talk to paving business owners throughout the country about Internet marketing and social media, I tend to get a puzzled look. The question is, "How in the world does all of this social media stuff apply to my business? How can I possibly use Facebook in a way that would help me increase my revenues, boost my estimates, and get more repeat business?"

I'd like to try and bridge the gap on where the "lowest-hanging fruit" for social media is in your business by asking, "What's your number one source of business today?" Just stop and think, where does most of your revenue come from? You'll quickly come to the conclusion that your number one source of revenue is repeated and referral business. The lifeblood of many paving businesses is your existing customers returning for services over time, and your existing customers referring you to their network.

If social media is harnessed correctly, it gives you the ability to take that repeat and referral business, inject it with steroids, and take it to a whole new level. Let me explain why I feel that it's a great place for you to really connect with your customers and get more repeat and referral business.

Just a couple of Facebook stats gleaned from Google:

- Facebook currently has 2.37 billion users
- The average user has 338 friends
- Users check in an average of 14 times per day

If you can get your real customers, current and past (your sphere of influence) to connect with you on social media, such as Facebook and/or Instagram, your business is exposed to their 338 friends as soon as they "like" and follow your page. It's almost as if they'd sent an email, or they'd sent a text message out to all their friends saying, "I recently received a service from this service provider in our area. The next time you need their services, why don't you think about them?" It's extremely powerful to gain exposure to their sphere of influence.

Another major advantage is that they've given you permission to remain top-of-mind with them. The average user checks in 14 times per day. They log in to check out the updates on their Facebook wall and to see the updates of all the companies and people they have liked or are friends with. If you're posting updates to your social media profiles, the people who have liked your page are going to see that new content whenever they log in. They are going to see an update and your logo. They're going to see some special offer or promotion, and it's going to pique their interest. Next time they need your services, who do you think they're going to call?

People ask for recommendations all of the time. I'm not a huge Facebook user, but I check in maybe once a day. I'm a member of local groups — think people who live in the same area — and I've seen several people asking for paving company recommendations in those groups.

Platform Selection for Paving Companies

Not all social media platforms are created equal when it comes to marketing paving services. Based on our experience working with hundreds of paving contractors, here are the platforms that deliver the best results:

Facebook

Recommendation: Essential

Facebook remains the dominant platform for local service businesses, including paving contractors. With 2.93 billion active users and the average user having 338 friends, it's where your potential customers are spending their time.

Key advantages for paving companies:

- Demographic targeting capabilities (homeowners, age 30-65, specific locations)
- Local awareness ads and "Get Quote" call-to-action buttons
- Community groups where recommendations are frequently requested
- Business page showcasing your work and reviews
- Effective platform for both organic content and paid advertising

Instagram

Recommendation: Highly Recommended

Instagram is visually-oriented, making it perfect for showcasing before/after photos of your paving projects. It's particularly effective for residential projects that transform property appearance.

Key advantages:

- Highly visual platform perfect for project photos
- Owned by Meta (Facebook's parent company), allowing integrated advertising
- Appeals to younger homeowners planning renovations
- Stories feature allows behind-the-scenes glimpses of your crew at work
- Hashtags can help reach local audiences (#[YourCity]Paving, #DrivewayrResurfacing) * Reels feature for short-form video content showcasing dramatic transformations

The visual nature of paving work—the dramatic before and after transformations—makes Instagram particularly well-suited for paving contractors. Research shows that posts with before/after imagery generate 58% more engagement than standard posts in the home improvement category.

LinkedIn

Recommendation: Recommended for Commercial Focus

If your paving company targets commercial clients (property managers, businesses with parking lots), LinkedIn is valuable for B2B networking and lead generation.

Key advantages:

- Connect with property managers and commercial decision-makers
- Establish professional authority with industry-specific content
- Networking opportunities with complementary businesses
- Targeted B2B advertising options
- Company page showcases commercial projects and capabilities

For paving companies focusing on commercial projects, LinkedIn provides direct access to facility managers, property management companies, and commercial real estate professionals who make decisions about parking lot maintenance and upgrades. These business relationships typically lead to higher-value contracts and repeat business opportunities. According to industry data, B2B companies generate 277% more leads on LinkedIn than on Facebook, making it an essential platform for paving contractors with a commercial focus.

YouTube

Recommendation: Recommended for Educational Content

YouTube ranks as the second most used search engine, making it valuable for informational content. It's not necessary for all paving companies but can significantly enhance your marketing if done right.

Key advantages:

- Host educational videos about paving processes, materials, and maintenance
- Time-lapse videos of projects are popular and showcase your efficiency

- Videos can be embedded on your website to increase conversion
- Long-term visibility through search (videos can generate leads for years)
- Enhances professional credibility

Did you know YouTube is the second-most used search engine on the market? Would you guess it is even ahead of Bing and Yahoo? It's true! Millions of people conduct Youtubees on a daily basis. Most business owners are so focused on SEO they completely neglect the opportunities that video and YouTube provide. By implementing a Video Marketing Strategy for your business, you can get additional placement in search results for your keywords, enhance the effectiveness of your SEO efforts and improve visitor conversion. Don't think that you have to be a video pro to do it — it's as simple as taking your smartphone and recording a video with your camera. Letting future customers get to know you a bit by seeing you on video can go a long way towards building the trust that is needed to make the purchase.

TikTok

Recommendation: Emerging Opportunity

TikTok has emerged as a surprisingly effective platform for contracting businesses willing to showcase their work in creative ways. With over 1 billion active users and the fastest-growing social media platform, it represents an opportunity to reach younger homeowners and property managers with engaging content.

Key advantages for paving companies:

- Viral potential for dramatic transformation videos
- Opportunity to showcase specialized equipment and techniques

- Algorithmic distribution that doesn't rely solely on follower count
- Less saturated with competitors than established platforms
- Appeals to younger homeowners and future decision-makers

According to recent statistics, hashtags like #homeimprovement have generated over 6.8 billion views on TikTok, indicating significant interest in contractor services. Paving companies that showcase satisfying transformations—like power washing degraded concrete before repaving or the smooth finishing of a freshly laid asphalt driveway—have seen videos reach hundreds of thousands of views.

Effective TikTok Content for Paving Companies

The most successful paving contractors on TikTok focus on these content types:

- Satisfying Transformations: Before/after reveals in quick, dramatic format
- Educational "Did You Know" Content: Short facts about paving materials or processes * Equipment Showcases: Featuring specialized machinery in action
- Day-in-the-Life: Following your crew through a project from start to finish
- Process Videos: Breaking down complex paving processes into understandable steps

For example, one asphalt contractor gained over 100,000 followers by creating 15-30 second clips showing the mesmerizing process of applying sealcoat in timelapse format. This content not only entertained but educated potential customers about maintenance services they offer.

TikTok Best Practices for Paving Contractors

If you decide to explore TikTok marketing:

- Keep Videos Short: 15-30 seconds is optimal for maximum engagement
- Use Popular Audio: Trending sounds increase discovery potential
- Create a Content Series: "Paving Transformations," "Asphalt Facts," etc.
- Show Your Personality: Let crew members showcase their expertise and passion
- Include Local Hashtags: #DallasHomeImprovement, #ChicagoPaving, etc.
- Post Consistently: 2-3 times per week minimum for algorithm favor

Remember, TikTok is primarily an entertainment platform. Educational content should be engaging and visually interesting rather than technical or sales-focused.

X (Formerly Twitter)

Recommendation: Selective Engagement

While X (formerly Twitter) might not be a primary lead generation platform for most paving contractors, it can play a strategic role in your overall social media presence, particularly for networking, industry engagement, and local reputation building.

Key advantages for paving contractors:

- Quick updates on project completions and availability

- Connection with local business networks and community leaders
- Engagement with industry associations and suppliers
- Responsive customer service channel
- Monitoring of local conversations and trending topics

For paving companies, X works best as a supplementary channel rather than a primary marketing focus. Its real-time nature makes it ideal for:

- Local Weather Response: Post about how you're adjusting to weather events that affect paving (e.g., "Our crews are working extended hours this week to make up for last week's rain delays")
- Community Involvement: Share your participation in local events, sponsorships, or community improvement projects
- Industry Insights: Comment on trends, regulations, or innovations in paving materials and techniques
- Business Networking: Connect with complementary businesses, suppliers, and industry organizations
- Customer Service: Respond quickly to inquiries or mentions of your company

X requires less time investment than other platforms—posting 2-3 times per week can maintain an effective presence. Focus on sharing quick updates, responding to mentions, and engaging with local business conversations rather than creating elaborate content strategies.

Reddit

Recommendation: Specialized Engagement

Reddit might not seem like an obvious choice for paving contractors, but several subreddits (topic-focused communities) offer unique opportunities to establish expertise and connect with potential customers researching paving projects.

Key advantages for paving contractors:

- Direct engagement with homeowners actively researching paving projects
- Opportunity to demonstrate expertise through helpful answers
- Access to niche communities focused on home improvement
- Building reputation as an industry authority
- Minimal competition from other contractors

Relevant subreddits for paving contractors include:

- r/HomeImprovement (3.5M+ members)
- r/landscaping (1.7M+ members)
- r/DIY (21.6M+ members)
- r/homeowners (446K+ members)
- Local community subreddits (e.g., r/Dallas, r/ChicagoSuburbs)

Reddit's unique value comes from its question-and-answer format. Homeowners frequently post questions about paving projects, seeking advice on everything from contractor selection to material choices and maintenance. By providing helpful, non-promotional responses, paving contractors can build credibility and occasionally receive direct inquiries.

Reddit Best Practices for Paving Companies

- Focus on Providing Value: Answer questions thoroughly and objectively without overt self-promotion
- Establish Expertise: Use your professional knowledge to explain

complex topics in accessible language
- Share Photos of Projects: When relevant, include images of similar work (while respecting client privacy)
- Be Transparent: Use a business-identified account and include your profession in your profile
- Follow Community Rules: Each subreddit has specific guidelines about commercial participation

Reddit requires a different approach than traditional social media. Direct promotion is typically unwelcome, but thoughtful participation can establish your company as a trusted resource. For example, one paving contractor reported receiving 5-10 qualified leads per month simply by answering questions about driveway materials and installation techniques on home improvement subreddits.

Research Findings: Facebook Ads Performance

Our research on social media advertising performance reveals compelling data for paving contractors considering Facebook ads:

- The average cost per click (CPC) for home improvement businesses on Facebook is **$2-3**, significantly lower than Google Ads for similar targeting
- In practice, well-optimized campaigns can deliver clicks for **under $2.00 each**
- The average click-through rate (CTR) for home improvement ads on Facebook is approximately **0.7%**
- Facebook lead generation ads in home services produce an average **cost per acquisition (CPA) around $40-45 per lead**
- Specifically, the average Facebook advertising cost per lead for Home Improvement services was measured at **$44.66**

These figures demonstrate why Facebook ads can be a cost-effective complement to more expensive search ads. While search ads capture high-intent prospects actively looking for paving services, Facebook ads can create demand by showing homeowners with deteriorating driveways that they should consider resurfacing.

Real-world case studies support these findings:

- One agency reported a 30-day campaign yielding **21 asphalt paving leads via Facebook Ads** (alongside 44 concrete leads) for a local contractor
- These leads helped generate **$32,000 in new jobs**
- Facebook's CPM (cost per thousand impressions) for home improvement typically ranges from **$10-20**, providing excellent reach on modest budgets

Facebook Ad Types for Paving Contractors

Facebook offers several ad formats particularly effective for paving companies:

1. Reach and Awareness Ads Reach ads are designed to show your ad to as many people in your target audience as possible, making them ideal for building local awareness of your paving company.

Best practices for paving reach campaigns:

- Target a 5-15 mile radius around your service area
- Use frequency capping (limit impressions to 2-3 per user per week)
- Showcase a variety of projects to appeal to different property types
- Include your service area in the ad copy
- Emphasize what makes your paving company unique

Example campaign structure:

- Objective: Reach
- Budget: $300-500/month
- Targeting: Homeowners within 10 miles of your location
- Ad content: Carousel of before/after transformations
- Call to action: "Learn More"

Example ad copy:

Is your driveway telling your neighbors you don't care about curb appeal? At [Company Name], we've transformed over 1,500 driveways in [City] with professional asphalt paving that lasts. ✓ Free estimates ✓ 5-year warranty ✓ Financing available ✓ Serving [Your Service Area] since [Year]

See what your neighbors are saying about us → [Learn More]

Reach campaigns typically achieve a CPM (cost per thousand impressions) of $10-15, making them an efficient way to build brand recognition in your local market.

2. Traffic and Conversion Ads Traffic campaigns direct users to your website with the goal of generating quote requests or calls. These campaigns work well for paving companies with strong website conversion pathways.

Best practices for paving traffic campaigns:

- Create dedicated landing pages for specific services (driveways, parking lots, etc.)
- Include testimonials and project photos on landing pages
- Add conversion tracking for form completions and phone calls
- Test different ad creative formats (single image, carousel, video)

- Use persuasive calls-to-action ("Get Your Free Estimate Today")

Example campaign structure:

- Objective: Traffic or Conversions
- Budget: $500-1,000/month
- Targeting: Homeowners with interest in home improvement
- Ad content: Video showing paving process with professional results
- Call to action: "Request a Quote"

Example ad copy:

WATCH: A Crumbling Driveway Transformed in Just 8 Hours

Your driveway is the first thing visitors see. Is yours making the right impression? Our [City] paving crews can transform your property in just one day with premium asphalt that resists cracking, fading, and weather damage. Summer special: 15% off all residential driveway projects booked this month. → Click to see how we can transform your property

According to our research, paving contractors typically see traffic campaign CPCs around $1.50-2.50 and landing page conversion rates of 3-8% when targeting well-qualified audiences.

3. Lead Generation Ads Lead ads allow users to submit their contact information directly within Facebook, eliminating the need to visit your website. This frictionless process often results in higher conversion rates for paving companies.

Best practices for paving lead generation campaigns:

- Keep form fields minimal (name, phone, email, project type)
- Pre-qualify leads with a "project timing" question
- Include a privacy statement to build trust

- Set up immediate notifications for new leads
- Create a follow-up process for lead responses

Example campaign structure:

- Objective: Lead Generation
- Budget: $500-1,000/month
- Targeting: Homeowners in specific neighborhoods, age 35-65
- Ad content: Before/after transformation with testimonial
- Form questions: Name, phone, email, project type, timeframe

Example ad copy:

"We should have done this years ago!"

- The Johnsons, [Neighborhood]

Stop patching that old driveway. Our [City] paving team can give you a beautiful, durable asphalt surface that enhances your home's value and curb appeal. ✓ Free no-obligation quotes ✓ Professional installation ✓ Premium materials with 5-year warranty ✓ Financing options available

⭑ Fill out this quick form for your custom estimate ⭑

Form questions:

- Full Name
- Phone Number
- Email Address
- What type of project are you interested in?
- Residential driveway

- Commercial parking lot
- Asphalt repair
- Sealcoating
- Other
- When are you looking to start this project?
- As soon as possible
- Within 1 month
- 1-3 months from now
- Just researching for now

Lead ads typically generate leads at $40-60 each for paving contractors, with higher quality leads coming from campaigns that include pre-qualification questions.

4. **Retargeting Campaigns** Retargeting shows ads to people who have previously visited your website or interacted with your business, making them highly effective for converting interested prospects.

Best practices for paving retargeting campaigns:

- Create separate campaigns for different website sections (driveways, commercial, etc.)
- Use a compelling offer for retargeting ads ("Limited Fall Discount")
- Set frequency caps to prevent ad fatigue (max 3-4 impressions per day)
- Exclude recent conversions from targeting
- Use a stronger call-to-action than awareness ads

Example campaign structure:

- Objective: Conversions
- Budget: $200-400/month
- Targeting: Website visitors in the past 30-60 days

- Ad content: Specific service they viewed with special offer * Call to action: "Get Your Quote"

Example ad copy:

Still thinking about that new driveway? We noticed you were exploring our paving services recently. Have any questions we can answer? For this week only, mention this ad for $200 off your project. Our schedule is filling up for the season - secure your spot now. → Get Your Free Estimate

Retargeting campaigns typically achieve 2-3x higher conversion rates than cold traffic campaigns, making them one of the most cost-effective advertising options for paving contractors.

5. Custom Audience Targeting Custom Audiences allow you to reach existing customers or leads with tailored messaging, creating opportunities for upsells, referrals, and reactivation.

How to leverage Custom Audiences:

- **Upload Customer Lists**
- Export contacts from your CRM or customer database
- Segment by service type, project value, or recency * Create separate audiences for past customers vs. unconverted leads
- **Target Similar Audiences**
- Create Lookalike Audiences based on your best customers
- Use 1% lookalikes for highest similarity
- Target homeowners similar to your highest-value clients
- **Sequential Messaging**
- Show different ad content based on previous engagement
- Progress prospects through awareness to consideration to decision
- Increase offer value for highly engaged non-converters

Example customer list campaign:

- Upload list of past sealcoating customers from 2-3 years ago
- Create campaign promoting maintenance services
- Target this specific audience with messaging about protecting their investment
- Include special "returning customer" offer

Example ad copy for past customers:

[First Name], your driveway needs protection!

It's been 2 years since we sealcoated your driveway at [Address]. To maintain its appearance and prevent costly repairs, experts recommend resealing every 2-3 years. As a valued customer, we're offering 20% off sealcoating services this month. → Schedule Your Maintenance Service

Custom audience campaigns typically produce the lowest cost per lead of any Facebook advertising approach, often 30-40% lower than cold targeting, with CPLs as low as $25-35 for paving contractors.

Content Strategy for Social Media Success

For paving companies, the right content strategy can transform social media from a time-waster to a lead generator. Here's a framework for effective content:

Types of Content That Work for Paving Companies

Before/After Project Showcases (Highest Performing)

- Photos showing dramatic transformations
- Include brief descriptions of the project scope and materials used

- Tag the location to enhance local relevance
- Example: "Completed this driveway resurfacing in Cedar Hills neighborhood today. Transformed a cracked, 15-year-old asphalt driveway into a smooth, sealed surface that will last for years."

Process Videos

- Time-lapse videos of projects from start to finish
- Explain the steps involved in professional paving
- Showcase your equipment and team expertise
- Example: "Watch our crew transform this commercial parking lot in just 48 hours. From milling the old surface to applying the final striping, here's the entire process condensed to 60 seconds."

Educational Content

- Signs it's time to repave your driveway
- How to maintain asphalt in different seasons
- Different material options and their benefits
- Cost factors that influence paving projects
- Example: "Winter can be harsh on asphalt. Here are 5 signs of winter damage to look for on your driveway this spring, and what you should do about each one."

Customer Testimonials

- Video testimonials from satisfied customers
- Featured reviews with photos of completed work
- "Customer of the Month" spotlights
- Example: "Hear what the Johnson family had to say about their new driveway installation and why they chose [Your Company] over other local contractors."

Team and Company Culture

- Introduce crew members and their expertise
- Share company milestones and celebrations
- Show community involvement and charitable work
- Example: "Congratulations to Mike on 10 years with our paving crew! His attention to detail has helped us deliver perfect driveways to over 1,000 happy customers."

Seasonal Content

- Spring maintenance tips
- Winter preparation advice
- Summer heat warnings and care instructions
- Fall cleanup recommendations
- Example: "Fall is the perfect time to sealcoat your asphalt before winter weather arrives. Here's why protecting your pavement now can save you thousands in repairs later."

Content Mix Ratio: The 80/20 Rule

Follow the 80/20 rule for your content mix:

- **80% informational, educational, and entertaining content**
- **20% promotional content** (special offers, direct calls to action)

This balance keeps your audience engaged without feeling constantly sold to. When you do promote, your audience will be more receptive because you've provided value with your other content.

Good
Company Logo, even better if you are a well known brand

Good
Mary Thompson
President
Mr. Rooter

Bad
Glad you like shaggy, and maybe it's your knick name. But it's not relevant to your business

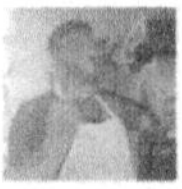

Very Bad
Drinking a beer while giving the middle finger, unbelievably common, but a poor choice

Don't be like our bad examples, "Shaggy" or the "drunk contractor." Don't put a picture of yourself in a T-shirt with a beard grown out. Be professional. Represent yourself as an important part of the business. Stick with the examples on the left — the logo and/or the professional head shot, as opposed to Shaggy or a weekend photo of you doing something crude and lascivious.

It's all about branding, so make sure that you're leveraging the header graphic and the image icon. If there is an option for you to customize the background, do it! You want to make sure that your elements marry up with the overall branding of your business. Make sure everything on your social media profiles is consistent with your website. On your website, you've got a color scheme, a logo, and maybe you have printed brochures. Be sure to keep a consistent flow, look, feel, and color scheme on all your social media profiles, website, and offline materials.

Community Engagement Tactics

Social media is about conversation, not just broadcasting. Here are tactics to foster engagement:

Local Community Engagement

Join and Participate in Local Facebook Groups

- Most communities have "Residents of [Town]" or similar groups
- Answer questions about paving without being salesy
- Share expertise when relevant topics arise

Engage with Local Businesses

- Follow and interact with other local businesses
- Cross-promote with complementary services (landscapers, home builders)
- Tag relevant local organizations in appropriate posts

Highlight Local Projects

- Showcase work in recognizable neighborhoods
- Tag local landmarks when working on commercial projects
- Create location-specific content that resonates with locals

Audience Building Techniques

Email Integration for Initial Following

- Send emails to past customers inviting them to follow your social pages
- Offer exclusive social-only promotions to incentivize following
- Include social handles on all customer communications

Referral and Sharing Incentives

- Run contests encouraging shares and tags

- Offer discounts for clients who share your content with friends
- Create "tag a neighbor who needs a new driveway" posts

Engage with Every Comment

- Respond promptly to all comments, questions, and messages
- Thank people for positive feedback
- Address concerns professionally and publicly

Use Engaging Questions

- "What's the worst driveway issue you've experienced?"
- "Which finish do you prefer for asphalt driveways? Smooth or textured?"
- "Can you guess how many tons of asphalt went into this parking lot?"

Proven Engagement Formats

"Ugliest Driveway Contest"

- Encourage followers to share photos of deteriorated driveways
- Offer a discount or free sealcoating as a prize
- Showcase the transformation when complete

Day-in-the-Life Content

- Give followers a behind-the-scenes look at your operation
- Show specialized equipment in action
- Highlight the skill and precision of your crew

Polls and Questions

- "What's your biggest concern about getting your driveway paved?"

- "How old is your current driveway or parking lot?"
- "Which project should we feature next: residential or commercial?"

Posting Schedules and Content Calendars

Consistency is key to social media success. Here's a framework for maintaining an effective posting schedule:

Optimal Posting Frequency

- **Facebook**: 3-5 times per week
- **Instagram**: 2-3 times per week, with additional Stories
- **LinkedIn**: 2-3 times per week (for B2B-focused companies)
- **YouTube**: 1-2 videos per month
- **TikTok**: 3-5 times per week (if using the platform)
- **X**: 2-3 times per week

Sample Weekly Content Calendar

Day	Content Type	Example
Monday	Educational	"Monday Maintenance Tip: How to spot early signs of driveway deterioration"
Tuesday	Project Showcase	Before/After transformation of recent project
Wednesday	Team Spotlight	Feature a crew member or behind-the-scenes look
Thursday	Customer Testimonial	Share a recent review with project photos
Friday	Weekend Special	Limited-time promotion or availability alert

Seasonal Content Planning

Align your content with the paving season and customer decision-making cycle:

- **Early Spring**: Educational content about winter damage, free estimate promotions
- **Late Spring/Summer**: Project showcases, capacity updates, maintenance tips
- **Fall**: Sealcoating promotion, winter preparation advice
- **Winter**: Planning content, early-bird specials for spring projects

Content Creation Efficiency Tips

Batch Creation

- Take photos and videos of multiple projects at once
- Write several posts in one sitting
- Schedule content in advance using scheduling tools

Repurpose Content

- Turn one before/after project into multiple posts with different angles
- Create Instagram posts from Facebook content
- Pull quotes from testimonials for standalone graphics

Delegate Responsibilities

- Assign crew members to take project photos
- Have office staff schedule and monitor social media
- Consider hiring a part-time social media coordinator

Managing Negative Comments

Every business occasionally faces negative feedback online. How you handle it can significantly impact your reputation.

Types of Negative Comments

Legitimate Customer Complaints

- Address these with the highest priority
- Take responsibility and offer solutions
- Follow up to ensure resolution

Misunderstandings

- Clarify information without being defensive
- Provide additional context or explanation
- Offer to discuss further privately

Trolls/Spam

- These are not legitimate engagement
- Can usually be hidden or removed
- Don't engage in arguments

Best Practices for Response

Respond Quickly

- Aim to reply within 1-2 hours during business hours
- Never let negative comments sit unaddressed for over 24 hours

Stay Professional

- Never argue or get defensive
- Maintain brand voice even when criticized
- Thank people for feedback, even negative

Take the Conversation Private

- Acknowledge publicly, then move to direct messages
- "Thank you for bringing this to our attention. We'd like to learn more about your experience. Please message us directly or call our office at [number]."

Follow Up Publicly

- Once resolved, follow up on the original thread
- “We’re glad we could resolve your concerns about the project timeline. Thank you for giving us the opportunity to make things right.”

Learn and Improve

- Use negative feedback to improve operations
- Update policies or training if the same issues recur

What NOT to Do

- Delete legitimate negative comments (this often escalates the situation)
- Argue with customers in comment sections
- Respond emotionally or defensively
- Ignore criticism, especially when valid
- Make excuses instead of offering solutions

Do’s and Don’ts of Social Media Marketing

Do’s:

Do Be Consistent

- Maintain regular posting schedules
- Keep branding consistent across platforms
- Respond to messages and comments promptly

Do Show Real Projects

- Feature actual work your company has completed
- Include before/after photos with permission
- Showcase the real people behind your company

Do Engage Authentically

- Respond to comments with personalized replies
- Ask questions to encourage interaction
- Thank customers who mention or tag your business

Do Provide Value

- Share helpful maintenance tips
- Educate followers about paving materials and processes
- Answer common questions about paving projects

Do Track Results

- Monitor which content performs best
- Track leads generated from social media
- Measure ROI from social media efforts

Don'ts:

Don't Post Only Promotional Content

- Avoid constant sales pitches
- Balance promotional posts with educational and engaging content
- Follow the 80/20 rule (80% informational, 20% promotional)

Don't Ignore Negative Feedback

- Address complaints publicly and professionally
- Never delete legitimate criticism
- Use negative feedback as an opportunity to demonstrate customer service

Don’t Post Low-Quality Media

- Avoid blurry or poorly lit photos
- Never use stock photos as your own work
- Ensure videos are stable and clearly show the work

Don’t Get Political or Controversial

- Keep business social accounts focused on business
- Avoid divisive topics that could alienate potential customers
- Maintain professionalism in all communications

Don’t Neglect Platform-Specific Best Practices

- Understand image sizing for each platform
- Use appropriate hashtags for each network
- Adapt content format to platform expectations

Conclusion: Building a Sustainable Social Media Presence

Social media marketing for paving companies isn’t about viral content or millions of followers. It’s about consistently showcasing your work, engaging with your local community, and leveraging both organic and paid strategies to generate qualified leads.

By selecting the right platforms, creating valuable content, implementing targeted advertising, and measuring your results, you can build a social media presence that drives real business growth.

Remember that social media is ultimately about relationships—with past customers, potential clients, and your local community. Focus on providing genuine value and building those connections, and the leads will follow.

The most successful paving companies on social media aren't necessarily the ones with the largest following—they're the ones who effectively convert that following into paying customers and brand advocates.

II

Part Two

Now we move into more advanced topics outside the "usual" digital marketing approach.

7

Email Marketing

Email marketing remains one of the most powerful and cost-effective tools in a paving company's marketing arsenal. While social media and paid ads often get more attention, email marketing consistently delivers the highest return on investment of any digital marketing channel.

Ever since there's been email, there's been email marketing. Email marketing is one of the oldest forms of advertising your business on the Internet. Although it gets a bad rap because of all the spam going around, it's still one of the most effective forms of marketing.

I am a big believer in email marketing. It's a powerful way to get instant traffic to your website and getting the telephone to ring, but there is a right way and a wrong way to use it.

Did you know the easiest customer to sell to is the customer you already have? Every self-proclaimed marketing expert will tell you that's nothing new. With that said, many paving business owners hardly ever market or keep in touch with their existing client base. Companies will spend thousands of dollars trying to get new customers but never think to market to the clients who already buy from them.

Why is that? I have a lot of ideas about this. I suspect business owners think that once a customer buys from them, they will just keep coming back on their own. Or maybe they simply don't want to bother their customers. The truth is customers want to hear from you and they want to be touched by your business. If you don't, your competition will.

The Power of Email for Paving Companies

The numbers speak for themselves when it comes to email marketing effectiveness:

For every $1 spent on email marketing, the average return is about **$40** in revenue. That's a 4,000% ROI—far exceeding what you'll typically achieve with other marketing channels.

- **60% of consumers make a purchase within a month of receiving a marketing email** from a business they know.
- Businesses that stay in touch with their ideal customers via email generate **50% more sales-ready leads and spend 33% less on sales** on average.
- Studies show that **email marketing delivers an ROI that's 40 times higher than Facebook and Twitter combined**.

For paving companies specifically, email marketing is especially valuable because:

- **Long buying cycles**: Most paving jobs are significant investments that customers research before committing. Email helps you stay top-of-mind during their consideration period.
- **Seasonal business**: Email allows you to reach out at optimal times for maintenance and new projects based on weather patterns in your area.
- **Repeat business opportunities**: From initial paving to sealcoating,

crack repair, and eventual replacement, each customer has multiple lifetime service needs.

- **High customer value**: The average paving job is worth thousands of dollars, making the investment in email marketing minuscule compared to the potential return.
- **Referral potential**: Satisfied paving customers often know other property owners who may need similar services.

How Do We Start an Email Marketing Campaign?

The first thing you need is an email marketing service. You shouldn't do this yourself for several reasons:

- Your Internet Service Provider (ISP) will blacklist you for sending bulk mail.
- You would have no stats for tracking your open emails.
- It would look unprofessional coming from your Microsoft Outlook box.

With that said, let's take a look at some of the popular email marketing services, all of which are paid services and are priced based on the amount of emails you send.

Email Marketing Service Providers

There are many email service providers to choose from, but here are the ones we recommend for paving companies:

Constant Contact I have used Constant Contact in the past and I like it for several reasons. It has great tracking stats, the ability to post to your social networks and a relatively user-friendly interface. Constant Contact has many templates available for use. You can also add your own custom templates. I think custom templates are a MUST for any business wanting to promote their brand. You will have to know a bit of HTML but if you don't, you can have a web designer create one for you at a fairly inexpensive cost.

Key features:

- Easy-to-use drag-and-drop editor
- Industry-specific templates (including contractor templates)
- List management and segmentation tools
- Automated email series
- Social sharing capabilities
- Detailed reporting

Ideal for: Paving companies that want a straightforward, reliable platform with good customer support.

Mailchimp Mailchimp is another service I have personally used and recommend. It's relatively easy to use and offers similar features to Constant Contact. The interface is clean and easy to use.

Key features:

- Free plan for up to 2,000 contacts (with limited features)
- Behavioral targeting
- A/B testing capabilities
- Landing page creation
- Customer journey mapping
- Integration with many other platforms

Ideal for: Paving companies just starting with email marketing or those with tight budgets.

Revenue Commander Email Capabilities For our clients, we offer comprehensive email marketing capabilities through our Revenue Commander platform. This tightly integrated system allows you to manage your email marketing alongside your other digital marketing efforts, with specific features designed for paving contractors:

Key features:

- Customer database integration with your CRM
- Automated campaign sequences based on customer behavior
- Pre-designed templates for paving companies
- Segmentation based on service history and property type
- Performance tracking and ROI calculation
- A/B testing of subject lines and content

The platform connects your email marketing with your other marketing channels, creating a unified customer experience and centralized data tracking.

I think all of these services are a good solution for any business looking to add email marketing to its Internet marketing strategy.

Building Your Email List

I am asked on a regular basis about how to get email addresses. It's not as easy as sending a letter in the USPS mail to anyone you want to. The reality of it is that just because they are your customer and you have their email address doesn't mean you can send them anything if you don't have their permission. This certainly is a fine line, because you somehow already have their email address, and they have used your services before, so is it really considered spam? Technically, yes. You didn't ask them if you could send them specials or a newsletter in email form.

Permission-Based List Building

The first thing you really want to do is get your clients' permission to add them to your email list. There are a variety of ways to do this, including placing a form on your website, putting a sign-up sheet on your counter or even a putting a space on your job ticket that they sign when you complete your service. Explain that you send out tips about your industry or specials on a monthly basis and would love to have them on your mailing list. You might even offer a discount coupon off your services if they sign up. Getting that email address is valuable, so if it cost you 5%, go for it. Remember, you want the opportunity to have your company's name in front of your customers every single month. You want to remain top-of-mind if one of their friends is looking for services like yours or if they run into an emergency.

Effective List-Building Strategies

Here are proven methods to build your email list organically:

1. **Capture During Project Lifecycle** Every customer interaction is an opportunity to build your list:

- **Pre-project consultations**: Include email field on assessment forms
- **Quote/estimate requests**: Make email a required field, with clear opt-in language
- **Contract signing**: Include an opt-in checkbox for "maintenance tips and special offers"
- **Project completion**: Have a "stay in touch" card that outlines benefits of joining your email list

Always frame email subscription as a benefit to the customer—exclusive offers, maintenance reminders, warranty information, etc.

2. Website Opt-in Opportunities Your website should have multiple email capture points:

- **Homepage banner**: Prominent signup form offering a lead magnet (like "7 Ways to Extend Your Driveway's Life")
- **Pop-up for exit intent**: Appears when someone is about to leave your site
- **Service pages**: Specific offers related to each service (e.g., "Driveway Maintenance Calendar" on your residential paving page)
- **Contact form**: Include an opt-in checkbox
- **Blog posts**: Inline signup forms within relevant content

3. Offline Collection Methods Don't forget traditional methods:

- **Business cards**: Include a QR code linking to your signup form
- **Printed materials**: Add a text code system (e.g., "Text PAVING to 12345 to join our list")
- **Job site signage**: QR codes or text-to-join options
- **Local events**: Tablet-based signup at community events, home shows, etc.
- **Referral incentives**: "Refer a friend and you both get $X off your next service"

I had a pest control service provider come to my home several years ago. He did a good job and was very professional. Four or five years later, I needed the services of the company again. I lost his business card and could not remember the name of the company. I had to find another pest removal service. He lost the business because he never stayed in contact with me. It was a big job that he lost, $1,500.00 to be exact. Start building your list today.

Email Marketing Content Strategy

First, what do I send? You must use the **80/20 rule, 80 percent good information and 20 percent sales.** If all you send is emails about what services you offer, no one will ever read it. It's a great way to kill your list.

Draft up some information about your industry, give good homeowner tips, throw in some DIY tips, and make sure it's information that will help your customers. For the 20% sales, add a coupon or a special you are having, or offer something for your customers' friends and family.

Types of Email Campaigns for Paving Companies

Different types of emails serve different purposes in your overall strategy. Here are the most effective campaign types for paving contractors:

1. **Welcome Sequence** New subscribers should receive an automated series of welcome emails:

Email 1: Immediate Welcome

- Thank them for subscribing
- Set expectations (what they'll receive and how often)
- Provide immediate value (useful tip or resource)
- Introduce your company briefly

Email 2: Education (2-3 days later)

- Share information about different paving materials
- Include photos of different finishes and styles
- Position your company as an expert

Email 3: Social Proof (5-7 days later)

- Share customer testimonials and before/after photos
- Include any awards or certifications
- Highlight your team's experience

Email 4: Offer (10-14 days later)

- Present a limited-time special offer
- Create urgency with a clear deadline
- Make it easy to respond (clear call-to-action)

2. Seasonal Maintenance Reminders Paving is inherently seasonal in many regions. Use these email campaigns to educate customers and generate off-season work:

Spring (March-April)

- Winter damage assessment recommendations
- Early booking incentives before peak season
- Pothole and crack repair promotions

Summer (June-August)

- New installation promotions during prime weather
- Community project spotlights
- Heat-related maintenance tips

Fall (September-October)

- Sealcoating before winter promotions
- Pre-winter maintenance checklists
- End-of-season discounts

Winter (November-February)

- Planning and budget guides for spring projects
- Early-bird specials for next season
- Indoor concrete work promotions (for relevant businesses)

3. Educational Content Series Position yourself as an expert by sharing valuable information:

- "Understanding Asphalt vs. Concrete: Which is Right for Your Property?"
- "How to Spot Early Signs of Driveway Deterioration"
- "The Real Cost of Delaying Pavement Maintenance"
- "Commercial Parking Lot ADA Compliance Guide"
- "How Weather Affects Your Paving Project: Planning Guide"

These educational emails should be minimally promotional and focus primarily on delivering valuable information that helps property owners make informed decisions.

4. Customer Retention Campaigns Nurture existing customers to encourage repeat business:

- Annual maintenance reminders based on their last service date
- Service anniversary recognition ("Your driveway is turning 3 this month!")
- Customer loyalty rewards
- Referral requests and incentives
- Feedback requests with improvement focus

5. Commercial Client Campaigns For B2B paving companies, create separate campaigns for commercial property managers:

- Budget planning guides for fiscal year maintenance
- Parking lot liability prevention tips

- Traffic flow optimization ideas
- Case studies of similar commercial projects
- Multi-property maintenance package options

Email Content Ideas

What should you actually write about in these emails? Here are specific content ideas that work well for paving companies:

Educational Topics

- Signs your driveway needs replacement vs. resurfacing
- How to prevent water damage to your pavement
- The importance of proper drainage for pavement longevity
- Understanding the sealcoating process and benefits
- How to remove oil stains from your driveway
- Winter maintenance tips to prevent damage
- Commercial parking lot compliance requirements
- Proper snow removal techniques to protect pavement

Before & After Showcases

- Dramatic transformations of deteriorated driveways
- Commercial parking lot renovations
- Decorative concrete installations
- Pothole and major repair projects
- Property value enhancement projects

Company Updates

- New equipment or technology you've added
- Team member spotlights
- Certifications or training achievements

- Community involvement and events
- Awards or recognition

Seasonal Information

- Spring damage assessment guide
- Summer heat precautions for new asphalt
- Fall winterization checklist
- Winter damage prevention tips

How Often to Send Emails

How often you send your emails is very important. I always go with once per month, around the same time every month. It is important to commit to a date. More than once a month is too much and annoys people. I get an email from a company I purchased from in the past and get 3-4 emails a week from them, 100% sales, sometimes several times a day. I HATE IT and it drives me nuts. I removed myself from that list very quickly as I'm sure others have as well.

While monthly is a good starting point, your optimal frequency may differ based on your specific audience and content. Here are some guidelines:

Email Frequency Guidelines

Minimum recommended frequency: Once per month

- Maintains top-of-mind awareness
- Provides seasonal relevance
- Doesn't overwhelm subscribers

For active sales periods: Twice monthly

- Extra email during peak seasonal demand
- Special promotion announcements
- Limited-time offer follow-ups

For educational sequences: Weekly for a limited period

- 4-6 week educational series on specific topic
- Return to normal frequency afterward
- Always set proper expectations with subscribers

For commercial clients: Monthly or bi-monthly

- Focuses on longer-term planning
- Respects busy schedules of property managers
- More in-depth, valuable content

The right frequency balances staying visible without becoming annoying. Pay close attention to your open rates and unsubscribe rates to gauge if you're hitting the right balance.

Email Design Best Practices

Your email design significantly impacts engagement and conversion rates. Follow these best practices for paving company emails:

Visual Elements

Before/After Photography: The single most powerful visual element for paving companies is high-quality before/after project photography. This immediately demonstrates your value proposition and quality of work.

Tips for effective project photos:

- Use consistent angles and lighting for fair comparison
- Include close-ups of problem areas in "before" shots
- Show the completed project from multiple angles
- Use real projects, not stock photos

Mobile-First Design: Over 60% of emails are now opened on mobile devices. Ensure your emails look great on smartphones:

- Single-column layouts work best
- Minimum 16px font size for body text
- Large, tap-friendly buttons (minimum 44x44 pixels)
- Properly sized images that don't require horizontal scrolling

Branded Elements: Maintain consistent branding across all emails:

- Same header design with logo
- Consistent color scheme matching your website
- Standardized fonts and button styles
- Professional footer with complete contact information and physical address

Content Structure

Subject Lines: The subject line determines whether your email gets opened. Effective subject lines for paving companies:

- Highlight a specific value ("Increase Your Property Value with Professional Paving")
- Create urgency when appropriate ("Last Chance: Schedule Before Winter Weather")
- Ask engaging questions ("Is Your Driveway Hurting Your Curb Appeal?")
- Keep under 50 characters when possible

- Avoid EXCESSIVE CAPS or multiple exclamation points!!!

Preview Text: The preview text (snippet that appears after the subject line in most email clients) is often overlooked:

- Complement your subject line rather than repeating it
- Provide additional motivation to open
- Keep under 100 characters
- Test different approaches

Body Content: Structure your email content for easy scanning:

- Begin with a personalized greeting when possible
- Lead with your most important message
- Use short paragraphs (2-3 sentences maximum)
- Include subheadings for longer content
- Utilize bullet points for key benefits
- Incorporate white space for readability

Call-to-Action (CTA): Every email should have a clear, compelling call-to-action:

- Use button-style CTAs rather than text links
- Make the desired action absolutely clear ("Schedule Free Estimate")
- Create contrast with surrounding elements
- Limit to one primary CTA per email
- Consider secondary CTAs for additional options
- Place primary CTA above the fold

Technical Considerations

Load Time Optimization: Slow-loading emails frustrate subscribers and decrease engagement:

- Compress images appropriately
- Avoid excessive HTML or complex coding
- Test load time before sending

Deliverability: Ensure your emails actually reach the inbox:

- Use a reputable email service provider
- Maintain proper sender authentication (SPF, DKIM)
- Keep HTML-to-text ratio balanced
- Avoid spam trigger words and phrases
- Maintain list hygiene by removing inactive subscribers

Get Legal

Make sure you have allowed customers the option to Opt Out of receiving email messages at the bottom of every message. Make sure that it's easy because nothing is more annoying than receiving emails that you don't want. If someone does not want to receive your messages, then remove them from your list. They may be getting emails from too many sources and just want to clean out their email box. It does not mean they will never buy from you again. But I will tell you this, if they want out and you keep sending email to them, it's a sure-fire way to bother them and they will likely never buy from you again.

Email Legal Requirements

All commercial email must comply with the **CAN-SPAM Act**, which establishes requirements for commercial messages and gives recipients the right to opt out. Here are the key requirements:

Clear identification

- Your company name must be clearly identified
- Include your physical mailing address in every email
- Provide a valid reply-to email address

Honest subject lines

- Subject lines must accurately reflect email content
- Avoid deceptive or misleading subject lines

Obvious commercial nature

- Clearly indicate the message is an advertisement if applicable
- Be transparent about promotional content

Visible unsubscribe option

- Include a clear and conspicuous way to opt out
- Make unsubscribe process simple (one-click is ideal)
- Honor opt-out requests promptly (within 10 business days)
- Don't charge a fee or require anything beyond email address to unsubscribe

Permission compliance

- Only send to people who have given permission

- Maintain records of how and when permission was granted
- Never harvest email addresses or buy lists

Failure to comply with these regulations can result in penalties up to $43,792 per email. Beyond legal requirements, following these best practices builds trust with your audience and improves overall campaign performance.

What is the Best Time to Send an Email Campaign?

These general email send time tips are widely accepted by the email marketing community. They are great when you're starting off, but be sure to read on and see why they won't always work.

- **Day-time vs. Night-time.** While this one may be obvious, it's usually better to send out your email campaigns during the daytime. You know, when people are awake. Not asleep.
- **Mad Mondays.** The general consensus is that you should avoid sending out email blasts on Mondays. Why? People are already bummed out about the end of the weekend. They march into the office and are flooded with emails they've collected over the past few days. What's the first thing they do? Delete those emails of course!
- **Weekends.** Historically, weekends are the days when folks are out running errands and going on adventures. Weekends tend to have low open rates, so most marketers avoid them like the plague.
- **Fan Favorites: Tuesday, Wednesday, and Thursday.** Tuesday, Wednesday, and Thursday have traditionally been favorite days to send email campaigns, as email marketers seek to avoid the Monday angst and Friday's itchy feet. MailChimp confirms that Tuesday and Thursday are the two most popular days to send email newsletters.

Optimal Timing for Paving Emails

While these general guidelines are helpful, paving companies should consider these industry-specific timing factors:

For residential customers:

- Midweek evenings (6-8pm) often perform well as homeowners consider property improvements
- Saturday mornings can work well, contrary to general advice, as homeowners plan weekend projects
- Early spring timing (February-March) for maintenance education
- Early fall (September) for winterization information

For commercial clients:

- Tuesday-Thursday mornings (9-11am) typically see highest engagement
- First week of a new quarter when budgets are being planned
- Send budget-related information 1-2 months before typical fiscal year planning

The best way to determine optimal timing for your specific audience is to test different times and days, then analyze the results. Most email platforms allow you to segment your list and test different sending times to identify what works best for your unique audience.

Measuring Email Marketing Performance

To optimize your email marketing efforts, you need to track key performance metrics:

Essential Email Metrics

Open Rate: The percentage of recipients who open your email.

- Industry average for construction/contractors: 18–23%
- Low open rates often indicate weak subject lines or poor list quality
- Test different subject lines to improve open rates

Click-Through Rate (CTR): The percentage of email recipients who clicked on one or more links in your email.

- Industry average for construction/contractors: 2.5–4%
- Low CTR suggests content isn't compelling or CTAs aren't clear
- Test different content approaches and CTAs to improve

Conversion Rate: The percentage of email recipients who clicked on a link and completed a desired action (like requesting a quote).

- Goal for paving companies: 0.5–2% of total recipients
- Track using UTM parameters and website analytics
- Measures ultimate effectiveness of your email marketing

Unsubscribe Rate: The percentage of recipients who opt out of your emails after opening.

- Industry average: Below 0.5%
- Spike in unsubscribes indicates content mismatch or excessive frequency
- Monitor closely after changing content approach or frequency

List Growth Rate: The rate at which your email list is growing.

- Healthy rate: 3–5% monthly

- Calculate: (New subscribers - Unsubscribes) ÷ Total list size
- Indicates overall program health and acquisition effectiveness

Using Data to Improve Performance

Here's how to use these metrics to continuously improve your campaigns:

Establish baselines

- Track your metrics for 3-6 months to establish your own benchmarks
- Compare against industry averages for context
- Set realistic improvement goals based on your starting point

Test systematically

- Test one element at a time to identify impact
- A/B test subject lines with 10-20% of your list
- Send winner to remaining subscribers
- Document what works for future campaigns

Segment for relevance

- Divide subscribers based on service history
- Create separate content for residential vs. commercial
- Target by geographic area for location-specific offers
- Engagement-based segments (active vs. inactive)

Analyze engagement patterns

- Identify which topics generate highest engagement
- Note which days and times perform best for your audience
- Track seasonal variations in engagement
- Connect email engagement to actual sales

Practical Email Marketing Implementation

Here's a step-by-step approach to implementing email marketing for your paving company:

1. Start With the Basics Begin with these fundamental campaigns:

- **Welcome series** for new subscribers or customers
- **Post-project follow-up** emails to request reviews and referrals
- **Monthly newsletter** with seasonal tips and project showcases
- **Annual service reminder** based on previous work date

2. Develop a Sustainable Schedule Create a realistic email calendar based on your resources:

Minimum viable approach (1-2 hours per week):

- Monthly newsletter (sent same day each month)
- Automated welcome sequence
- Automated post-project emails
- Quarterly promotional campaign

Intermediate approach (3-4 hours per week):

- Bi-weekly emails alternating between educational and promotional
- Segmented content for residential vs. commercial
- Regular A/B testing of subject lines
- Seasonal campaigns based on weather patterns

Advanced approach (dedicated marketing person):

- Weekly valuable content
- Highly segmented campaigns

- Sophisticated automation workflows
- Continuous testing and optimization

3. Create a Content Bank Develop a library of content you can use throughout the year:

- 12 seasonal maintenance tips (one per month)
- 10 before/after project showcases with descriptions
- 5 customer testimonials with photos
- 3-5 educational articles about paving materials and processes
- 4 seasonal promotional offers

This content bank lets you plan emails in advance and maintain consistent sending even during busy periods.

4. Implement List Growth Tactics Continuously build your subscriber base:

- Add email signup to all forms on your website
- Train crew to collect emails during jobs
- Create valuable lead magnets (downloadable guides)
- Run quarterly list-building promotions
- Regularly import customer emails from your CRM (with permission)

5. Analyze and Refine Establish a regular review process:

- Weekly check of basic metrics (opens, clicks)
- Monthly performance analysis and adjustment
- Quarterly strategy review
- Annual program assessment and planning

This systematic approach ensures continuous improvement over time.

Conclusion

Again, you want to leverage email marketing as part of your overall Internet marketing strategy. The best way to use it is to be sure you're collecting the email address from all your customers and prospects. From there, use email marketing to get online reviews, engagement on your social media accounts and remain top-of-mind as a strategy to get more repeat and referral business.

Email marketing has "stuck around so long" for one simple reason: it works. With an average return of $40 for every $1 spent, it's one of the most cost-effective marketing channels available to paving companies. When implemented correctly, email marketing helps you:

- **Maintain relationships** with past customers, keeping your company top-of-mind
- **Educate prospects** about paving options and maintenance requirements
- **Generate referrals** from satisfied customers
- **Fill schedule gaps** with timely promotions
- **Position your company as an expert** in the paving industry

The key to success is consistency—both in collecting email addresses and in sending valuable content. Whether you're just starting with a monthly newsletter or implementing sophisticated automated sequences, your email marketing program will build value over time, creating a vital asset for your business.

Remember that email marketing works best as part of an integrated strategy. Use it alongside your website, SEO efforts, paid advertising, and social media to create multiple touchpoints with prospects and customers. Each channel reinforces the others, creating a cohesive marketing ecosystem that drives sustainable growth for your paving company.

8

Cold Email Marketing

While email marketing to your existing customer database is essential, cold email outreach to potential customers can be a powerful lead generation tool for paving companies. Cold email marketing involves sending targeted emails to prospects who haven't previously engaged with your business. When executed correctly, it can open doors to new commercial opportunities and residential projects. However, cold email requires a different approach than marketing to your existing list. This chapter covers the essential strategies for creating a compliant, effective cold email campaign that generates quality paving leads.

Legal Compliance Requirements

Before launching any cold email campaign, you must understand and follow applicable laws. Non-compliance can result in significant penalties, damage to your reputation, and delivery problems.

CAN-SPAM Act Compliance

The CAN-SPAM Act is a U.S. law that sets rules for commercial email. Every email must comply with these requirements:

Don't use false or misleading header information

- Your "From," "To," and "Reply to" information must accurately identify your business.

Don't use deceptive subject lines

- Subject lines must accurately reflect email content. For example, don't use a subject line like "Your Invoice" when you're actually sending a sales pitch.

Identify the message as an advertisement

- Be transparent that you're reaching out with a commercial offer. You don't need to use the word "advertisement," but the commercial nature should be clear. For paving companies, this might be as simple as introducing yourself as a paving contractor in the first sentence.

Include your physical business address

- Every email must contain your current postal address. This can be a street address, post office box, or private mailbox registered with a commercial mail receiving agency. This is typically included in your email signature or footer.

Provide a clear way to opt out

- Include an obvious unsubscribe method in every email. This can be a link or simple reply instructions (e.g., "Reply with 'REMOVE' to unsubscribe"). Make this process simple—complex unsubscribe procedures can result in penalties.

Honor opt-out requests promptly

- Process opt-out requests within 10 business days. You cannot charge a fee, require additional information, or make the process complicated. Once someone has unsubscribed, that email address should be permanently removed from your cold outreach lists.

Monitor what others do on your behalf

- Even if you hire another company to handle your email marketing, you're legally responsible for compliance. Know what your marketing partners are doing on your behalf and ensure they follow all regulations.

Canada's Anti-Spam Legislation (CASL)

If you market to Canadian prospects, be aware that CASL is stricter than CAN-SPAM and requires:

Express or implied consent before sending messages

- This is the biggest difference from U.S. law. You need either express consent (direct permission) or implied consent, which can come from existing business relationships or publicly available contact information, but time limits apply. For example, if you find an email on a company's website, you may have implied consent to contact them about business matters related to their role.

Clear identification information

- Similar to CAN-SPAM, but with additional requirements for clearly identifying yourself and your business.

Simple unsubscribe mechanism

- Must remain active for at least 60 days after sending and be processed without delay.

The penalties for CASL violations can exceed $1 million for individuals and $10 million for businesses, making compliance critical. If you're targeting Canadian prospects, it's worth consulting with a legal expert familiar with CASL requirements.

European GDPR Considerations

If targeting European prospects, the General Data Protection Regulation (GDPR) imposes stricter requirements:

Lawful basis for processing data

- You need a legal basis such as consent or legitimate interest. B2B marketing may qualify under legitimate interest in some cases, particularly if you're contacting a business person about a service relevant to their professional role.

Right to be informed

- You must explain how you obtained their data and how you'll use it. Include a link to your privacy policy that details your data practices.

Right to object

- Recipients must be able to easily object to processing their data. Similar to unsubscribe requirements but broader in scope.

Best Practices for Compliance

To stay on the right side of these regulations:

Document your compliance measures

- Keep records of how contacts were sourced, document consent where applicable, and maintain unsubscribe records. This documentation can be crucial if your practices are ever questioned.

Include proper legal footers

- Use consistent, compliant footers in all emails that include all required elements (address, unsubscribe option, etc.). Consider having a legal professional review your email templates.

Use a reputable email service provider

- Many ESPs have built-in compliance tools that can help manage unsubscribes automatically and ensure your emails meet basic requirements.

Create a privacy policy

- Have a clear privacy policy on your website and link to it in your cold emails. This should explain how you collect and use data and outline recipients' rights regarding their information.

List Building and Verification

The quality of your email list directly impacts your campaign success. Here's how to build an effective list:

Target Audience Definition

Before collecting emails, clearly define who should receive your messages. For paving companies, potential targets include:

Commercial Prospects

- **Property managers** of office buildings, shopping centers, and apartments are often responsible for maintaining parking lots and access roads.
- **Facility managers** at industrial sites must ensure safe vehicle access for employees and deliveries.
- **HOA board members** make decisions about community roads and parking areas, while business owners with aging parking lots may be considering renovation.
- **General contractors** frequently need paving subcontractors for their projects.

Residential Prospects

- **Homeowners in specific neighborhoods** or subdivisions with aging infrastructure are prime targets.
- **Residents of older developments** with deteriorating driveways often need replacement or major repairs.
- **New construction homeowners** may need driveway installation once construction is complete.

Geographic Focus

- Stay within your **service radius** (typically 25-50 miles maximum) to ensure you can profitably service the leads you generate.
- Prioritize areas with **higher concentrations** of your ideal customers, such as business districts for commercial leads or upscale neighbor-

hoods for residential work.

- Consider **seasonal factors** for different regions you serve, as paving needs often fluctuate with weather patterns.

Ethical List Building Methods

There are several ways to build your cold email list ethically:

Public Records and Directories

- **Commercial property tax records** can identify owners of properties with parking lots. These records are typically available through county assessor offices and can reveal who owns commercial properties in your area.
- **Business directories and association memberships**, such as your local chamber of commerce, often provide member contact information.
- **Government procurement registries** list contacts for public works opportunities, which can be valuable for paving companies seeking municipal contracts.

LinkedIn Prospecting

- Search for relevant job titles like **Facility Manager, Property Manager, or Maintenance Director**.
- Join **industry groups** where potential clients participate, such as property management associations or commercial real estate networks.
- You can export connections (where permitted) who fit your criteria, though always respect LinkedIn's terms of service when doing so.

Data Providers and List Services

- **Industry-specific database providers** offer targeted lists of property managers and facility directors.

- **Commercial real estate databases** can identify recent property transactions that might trigger renovations or improvements.
- **List brokers** with property owner information can provide targeted lists, though you should verify their data collection practices meet legal requirements.

List Verification and Cleaning

Before sending emails, verify your list to reduce bounces and improve deliverability:

Email Verification Services

- Use tools like **NeverBounce, ZeroBounce, or BriteVerify** to identify invalid, toxic, or risky addresses. These services typically charge between $0.003-$0.01 per email verified, but the cost is justified by the improved deliverability and sender reputation they provide.

Manual Verification Steps

- Check for obvious errors like typos in domain names or formatting issues.
- Remove **role-based emails** (info@, admin@, etc.) as these rarely reach decision-makers and often have spam filters.
- Eliminate **duplicate entries** to avoid sending multiple messages to the same person.

Progressive Data Enhancement

- Add **company size, industry, and other relevant data points** to help personalize your outreach.
- Include **property information** where applicable, such as parking lot size or age if available.

- Note **potential pain points** like aging facilities or recent development that might create paving needs.

Segmentation for Targeting

- Divide your list by **prospect type and property characteristics** to allow for more personalized messaging.
- Group prospects by **estimated project value or potential need** so you can prioritize your outreach.
- Separate **decision-makers from influencers** to tailor your approach appropriately.

Data Management Best Practices

To maintain your list effectively over time:

Centralized Database

- Store all prospect information in your **CRM** to maintain a single source of truth.
- Track every touchpoint and response to build a **comprehensive history** for each contact.
- Maintain detailed contact histories so anyone on your team can see past interactions.

Regular List Maintenance

- Remove **hard bounces** immediately to maintain good sender reputation.
- **Update contact information** when notified of changes, such as when you receive an automated reply about a staff change.
- **Purge unresponsive contacts** after multiple attempts—if someone hasn't engaged after 4-5 emails, they're unlikely to convert.

Documentation of Data Sources

- Record **how and when** each contact was acquired to ensure compliance with regulations.
- Note any **existing relationships or connections** that might help with personalization.
- Track **consent** where applicable, especially for prospects in regions with stricter privacy laws.

Cold Email Templates for Paving Leads

Effective cold emails for paving companies need to be concise, valuable, and focused on customer needs. The templates below provide frameworks you can adapt to your specific situation.

Commercial Property Manager Approach

When reaching out to property managers, focus on maintenance issues and potential cost savings. Here's an effective template:

> **Subject Line:** [Property Name]'s Parking Lot - Quick Question
>
> Hi [First Name],
>
> I noticed while driving by [Property Name] that your parking lot is showing some early warning signs of deterioration (alligator cracking near the entrance and several potholes forming in the north section). These issues typically develop into more serious problems during the freeze/thaw cycles of winter, potentially creating liability concerns and more expensive repairs down the road.

> As the [Property Manager/Owner], you're probably focused on maintaining property value while controlling maintenance costs.
>
> Would you be open to a 15-minute discussion about cost-effective options to address these issues before they worsen? We've worked with several similar properties in [Location] and could provide some valuable insight whether you use our services or not.
>
> Best regards,
>
> [Your Name] [Your Company] [Phone Number] [Address]
>
> P.S. Here's a recent project we completed for [Similar Business] in [Location]: [Link to before/after photos]
>
> [Unsubscribe Option]

This approach works because it:

- Opens with a specific observation about their property (not a generic pitch)
- Identifies potential problems and consequences
- Addresses what matters to property managers (maintaining value while controlling costs)
- Offers value even if they don't hire you
- Includes social proof with a similar project

HOA Board Member Approach

Homeowners Associations often struggle with road and parking area maintenance. This template addresses their specific concerns:

> **Subject Line:** [Neighborhood Name] Road Maintenance Options
>
> Hi [First Name],
>
> As a board member for [HOA Name], you're likely concerned about maintaining the roads in your community while managing the association's budget responsibly. I recently drove through [Neighborhood Name] and noticed some developing issues with your community roads, particularly near [Specific Area].
>
> These types of problems typically worsen over time and can lead to more significant repair costs if not addressed.
>
> We've helped several HOAs in [Region] develop phased maintenance plans that spread costs over multiple budget years while addressing critical areas first. Would you be interested in receiving a complimentary assessment of your community roads with recommendations that could be presented at your next board meeting?
>
> Best regards,
>
> [Your Name] [Your Company] [Phone Number] [Address]

> P.S. Here's a testimonial from another HOA we worked with recently: [Brief testimonial quote]
>
> [Unsubscribe Option]

The strength of this template comes from understanding the HOA board's dual responsibility to maintain quality while managing member dues carefully. The offer of a phased approach acknowledges budget constraints, and the free assessment with board presentation materials adds immediate value.

General Contractor Partnership Template

Building relationships with general contractors can provide a steady stream of subcontract work:

Subject Line: Reliable Paving Subcontractor for Your Projects

> Hi [First Name],
>
> I see that [Company Name] has been awarded the contract for the new [Development Project] in [Location]. Congratulations on securing this project.
>
> As you finalize your subcontractor teams, I wanted to introduce our paving company as a potential partner for the parking and roadwork portions. We've worked with several general contractors including [Name if applicable] on similar projects and pride ourselves on:

> Meeting deadlines consistently (98% on-time completion rate) · Transparent pricing with no surprise change orders · Full compliance with all specifications and regulations · Dedicated project managers assigned to each job
>
> Do you have 10 minutes this week to discuss your upcoming paving needs and how we might be able to support your team?
>
> Regards,
>
> [Your Name] [Your Company] [Phone Number] [Address]
>
> [Unsubscribe Option]

This template works because it identifies a specific project the contractor is working on, demonstrates understanding of their needs, provides clear differentiators with specifics (not just vague claims), and asks for a small, specific next step.

Residential Neighborhood Campaign Template

When targeting homeowners, neighborhood-specific approaches with social proof are most effective:

> **Subject Line:** Driveway Restoration for [Neighborhood] Homes
>
> Hi [First Name],
>
> We recently completed a driveway replacement for your neighbor at [Nearby Address], and I noticed while in the area that several

> homes in [Neighborhood], including yours, were built around the same time. Asphalt driveways in [City] typically show significant wear after 15-20 years due to our climate conditions, and homes in your neighborhood are approaching that age range.
>
> We're offering a neighborhood discount for [Neighborhood] residents this season:
>
> 15% off when you and at least one neighbor book together • Complimentary sealcoating one year after installation • Extended 5-year workmanship warranty (our standard is 3 years)
>
> Would you be interested in a free assessment of your driveway's condition and a no-obligation estimate?
>
> Best regards,
>
> [Your Name] [Your Company] [Phone Number] [Address]
>
> P.S. You can see the before and after of your neighbor's driveway here: [Link to photos]
>
> [Unsubscribe Option]

This approach leverages social proof (work completed for a neighbor) and understanding of neighborhood-specific conditions. The group discount incentivizes word-of-mouth sharing and creates efficiency for your crew by clustering projects.

Key Elements of Effective Cold Emails

Regardless of which template you adapt, ensure your cold emails include these critical elements:

Personalization Beyond First Name

- Reference specific property details you've observed, like "cracking in the southwest corner of your parking lot" or "the uneven section of your driveway near the basketball hoop."
- Mention their exact neighborhood or business location to demonstrate local knowledge.
- Acknowledge their role or responsibilities to show you understand their specific challenges.

Value-First Approach

- Begin with an observation or insight relevant to them, not with your company history or capabilities.
- Offer educational content before pitching services, like maintenance tips or warning signs of pavement failure.
- Position yourself as an advisor, not just a vendor by sharing expertise whether they hire you or not.

Clear, Specific Call to Action

- Ask for a small, specific next step like a 15-minute call or quick property assessment.
- Make it easy to respond with a simple question or direct phone number.
- Give time parameters such as "this week" or "before the rainy season starts" to create gentle urgency.

Social Proof Elements

- Mention nearby projects to create relevance and establish local presence. Include brief, relevant testimonials that address common concerns.
- Reference similar clients you've helped to demonstrate experience with their specific type of property.

Follow-up Sequences

Most prospects won't respond to your first email. In fact, research shows that 80% of sales require at least five follow-ups, yet 44% of salespeople give up after just one attempt. A strategic follow-up sequence dramatically increases response rates.

Optimal Sequence Structure

An effective follow-up sequence maintains contact without becoming annoying. Here's a proven structure:

Initial Outreach

- Your value-focused email using templates above should focus on starting a conversation, not making a hard sell.
- Include a clear but low-pressure call to action that makes it easy for the prospect to engage.

Follow-up #1 (3 business days later)

- Send a brief reminder referencing your first email.
- Add new value with an insight, tip, or industry information they might find useful.
- Restate your call to action, perhaps from a slightly different angle.

Follow-up #2 (5 business days later)

- Share a relevant case study or success story that demonstrates your expertise.
- Address a potential objection or concern they might have about moving forward.
- Position yourself as trying to be helpful, not pushy.

Follow-up #3 (7 business days later)

- Take a different angle or value proposition that might resonate better.
- Include a new insight about their property or business to show continued attention to their specific situation.
- Use a "Is this still relevant?" approach to make it easy for them to respond.

Break Sequence (14 business days later)

- Provide a final value-add like an article, guide, or industry report as a parting gift.
- Use a "closing the loop" message that acknowledges you'll stop reaching out.
- Leave the door open for future contact if their needs change.

Commercial Property Manager Follow-up Example

Here's how a complete sequence might look for a commercial property manager:

Follow-up #1:

> **Subject Line:** Re: [Property Name]'s Parking Lot
>
> Hi [First Name],
>
> I wanted to follow up on my email from earlier this week about the parking lot issues I noticed at [Property Name]. I've prepared a quick reference guide on "5 Early Warning Signs of Parking Lot Failure" that many property managers find helpful for identifying problems before they require major repairs. You can view it here: [Link]
>
> Would you still be interested in that 15-minute discussion about cost-effective maintenance options?
>
> Best regards, [Your Name]

Follow-up #2:

> **Subject Line:** Maintenance Options for [Property Name]
>
> Hi [First Name],
>
> I'm reaching out once more about your parking lot at [Property Name]. We recently helped [Similar Property/Business] reduce their maintenance costs by 22% through preventative treatments that extended their lot's lifespan by 5-7 years. The property manager was particularly concerned about managing expenses while ensuring visitor safety.
>
> If budget-friendly maintenance solutions would be valuable to

> you, I'm happy to share specific approaches that have worked for similar properties.
>
> Best regards, [Your Name]

Follow-up #3:

> **Subject Line:** Quick Question About [Property Name]
>
> Hi [First Name],
>
> I've tried to reach you regarding the parking lot conditions at [Property Name], but understand you're likely busy managing multiple priorities. Just a quick question: Are you currently working with a paving contractor you're happy with, or would you be open to learning about our maintenance programs that could prevent more costly repairs in the future? A simple yes/no is fine, and I'll respect your preference either way.
>
> Regards, [Your Name]

Break Sequence:

> **Subject Line:** Last Note Re: [Property Name] Maintenance
>
> Hi [First Name],
>
> I'll make this my final note regarding [Property Name]'s parking

> lot maintenance. Based on what I observed, you might find our seasonal maintenance checklist useful for your property management planning: [Link to Resource]
>
> If your needs change in the future or you have questions about asphalt maintenance, please don't hesitate to reach out. My direct line is [Phone Number].
>
> All the best, [Your Name]

Best Practices for Follow-up Sequences

To maximize the effectiveness of your follow-up efforts:

Timing and Cadence

- Space your follow-ups appropriately, typically 3-7 days apart for the first few touches.
- Avoid sending on weekends or outside business hours, as these emails may get buried.
- Consider seasonal timing—don't follow up about paving during winter in cold-weather regions when projects can't be completed.

Value in Every Message

- Each follow-up should contain new information or insights, not just a reminder.
- Avoid generic phrases like "just checking in" or "following up" as the primary content.
- Instead, provide useful resources or information even if they don't respond, positioning each touchpoint as valuable regardless of whether they hire you.

Respecting Boundaries

- Have a clear endpoint to your sequence, typically 4-5 touches maximum.
- Honor opt-outs immediately by removing the contact from all future communications.
- Never use guilt or pressure tactics, which can damage your brand reputation and violate regulations in some jurisdictions.

Thread Building

- Keep all follow-ups in the same email thread to make previous communications easily accessible.
- Reference previous communications naturally to maintain context. This makes it easy for prospects to find the entire conversation if they decide to respond later.

Revenue Commander Automation Capabilities

Our Revenue Commander platform streamlines cold email campaigns with powerful automation features designed specifically for paving companies:

Campaign Setup and Management

Automated Sequence Building

- Create professional email sequences using our drag-and-drop sequence builder, which makes it easy to set up complex follow-up patterns without technical expertise.
- Choose from pre-built templates specifically designed for paving companies that address common pain points and objections.
- Use dynamic content insertion based on prospect attributes to personalize at scale.

List Management Tools

- Segment and filter your lists based on multiple criteria like property type, location, and estimated project value.
- Our system automatically verifies and cleans your contact lists, removing bounces and problematic addresses.
- Duplicate detection and merging features prevent sending multiple messages to the same prospect.

Compliance Safeguards

- The platform automatically inserts CAN-SPAM compliant footers with all required elements.
- It processes unsubscribe requests instantly to maintain compliance with regulations.
- Bounce and complaint handling is automated to maintain your sender reputation and deliverability.

Personalization Features

Dynamic Field Insertion

- Our system automatically populates emails with prospect details beyond just first name and company.
- You can include property-specific information gathered from your observations or database.
- The platform can even reference location-based weather patterns or conditions ("With the heavy rainfall we've experienced in [City] this spring...").

Conditional Content

- Show different content based on prospect attributes, such as different testimonials for commercial versus residential prospects.

- You can customize messages for different property types, showing parking lot examples to commercial properties and driveway examples to residential prospects.
- The system can even adjust offerings based on property characteristics like age, size, or condition.

AI-Powered Personalization

- Our advanced AI can analyze prospect websites and social profiles to gather insights for personalization.
- It generates custom insights for each recipient based on available data.
- The system can even recommend the best messaging approach based on prospect characteristics and behavior patterns.

Delivery Optimization

Sending Time Optimization

- The platform analyzes when prospects are most likely to engage based on their past behavior.
- It automatically adjusts sending times for the best results based on open and response data.
- The system accounts for time zone differences to ensure emails arrive during business hours.

Deliverability Monitoring

- Revenue Commander tracks inbox placement rates to ensure your messages aren't going to spam.
- It monitors domain reputation and alerts you to potential issues before they impact your campaigns.
- The platform provides deliverability dashboards with actionable

recommendations for improvement.

Throttling and Warming

- To maintain inbox placement, the system gradually increases sending volume when you start new campaigns.
- It prevents triggering spam filters by managing sending patterns and volume.
- These healthy sending practices protect your domain reputation over time.

Integration with Sales Processes

CRM Synchronization

- The platform automatically logs all email activity in your CRM, creating a complete record of the customer journey.
- It updates prospect records with engagement data like opens, clicks, and replies.
- The system creates tasks for your sales team when leads respond, ensuring prompt follow-up.

Sales Handoff Automation

- Revenue Commander alerts sales reps when prospects engage with your emails, enabling quick response.
- It provides the full conversation history so reps have complete context for their outreach.
- The platform can even schedule follow-up calls directly when prospects express interest.

Task Management

- Create follow-up tasks based on different response types, assigning different actions for positive versus neutral responses.
- The system assigns leads to appropriate team members based on territory, expertise, or capacity.
- It sends reminders for pending follow-ups to ensure no opportunities slip through the cracks.

Measuring Campaign Performance

Tracking the right metrics ensures your cold email campaigns deliver a positive ROI. Here's what to measure and how to interpret the results:

Key Performance Indicators

Delivery Metrics The foundation of any email campaign is successful delivery.

- Track your **delivery rate** (percentage of emails successfully delivered), which should be above 95% for a healthy campaign.
- Monitor **bounce rate** (percentage of emails that couldn't be delivered), aiming to keep it below 5% through regular list cleaning.
- Also track **inbox placement** (percentage of emails reaching inbox vs. spam folder), as emails in spam folders rarely generate responses.

Engagement Metrics Once delivered, you need to know if recipients are engaging with your messages.

- **Open rate** (percentage of recipients who opened your email) indicates subject line effectiveness and sender reputation. For cold emails, 15-25% is a reasonable benchmark.
- **Click rate** (percentage who clicked links in your email) shows content relevance, while **reply rate** (percentage who responded) is often the most important engagement metric for cold outreach. For cold emails

to businesses, a 1-5% reply rate is considered good performance.

Conversion Metrics These metrics track how many prospects take meaningful next steps.

- **Meeting conversion** (percentage of recipients who scheduled a meeting) is a key milestone, with 10-20% of replies converting to meetings being a good target.
- **Quote rate** (percentage who requested a quote) and **sales conversion** (percentage that became customers) are the ultimate measures of campaign success.

Financial Metrics To determine ROI, track cost per lead (total campaign cost divided by number of leads generated), cost per acquisition (total campaign cost divided by number of new customers), and return on investment (revenue generated divided by campaign cost). For cold email campaigns, aim for at least 3x ROI to justify the investment.

Revenue Commander Reporting Features

Our platform provides comprehensive analytics to track and improve campaign performance:

Campaign Dashboard

- Get a real-time performance overview with key metrics at a glance.
- The dashboard shows trend analysis over time, allowing you to spot patterns and improvement opportunities.
- You can drill down into specific metrics for deeper understanding.

Sequence Performance Analysis

- Break down performance by sequence to identify which follow-up patterns work best.

- Identify which follow-ups generate most responses to refine your approach. Compare different sequence structures to optimize your cadence and content.

Message Testing Results

- Get detailed A/B test comparison data to identify winning approaches.
- The platform provides subject line performance analysis to help improve open rates.
- Content effectiveness metrics show which messages resonate most with your audience.

ROI Calculator

- Track costs against results with automated calculations.
- Calculate key financial metrics like cost per lead, cost per acquisition, and ROI.
- Project long-term value of campaigns based on average customer lifetime value.

Continuous Improvement Process

Use performance data to refine your approach over time:

Regular Testing Protocol

- Test one element at a time (subject line, CTA, etc.) to clearly understand what impacts results.
- Implement consistent A/B testing on new campaigns to find winning formulas. Document learnings for future campaigns to build institutional knowledge.

Messaging Refinement

- Analyze which value propositions resonate best with different segments.
- Identify the most effective pain points to address in your initial outreach. Refine personalization approaches based on engagement data.

List Optimization

- Identify most responsive segments to focus your efforts on high-potential prospects.
- Refine targeting criteria based on results to improve future list building. Continuously improve list quality through verification and cleaning.

Sequence Adjustments

- Optimize timing between touches based on response patterns. Remove or replace underperforming messages that don't generate engagement.
- Test different sequence lengths to find the optimal number of touches.

Implementation Strategy

To implement cold email marketing for your paving company effectively:

Start Small and Focused

- Begin with a highly targeted list of 50-100 prospects who match your ideal customer profile.
- Focus on one segment (e.g., commercial property managers) rather than attempting to reach everyone at once.

- Create a simple 3-4 email sequence based on the templates above.
- Use results from this initial campaign to refine your approach before scaling to larger lists or additional segments.

Establish Clear Processes

- Develop clear guidelines for list building, including criteria for inclusion and verification steps.
- Create standard templates and sequences that your team can use consistently.
- Establish response handling protocols so prospects receive prompt attention when they reply.
- Define lead qualification criteria to ensure sales time is focused on the most promising opportunities.

Train Your Team

- Ensure anyone responding to replies understands the campaign context and messaging.
- Provide scripts for common questions and objections to maintain consistency.
- Set response time expectations (ideally within 1-2 hours) as quick follow-up dramatically increases conversion rates.
- Create a smooth handoff process from marketing to sales to prevent leads from falling through the cracks.

Scale Strategically

- Expand to additional segments once initial results prove positive. For example, if your commercial property manager campaign succeeds, add HOA boards or general contractors next.
- Gradually increase volume while maintaining quality rather than rushing to massive scale.

- Create segment-specific messaging for each target audience that addresses their particular challenges and needs.
- Develop seasonal campaigns aligned with paving needs in your region.

Integrating Cold Email with Other Marketing Channels

Cold email is most effective when integrated with your overall marketing strategy. Here's how to create a cohesive approach:

Coordinate with LinkedIn Outreach

- Connect with prospects on LinkedIn before or immediately after sending initial cold emails.
- Share relevant content on LinkedIn that supports your email messaging.
- Reference your connection request in your email or vice versa to create multiple touchpoints.

Retargeting Campaign Integration

- Set up custom audience retargeting for email recipients who visit your website.
- Create ads that reinforce your email messaging to build familiarity. Use similar visual elements in both channels for consistent branding.

Direct Mail Follow-up

- For high-value prospects who engage but don't convert, consider targeted direct mail.
- Send capability brochures or printed case studies to stand out from digital-only competitors. Use handwritten notes for executive-level decision makers.

Event and Webinar Invitations

- Use cold email to invite prospects to industry events or educational webinars.
- Create valuable content that addresses pain points identified in your email campaigns.
- Follow up with attendees to continue the conversation started via email.

This multi-channel approach creates multiple touchpoints with prospects, dramatically increasing the likelihood of response and conversion.

Conclusion

Cold email marketing, when executed professionally and ethically, can be a valuable lead generation channel for paving companies. By focusing on providing value, maintaining strict compliance with regulations, and using Revenue Commander's powerful automation tools, you can create campaigns that connect you with prospects you might otherwise never reach.

Remember that cold email works best as part of an integrated marketing strategy. Use it to complement your other outreach efforts, particularly for commercial prospects who may not find you through traditional search channels.

With proper targeting, personalized messaging, and persistent (but respectful) follow-up, cold email can help you fill your project pipeline with valuable commercial and residential paving opportunities. The key is consistency and quality over quantity. A well-crafted email to 100 perfectly targeted prospects will outperform a generic message sent to thousands. Take the time to research your prospects, personalize your outreach, and provide genuine value in every communication. This approach not only generates more responses but builds your reputation as a professional, customer-focused paving contractor.

9

Online Directories and Lead Aggregators

Online directories and lead aggregation services can be a significant source of potential customers for paving companies. These platforms connect homeowners and businesses actively searching for paving services with contractors in their area. While your own website and marketing efforts should be the foundation of your lead generation strategy, directories and aggregators can supplement your pipeline with additional opportunities.

Understanding the Directory and Lead Aggregator Landscape

There are several types of online platforms where potential customers might find your paving business.

Business directories are general listing sites where your business information appears alongside competitors. These include **Google Business Profile** (formerly Google My Business), **Yelp**, **Yellow Pages**, **Better Business Bureau (BBB)**, local **Chamber of Commerce** directories, and **Bing Places for Business**. Business directories typically offer free basic listings with paid upgrade options. They focus on providing business information rather than actively generating leads.

Lead generation platforms actively collect and sell leads to contractors.

Important players in this space include **Angi** (formerly Angie's List), **HomeAdvisor** (now part of Angi), **Thumbtack**, **Porch**, **Networx**, and **CraftJack**. These platforms actively market to consumers looking for contractor services, then sell those leads to multiple contractors in the area. They tend to be more expensive than directories but can provide a steady stream of inquiries.

Industry-specific directories focus on contractors and construction services. Examples include **BuildZoom**, **The Blue Book**, **Houzz Pro**, **National Asphalt Pavement Association** directory, and local contractor associations. These directories typically have more targeted audiences and may provide higher-quality leads, though often at lower volume than general platforms.

Research Findings on Lead Generation Platforms

Our research into lead aggregation platforms has revealed important insights about their cost structures and effectiveness for paving contractors. According to our analysis of industry data, lead generation platforms like HomeAdvisor and Angi typically charge **$15 to $85+ per lead** depending on the project type and location. For larger paving projects (commercial parking lots, for example), lead fees trend toward the higher end of that range. HomeAdvisor specifically sends lists of leads that contractors pay **$15 to $100 per lead** to be able to quote.

Most platforms operate on one of four payment models. The **pay-per-lead** model requires you to pay for each lead you receive, regardless of quality or whether you win the job. This is the most common model for platforms like HomeAdvisor and Angi. **Subscription models** charge a monthly fee for access to leads or enhanced visibility. Some platforms like Houzz Pro use this model, charging a set monthly fee regardless of lead volume. **Hybrid models** combine a base membership fee plus additional per-lead charges, requiring an upfront investment with ongoing per-lead costs. Finally, the **pay-per-quote** model, used by platforms like Thumbtack, requires you to pay to submit a quote to a homeowner or business that has posted a project. This differs slightly from pay-per-lead as you're bidding on already-posted jobs.

One major finding from our research is the **inconsistent lead quality** from these platforms. Leads are typically shared with 3-4 other contractors, creating immediate competition and reducing win rates. Many users are in the early research phase and contacting multiple companies to compare prices, not necessarily ready to commit. Some leads may be outside your service area or mismatched with your services despite platform filtering options. According to industry data, conversion rates on these leads tend to be lower than those from your own website or referrals. Lead quality can vary significantly between platforms and even within the same platform over time.

As one industry source noted: "While they might deliver a lot of leads to your paving business, the quality often isn't up to par... lead generation services like HomeAdvisor and Angi just don't deliver on quality."

That said, many paving companies do successfully use these platforms as part of their marketing mix, particularly when they respond very quickly to new leads (ideally within minutes), have competitive pricing or clear value differentiation, present a professional image with strong reviews, have capacity to handle additional work, and implement effective follow-up processes to nurture leads. The key is understanding that these leads typically require more effort to convert compared to direct inquiries or referrals.

Comparing Top Lead Generation Platforms

Each lead generation platform has different strengths and weaknesses. Here's a comparison of the major platforms based on our research and feedback from paving contractors.

HomeAdvisor/Angi Since these companies merged, they now operate under the same parent company but maintain separate platforms.

- **Advantages**: High lead volume potential, established brand with consumer recognition, detailed profile options to showcase your work, and potential for reviews to boost visibility.
- **Disadvantages**: Leads are shared with multiple contractors (typically 3-5), higher cost per lead for premium services, variable lead quality reported by contractors, and aggressive upselling to contractors for better placement.
- **Cost Structure**: Annual membership fee ($300-500), per-lead costs ranging from $15-100 depending on project size, and optional profile enhancements and featured listing fees.
- **Best For**: Companies with capacity to handle high volume, businesses with strong follow-up processes, and contractors who can respond very quickly to leads.

Thumbtack Thumbtack operates differently, allowing customers to post specific projects and contractors to bid on them.

- **Advantages**: More detailed project specifications upfront, paying only for leads you choose to pursue, direct messaging with potential customers, and ability to set your own pricing.
- **Challenges**: Competitive bidding environment, need to actively moni-

tor for new projects, less brand awareness than HomeAdvisor/Angi, and can be time-consuming to manage effectively.

- **Cost Structure**: No membership fee, pay-per-quote model with costs varying by project value, and credits purchased in advance and used to bid on jobs.
- **Best For**: Selective contractors looking for specific project types, companies with competitive pricing, and businesses willing to actively manage their platform presence.

Porch Porch partners with major retailers and service providers to generate leads.

- **Strengths**: Partnership with Lowe's and other retailers providing unique lead sources, often fewer contractors competing for each lead, homeowner project history sometimes available, and more data-driven matching.
- **Drawbacks**: Lower lead volume in some markets, less consumer awareness, inconsistent quality, and limited control over lead flow.
- **Cost Structure**: Subscription-based pricing in some areas and pay-per-lead in others, with costs generally comparable to HomeAdvisor.
- **Best For**: Contractors seeking alternative lead sources, companies in markets where Porch has strong retail partnerships, and businesses looking to diversify lead generation.

Networx Networx focuses specifically on contractor leads.

- **Benefits**: Focused specifically on home service leads, often less competition than larger platforms, flexible lead purchasing options, and typically lower cost per lead than market leaders.

- **Limitations**: Lower brand recognition means fewer consumer users, inconsistent lead volume in many markets, variable lead quality, and less robust contractor profiles.
- **Cost Structure**: Monthly subscription options and pay-per-lead options, generally at lower costs than HomeAdvisor/Angi.
- **Best For**: Cost-conscious contractors, companies in markets where larger platforms are saturated, and businesses looking for supplemental lead sources.

Optimizing Your Presence on Key Platforms

To maximize results from directories and lead platforms, your listings must be complete, accurate, and compelling.

Google Business Profile

Google Business Profile is arguably the most important directory for local paving companies because it powers both Maps results and the local pack in search results. For **Google Business Profile optimization**, start by claiming and verifying your business if you haven't already. This fundamental step establishes your ownership of the listing and allows you to make changes. Verification typically happens via postcard, phone, or email, depending on your business type.

Complete every section of your profile thoroughly. Use your exact business name (no keyword stuffing), choose the most accurate primary category ("Paving Contractor") and relevant secondary categories, add your complete address and service area boundaries, include your phone number, website URL, and business hours, add a complete business description that includes your key services and unique selling points, and list all services you offer using Google's services list feature.

Add high-quality photos (at least 10-15) showing the exterior of your business location, team members/staff in branded uniforms, equipment and vehicles with your logo visible, before/after project photos showing dramatic transformations, and action shots of your crew working. The quality of your images matters significantly. Professional photos generate more engagement than casual smartphone pictures, though authentic job site photos are still valuable even if not professionally shot.

Create Google Posts regularly (weekly if possible) featuring recent projects with before/after comparisons, special offers or seasonal promotions, company news or team highlights, seasonal maintenance tips for pavement, and community involvement or charitable work. These posts appear directly on your profile and in search results, providing fresh content that keeps your listing active.

Answer questions that appear in the Q&A section promptly by monitoring for new questions daily, providing thorough, helpful answers, addressing common objections or concerns, and adding your own FAQs to preemptively answer common questions.

Set up messaging for direct customer inquiries by configuring business messaging hours, setting up automatic responses for after-hours inquiries, ensuring messages are checked and answered promptly, and training staff on proper message response protocols.

Actively solicit reviews by implementing a systematic review request process, responding to all reviews (positive and negative), featuring reviews that highlight your key differentiators, and maintaining a steady flow of new reviews over time.

Yelp

While Yelp's influence varies by market, it remains a significant platform for service businesses. For **Yelp optimization**, claim your business and complete your profile by verifying ownership through Yelp's process, uploading a professional logo and cover image, adding all relevant contact information, and including your website URL and direct contact details.

Select appropriate categories (Asphalt & Paving, Contractors, etc.) by choosing the most specific categories that apply to your services, adding secondary categories for related services you offer, and ensuring categorization matches your actual service offerings.

Upload high-quality photos showing your best work. Before/after comparisons have the highest impact. Include action shots of your team working, show a variety of different project types, and update photos seasonally to keep content fresh.

Consider **Yelp's enhanced profiles** if they work financially. Yelp for Business packages provide enhanced visibility, enhanced profiles with slideshow features and call-to-action buttons, competitor ad removal on your listing prevents other companies from advertising on your profile, and featured placement in search results can increase visibility.

Respond to all reviews, both positive and negative. Thank positive reviewers specifically for their feedback, address negative reviews professionally and offer solutions, demonstrate your commitment to customer satisfaction, and show potential customers how you handle problems.

Add detailed business information including years in business to establish credibility, specialties that differentiate you from competitors, credentials and certifications that verify your expertise, insurance information to build trust, and payment methods accepted for customer convenience.

Better Business Bureau (BBB)

BBB accreditation signals credibility to potential customers. To **optimize your BBB presence**, achieve and maintain BBB accreditation if possible by applying for accreditation through your local BBB, meeting their standards for trust and transparency, paying the annual accreditation fee, and maintaining compliance with BBB requirements.

Complete your profile with detailed company information by adding comprehensive business description, listing all services offered, including history and ownership information, uploading business photos, and providing complete contact information.

Respond promptly to any complaints filed through BBB by setting up alerts for BBB complaints, addressing issues professionally and thoroughly, documenting resolution processes, and following up to ensure customer satisfaction.

Display your BBB rating on your website and marketing materials by adding the BBB logo to your website footer, including accreditation status in proposals, mentioning BBB rating in marketing materials, and linking to your BBB profile from your website.

Request reviews from satisfied customers through the BBB platform by asking happy customers to share experiences, following BBB guidelines for review solicitation, thanking customers who leave positive reviews, and using reviews as testimonials (with permission).

HomeAdvisor/Angi/Lead Platforms

If you decide to use lead generation platforms like HomeAdvisor/Angi, **complete your profile thoroughly** with detailed service descriptions explaining your processes and materials, project photos and videos showcasing your best work, team member information highlighting experience and expertise, licensing and certification details to establish credibility, service area information with specific boundaries, and pricing information (general ranges) to pre-qualify leads.

Set precise service categories and geographic parameters to receive better-matched leads by selecting only services you actually provide, defining service area boundaries accurately, specifying minimum project sizes if applicable, indicating specialties and preferences, and being transparent about limitations.

Respond to leads within minutes for best results by setting up mobile notifications for new leads, creating templated initial responses that can be quickly personalized, establishing a 24/7 monitoring system during peak seasons, and tracking response times and conversion correlation.

Configure lead budget caps to prevent overspending by setting daily and weekly spending limits, adjusting budget based on conversion rates, increasing during high-converting periods, and decreasing during low-quality lead periods.

Track lead quality meticulously to determine ROI by documenting source platform for each lead, recording qualification rate by platform, calculating conversion rate by source, and determining average job value by source.

Generate positive reviews to rise in their ranking algorithms by requesting reviews from satisfied customers, responding to all reviews promptly, addressing negative reviews professionally, and building a steady stream of positive feedback.

Consider upgrading to premium placement only after testing basic service by testing standard placement first to establish baseline, calculating

ROI before upgrading, testing premium placement for limited periods, and comparing conversion rates between levels.

Managing Online Reputation

Your reputation on directories and lead platforms directly impacts your visibility and conversion rates. Building a strong review profile doesn't happen by accident. You need a systematic approach that begins with **creating a systematic review request process**. Send follow-up emails after project completion when satisfaction is highest, include direct links to your preferred review platforms to make it easy, make printed cards with QR codes linking to review sites for in-person requests, and offer guidance on how to leave a review, as many customers aren't familiar with the process.

For example, you might create an email template like this:

> **Subject:** How was your experience with [Your Company]?
>
> Hi [Customer Name],
>
> Thank you for choosing [Your Company] for your recent paving project. We hope you're enjoying your new [driveway/parking lot/etc.].
>
> We'd greatly appreciate it if you could take a moment to share your experience with us by leaving a review. Your feedback helps us improve our service and helps other property owners find quality paving services.
>
> You can leave a review by clicking this link: [Direct link to Google

> review page]
>
> Thank you again for your business!
>
> Best regards, [Your Name] [Your Company]

Prioritize platforms based on your market analysis. Google Business Profile should be your highest priority for most markets, followed by platform-specific reviews (HomeAdvisor, Angi, etc.) if you're active on those services, Yelp (especially important in some markets where it has strong user adoption), and BBB reviews for establishing credibility with certain customer segments. While you want reviews on all platforms, focus your efforts on getting a critical mass of reviews on your primary platform before diversifying.

Timing is critical in review acquisition. Request reviews when customer satisfaction is highest, typically right after project completion when the transformation is most visible. Follow up if no review is posted with a gentle reminder, and avoid asking for reviews when issues are still being resolved.

How you **respond to reviews** is almost as important as the reviews themselves.

For positive reviews, respond within 1-2 business days to show attentiveness, thank the customer specifically by name to personalize your response, mention a detail from their project to show that you remember them specifically, express appreciation for their business and taking time to review, and invite them to contact you for future needs.

Example: "Thank you so much, John! We really appreciated the opportunity to work on your driveway project. It was a pleasure transforming your property entrance, and we're thrilled that you're happy with the results. Please don't hesitate to reach out if you need any maintenance tips or have questions about your new asphalt. We look forward to serving you again in the future!"

For negative reviews, respond quickly (within 24 hours if possible) to demonstrate responsiveness, thank them for their feedback, even if critical, apologize for their disappointing experience without being defensive, offer to resolve the issue offline to show willingness to make things right, provide your direct contact information for immediate communication, follow up privately to address concerns thoroughly, and if resolved, politely ask if they would consider updating their review.

Example: "Thank you for your feedback, Sarah. We sincerely apologize that your driveway project didn't meet your expectations. At [Your Company], we pride ourselves on quality workmanship, and we're disappointed to hear about your experience. We'd like to understand more about the issues you've encountered and make things right. Please contact me directly at [phone number] or [email] so we can address your concerns immediately. We appreciate the opportunity to resolve this situation to your satisfaction."

Implement review monitoring alerts by setting up alerts to notify you of new reviews immediately. Revenue Commander can automate this monitoring across platforms. Never let negative reviews sit unaddressed, and create a response protocol so everyone knows how to handle reviews.

The **quantity of reviews** matters as much as quality. Our data indicates that businesses with more than 40 reviews tend to overcome the occasional negative review without significant impact. Consider this example from a paving contractor with 46 five-star reviews and one negative review: with such a positive overall rating, most prospects won't be deterred by a single negative experience. The goal should be to generate a steady stream of reviews to build this buffer of positive sentiment.

Implement effective review generation tactics by making it part of your project completion process, training all customer-facing staff to request reviews, setting monthly goals for new review acquisition, tracking review generation performance, and celebrating when you reach review milestones. Remember that consistency matters more than volume. A steady stream of 4-5 new reviews per month is more beneficial than 20 reviews all at once followed by months of silence.

Cost-Benefit Analysis of Paid Lead Services

Before investing in paid lead services, conduct a thorough cost-benefit analysis to determine if they make financial sense for your business. The advertised cost per lead is just the starting point.

To determine the **true cost**, consider the cost per qualified lead: True Lead Cost = Cost per Lead ÷ Qualification Rate For example: If HomeAdvisor charges $50 per lead and only 60% are qualified: $50 ÷ 0.6 = $83.33 per qualified lead This calculation accounts for the fact that some leads will be unqualified—perhaps outside your service area, looking for services you don't offer, or simply not serious about moving forward.

Next, calculate the **cost per acquired customer**: Customer Acquisition Cost = True Lead Cost ÷ Conversion Rate For example: If you convert 25% of qualified leads: $83.33 ÷ 0.25 = $333.32 per acquired customer This reflects what you're actually paying to acquire a new customer, accounting for all the leads that don't convert.

Finally, calculate your **ROI**: ROI = (Average Project Value × Profit Margin - Customer Acquisition Cost) ÷ Customer Acquisition Cost For example: If average project value is $5,000 with 30% profit margin: ($5,000 × 0.30 - $333.32) ÷ $333.32 = 3.5 or 350% ROI A positive ROI indicates the lead service is profitable for your business. Generally, you should aim for at least a 200-300% ROI to account for variables and ensure the channel is truly worthwhile.

When evaluating different platforms, create a **comparison process** that includes an initial testing period. Allocate a specific budget (perhaps $500-1,000) to test each platform for a defined period (30-60 days). Track all metrics carefully and calculate the key performance indicators above.

Implement **lead quality assessment** by creating a scoring system for leads based on factors like project type match to your services, location within your service area, timeline alignment with your schedule, budget appropriateness, and decision-making authority of contact.

Document **conversion tracking** throughout the entire customer journey for each lead, including initial contact date and method, follow-up interactions, estimate presentation, close/no close decision, reasons for lost opportunities, and final project value if won.

Consider **long-term value** by calculating not just the immediate job value but also potential for repeat business, referral likelihood, maintenance opportunities, and upsell potential. This comprehensive approach will give you a much clearer picture of which platforms deserve your continued investment.

Use a **decision framework** to decide which platforms warrant investment.

- **Test before scaling** by starting with a limited budget on any new platform, setting a 30-60 day test period with specific success metrics, tracking all metrics meticulously using Revenue Commander, evaluating performance before increasing spend, and being prepared to cut underperforming platforms quickly.

- **Focus on platforms** with higher lead quality scores based on your assessment, better exclusivity (fewer competing quotes), lower acquisition costs relative to project value, more granular geographic targeting options, and stronger alignment with your ideal customer profile.
- **Consider your business needs**, as new businesses may benefit from any lead volume despite higher costs, established businesses should be more selective about lead quality, seasonal capacity fluctuations might warrant different approaches during busy/slow periods, and your specific service specialties may perform better on certain platforms.

Remember that what works for one paving company may not work for another. Your specific service mix, geographic location, pricing structure, and capacity will all influence which platforms perform best for your business.

Strategies for Converting Shared Leads

When using platforms that send leads to multiple contractors, you need strategies to stand out from your competition.

Speed to Lead The first contractor to make contact often has a significant advantage.

- Aim for **under 5 minutes response time**, as data shows contact rates drop dramatically after 5 minutes.
- The first contractor to respond often gains a **psychological advantage**.
- Configure instant notifications in Revenue Commander to alert you immediately, and create an emergency response protocol for new leads.
- According to research, leads contacted within 5 minutes are **21 times**

more likely to qualify than those contacted after 30 minutes. For shared leads, this advantage is even more pronounced since competitors are racing to make contact.

- Use **automated initial responses** by setting up text/email autoresponders confirming receipt immediately, including estimated timeframe for full response (ideally within hours, not days), providing your direct contact information for immediate questions, and personalizing with the customer's name and project details.
- **Example:**

Hi [Name],

Thanks for your inquiry about [specific project type] through [platform name]. We've received your request and are preparing a detailed response for you. One of our paving specialists will contact you personally within the next [timeframe, e.g., 2 hours] to discuss your project and answer any immediate questions. If you'd like to reach us directly in the meantime, please call [direct phone number].

Best regards, [Your Name] [Your Company]

- Implement **24/7 response systems** by using after-hours answering service for leads that come in outside business hours, considering chatbots for initial screening and basic information collection, ensuring weekend coverage during peak seasons, and creating a rotation schedule so someone is always monitoring leads.
- Remember that the customer is likely contacting multiple companies at once. If they hear back from your competitor first, they may have already formed a positive impression before you even make contact.

Professional Presentation How you present your company and services significantly impacts conversion rates.

- Create **branded quote documents** with your logo and branding, include your insurance information, certifications, and guarantees, use project visualization tools when possible to help customers envision the finished result, include options at different price points to provide choice, and detail your materials and process to demonstrate quality.
- Consider using **video responses** by sending personalized video messages addressing specific needs mentioned in their inquiry, recording quick walkthroughs of similar completed projects to show relevant experience, showing your face to build immediate trust and human connection, and keeping videos short (under 2 minutes) but informative and personalized. Tools like BombBomb, Loom, or even simple smartphone videos can dramatically increase engagement compared to text-only responses.
- Provide **detailed proposals** that include more information than competitors to demonstrate thoroughness, break down costs transparently to build trust, include multiple options/packages to accommodate different budgets and needs, add value through educational content about materials and processes, and use professional graphics and images to illustrate concepts.
- The goal is to position yourself as the thorough, professional choice compared to competitors who might send generic quotes with minimal detail.

Follow-up Strategy Most leads don't convert on first contact. A strategic follow-up sequence is essential.

- Use a **multi-channel approach** with initial call + text confirmation to establish immediate contact, email proposal with video walkthrough for detailed information, scheduled follow-up call to answer questions and build relationship, value-add communication (article, tip sheet) to provide useful information, and final check-in to close the loop. Using multiple channels increases the likelihood of connecting with the prospect in their preferred communication method.

- Implement a **timing strategy** with initial response and quote within hours of lead on Day 1, value-add follow-up (helpful information, not just sales pressure) on Day 2, check-in and answer questions that may have arisen on Day 4, alternative options or special offer if no decision yet on Day 7, and final "closing the loop" message with open invitation for future contact on Day 14. This persistent but respectful sequence ensures you stay top-of-mind without becoming annoying.
- Use **differentiation messaging** that focuses on unique value propositions that competitors likely don't offer, addresses likely competitor weaknesses without directly mentioning them, emphasizes guarantees and warranties that reduce customer risk, shares specific, relevant testimonials from similar projects, and highlights your local presence and commitment to the community. For example, if you know competitors often use subcontractors, emphasize that your crews are in-house employees. If others typically have long lead times, highlight your availability.

Pricing and Value Proposition Price is almost always a factor, but rarely the only factor. Don't compete solely on price.

- Instead, offer clear **value justifications** for your pricing, create **good-better-best options** to accommodate different budgets, **bundle services** for higher perceived value (e.g., include sealcoating with new installation), and **emphasize long-term cost savings** of quality materials and workmanship.
- Consider **strategic discounts** such as time-limited offers to create

urgency to decide quickly, conditional discounts (e.g., "if you decide within 48 hours") to reward prompt decisions, value-added extras instead of pure price cuts to maintain profit margins, and neighborhood discounts for multiple projects in same area.

- Offer **payment flexibility** through financing options via partners like GreenSky or Synchrony, multiple payment methods for convenience, deposits vs. payment plans to accommodate cash flow needs, and early payment discounts for cash flow advantages.
- The key is positioning your company as the best **value**—the intersection of quality, service, and price—rather than necessarily the lowest price.

Revenue Commander Lead Tracking

Revenue Commander provides comprehensive tools for tracking and managing leads from directories and aggregators.

Source Attribution Understanding where your leads and customers come from is crucial for optimizing your marketing. Revenue Commander offers automatic tracking with unique phone numbers for each lead source to show exactly which platforms generate calls, form tracking with source identification for online quote requests, UTM parameter capture from directory clicks for complete digital journey tracking, and full history maintenance for multi-touch attribution. The system includes a lead tagging system that categorizes leads by source platform automatically, applies quality scores based on predefined criteria, tags by service type and project value for segmentation, and creates custom tags based on your business needs. Revenue Commander's cost integration features track platform costs against leads generated for real-time ROI calculation, calculate real-time ROI by source to identify top performers, provide alerts for underperforming sources that aren't meeting targets, and forecast performance based on historical data. This comprehensive tracking allows you to identify exactly which platforms provide the best return on investment, rather than relying on gut feeling.

Lead Management The platform offers efficient lead management through a centralized lead inbox where all leads appear in one dashboard regardless of source, prioritization based on source quality and lead score, automated routing to appropriate team members based on criteria, and visual status indicators for at-a-glance management.

Automation Response automation features include instant acknowledgment messages tailored to lead source, customized responses by lead source and project type, follow-up sequence triggering based on lead behavior, and automated reminders for team members to maintain contact.

Status Tracking Status tracking provides visual pipeline management showing leads at each stage, stage transition tracking with timestamp documentation, conversion rate monitoring by source and stage, and aging alerts for leads without recent activity. This systematic approach ensures no lead falls through the cracks and each receives appropriate follow-up.

Reporting Data-driven decision making requires comprehensive reporting. Revenue Commander offers source comparison with side-by-side platform performance dashboards, cost per lead by source with trend analysis, conversion rates across platforms with benchmarking, and quality score comparison between sources. ROI calculation features include true cost per acquired customer calculation, profit margin by lead source for financial analysis, long-term customer value tracking for lifetime value assessment, and seasonality analysis for budget allocation planning. Optimization insights provide recommendations for budget adjustments based on performance, best performing days/times by source for scheduling, lead quality trend analysis to identify patterns, and competitive intelligence gathering from customer feedback. These reports provide actionable insights to continuously improve your marketing strategy.

Integrations Revenue Commander seamlessly connects with other systems through directory API connections that offer direct integration with HomeAdvisor, Angi, and other platforms, automatic lead importing without manual data entry, two-way status updates to maintain consistency, and centralized communication history. Call tracking integration allows you to record and transcribe lead calls for quality monitoring, implement quality scoring based on call content and outcome, generate performance reporting by team member for training purposes, and utilize keyword spotting for common questions and objections. Website synchronization updates your website with latest reviews from directories automatically, maintains consistent NAP (Name, Address, Phone) information across platforms, offers centralized profile management for all directories, and enables content syndication to multiple platforms. These integrations create a unified system that eliminates duplicate work and ensures consistency across all your marketing channels.

Implementation Strategy

To effectively leverage directories and lead aggregators, follow a phased implementation plan.

Phase 1: Foundation Building (1-2 months) Begin with the fundamentals before investing heavily in paid platforms.

- **Claim and optimize free listings** starting with Google Business Profile (highest priority), Yelp, BBB, local business directories, and industry association directories. Ensure each listing is complete, accurate, and includes high-quality photos and a compelling business description.
- **Set up tracking systems** by configuring Revenue Commander tracking for all platforms, establishing baseline metrics for current perfor-

mance, creating reporting templates for ongoing analysis, and implementing call recording for lead quality assessment. Proper tracking from the beginning allows you to accurately measure improvements.

- **Develop response protocols** by creating templates for different lead types and sources, training team on response procedures and timing expectations, establishing service standards for lead handling, and role-playing common scenarios to prepare staff. Having standardized processes ensures consistent, professional handling of all inquiries regardless of source.

Phase 2: Controlled Expansion (2-3 months) Once your foundation is solid, move to testing paid platforms.

- **Select 1-2 lead services** based on your market research, set modest initial budgets (perhaps $500-1,000 per platform), establish clear success criteria before starting, and document all interactions and outcomes meticulously. This controlled testing allows you to evaluate platforms without significant financial risk.
- **Implement a review generation system** by developing systematic review requests for all completed projects, creating monitoring procedures for new reviews across platforms, training staff on reputation management procedures, and setting goals for review quantity and quality. A strong review profile will improve your visibility and conversion rates on all platforms.
- **Optimize your conversion process** by refining proposal templates based on customer feedback, developing competitive analysis to understand market positioning, creating value-focused presentations that differentiate your company, and testing different follow-up sequences to identify the most effective approach. Continuously improving your sales process increases your return on marketing investment.

Phase 3: Analysis and Scaling (3-6 months) Based on your testing results, refine your strategy.

- **Analyze platform performance** by comparing test results across platforms using standardized metrics, calculating ROI by source with full cost accounting, identifying highest-performing options for continued investment, and documenting specific strengths and weaknesses of each platform. This analysis tells you exactly where to focus your ongoing resources.
- **Adjust budget allocation** by increasing investment in top performers that demonstrate positive ROI, reducing or eliminating underperformers that don't meet thresholds, setting performance thresholds for continued investment, and creating a dynamic budget that adjusts based on results. Your budget should follow performance, not be rigidly allocated regardless of results.
- **Refine targeting parameters** by narrowing geographic focus to areas with highest performance, specifying ideal project types based on profitability analysis, optimizing timing based on your capacity and seasonal patterns, and adjusting messaging based on customer feedback. Fine-tuning your targeting improves lead quality and reduces wasted spend.

Phase 4: Integration and Expansion (6+ months) With a proven system in place, look for opportunities to advance.

- **Integrate successful platforms** by developing seamless workflows between platforms and your CRM, creating unified reporting across all lead sources, implementing cross-platform lead nurturing sequences, and standardizing customer experience regardless of lead source.
- **Explore advanced features** by testing premium placements on platforms that demonstrate basic ROI, exploring retargeting options for leads that don't convert immediately, implementing automated bidding strategies where available, and leveraging platform-specific features like guaranteed leads.

- **Expand service offerings** by using platform analytics to identify demand for additional services, testing new service categories on proven platforms, creating specialized landing pages for emerging service opportunities, and developing expertise in high-margin services identified through platform data.

Measuring Long-Term Success

Beyond immediate lead generation, directories and aggregators can contribute to your business growth in several ways.

Brand Building Benefits

- **Expanded digital footprint** through multiple listings across the web that improve search presence
- **Consistent NAP information** that reinforces brand identity
- **Professional profiles** that communicate credibility
- **Reviews** that build social proof across multiple platforms

Trust Signals

- **Third-party validation** from established platforms
- **Verified reviews** from actual customers
- **Badges and certifications** displayed on profiles
- **Transparent pricing** and service information

Competitive Positioning

- **Direct comparison** with competitors on the same platforms
- **Opportunity to showcase** differentiators
- **Visibility into competitor** pricing and offerings
- **Strategic positioning** based on market research

Market Intelligence

- **Service demand trends** by tracking which services are most requested by season
- **Identify emerging service needs** in your market
- **Understand pricing expectations** of prospects
- **Discover customer pain points** and priorities

Geographical Insights

- **Map request patterns** across your service area
- **Identify high-potential** neighborhoods or zones
- **Discover underserved areas** with less competition
- **Optimize service routes** based on demand clusters

Customer Preference Data

- **Learn what factors** most influence hiring decisions
- **Understand communication** preferences
- **Identify decision timelines** for different project types
- **Determine most common questions** and concerns

To truly measure success, track the **full customer lifecycle**.

- **Initial acquisition metrics** include cost to acquire customer through the platform, first project value and profit margin, sales cycle length from first contact to project completion, and resources required to convert the lead.
- **Long-term relationship value** encompasses repeat business frequency and value, maintenance service adoption, cross-selling of additional services, and average customer lifespan.
- **Referral generation** measures the number of referrals generated per platform-acquired customer, value of referred projects, referral

close rate compared to other lead sources, and word-of-mouth amplification through social sharing.

- **Total ROI calculation** includes full customer lifetime value from all services, value of all referrals generated, less total acquisition and servicing costs, presented as return on initial investment.

This comprehensive view often reveals that even seemingly expensive leads can provide excellent long-term returns when the full customer value is considered.

Conclusion

Online directories and lead aggregators can be valuable components of your paving company's marketing strategy when approached strategically. While they shouldn't replace your own website and direct marketing efforts, these platforms can provide additional lead flow and increase your visibility in the marketplace.

By understanding the true costs, optimizing your presence, managing your reputation diligently, and using Revenue Commander to track performance, you can make informed decisions about which platforms deserve your investment and attention.

Remember that success with directories and lead services often comes down to execution—responding quickly, presenting professionally, and following up diligently can set you apart from competitors receiving the same leads. With the right approach, even shared leads can become profitable customers who generate referrals and repeat business for years to come.

The key is to view these platforms as one component of a comprehensive marketing strategy rather than a silver bullet solution. When integrated properly with your website, SEO efforts, social media, and traditional marketing, directories and lead services can help create a steady pipeline of opportunities that sustains and grows your paving business.

10

Video Marketing

Video marketing has emerged as a powerful tool for paving companies to showcase their expertise, demonstrate work quality, and build trust with potential customers. In an industry where visual transformation is at the core of your service, video provides the perfect medium to highlight the dramatic before-and-after results your company delivers.

Why Use Video Marketing?

There are a number of reasons to use Video Marketing for your paving business. First, it will increase your exposure on the search engines, giving you more placeholders for the keywords that are most important to you. Video marketing will enhance your SEO effort by driving visitors to your website and creating relevant links to your website, which will improve conversion. Once somebody gets to your website, if there is good video on the home page and the subpages, it will resonate deeper with your potential customers than a site without video. This helps convert those visitors from just Browse around pages to actually picking up the phone and calling your office.

Again, YouTube is the second most used search engine there is. Obviously, Google is number one. One would think that Bing and Yahoo would be the other major search engines, but that just isn't the case. There are significantly less videos than there are web pages on the Internet. So creating relevant and quality video content for YouTube and other video sharing sites is a really huge opportunity. These videos will help you to connect with people and answer their questions when they're looking for information on what you do.

I talked about the fact that you can show up in search engines with an image next to it, and you can obtain multiple placeholders on Google for the keywords that are most important to you. Here is a screenshot representing what this means:

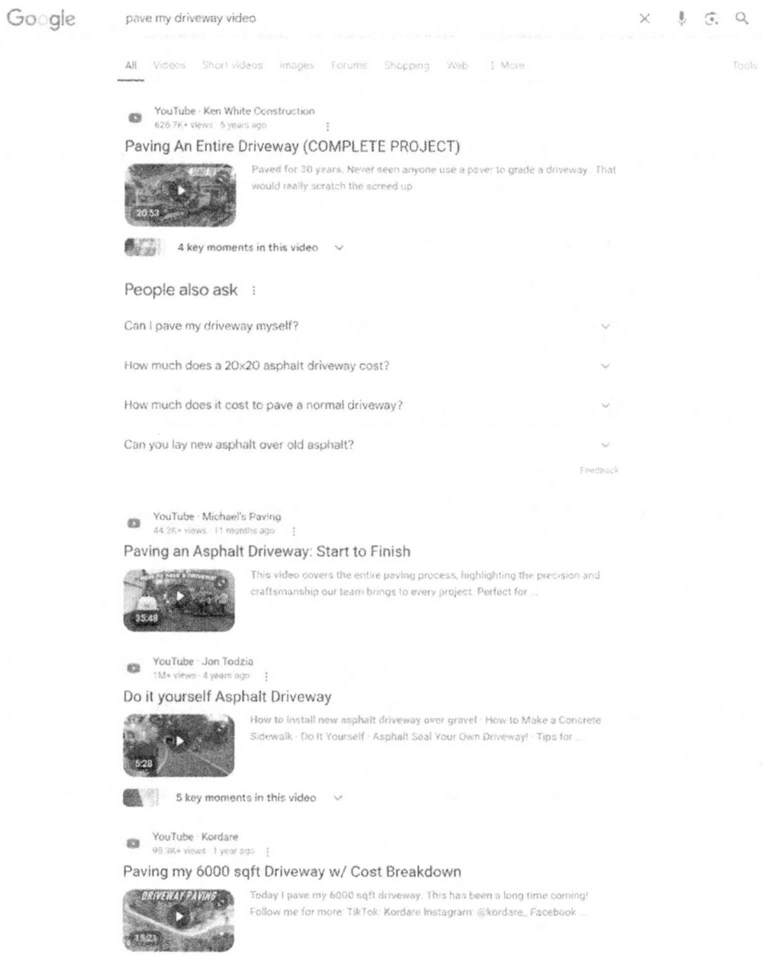

If we type in a search on Google for "pave my driveway video," you'll see that videos show up on page one with a few other listings. If you click a link, it takes you straight to a video. If you do this right and you optimize your videos correctly (I'm going to show you exactly how in this chapter), you can start to have your video show up in the natural search on Google, which is extremely powerful. It also gives you the opportunity to have more placeholders for the various services that you provide. Below that video, you see a blog post from a different site after a questions snippet, and then several more videos. Videos have taken over a large amount of "how to" queries, and those are smart ones to target.

Whether your video ranks number one, number two, or number three, most of the time you'll notice that the video gets a much higher click-through rate. This is because there is a large image displaying what that video is. Where are you going to click when you're searching? A static piece of text or the image? A lot of attention goes to those video results. This chapter explains how to incorporate these types of videos for your services and optimize them to show up just like this in your market.

Video Helps with Your Overall SEO Effort

The other thing that we can accomplish with video is the enhancement of our SEO efforts. As covered in the SEO chapter, links are critical for ranking. By creating good video content, you have the ability to drive inbound links to your website from high level video sites like YouTube and Vimeo. Again, you don't want to have just the generic Home, About Us, Our Services, Contact Us pages on your website. You want to have a page for each of your core services and products. Videos that link to those pages is going to help with that SEO effort.

Also, you're going to find that video content on your website, and on the pages of your site, actually reduces your bounce rate and increases visitors' time on your site. These are SEO factors. 'Bounce rate' refers to somebody getting to your page and clicking back immediately or Browse away. Google understands those actions as the page not being relevant to that search. If the majority of the people that get to your site click off and leave right away, your bounce rate is high, and Google is going to start to show you less prominently in their results. That's part of the Google algorithm. The other factor is the amount of time spent on the site. If somebody gets to your page, stays there for ten seconds, and then moves on, the visit might not get treated like a bounce, but Google is still looking at the length on the site. If you have a video and a visitor takes the time to watch it in its entirety, that's improving your website visit length statistics. Even if they only watch a couple seconds of the video, you have captured their attention long enough that Google is going to see your site is relevant.

Don't get confused by the notion that having video on your page automatically improves your SEO. That's not necessarily the case. But having people stay on your page longer and not bounce off does impact SEO.

Here's an example of how you can drive some links with your videos. Let's look at Stanley "Dirt Monkey" Genadek, one of the most successful construction YouTube channels. With over 1,000,000 subscribers, his channel covers everything from excavation to paving, and he uses it masterfully to promote his landscaping and excavation business.

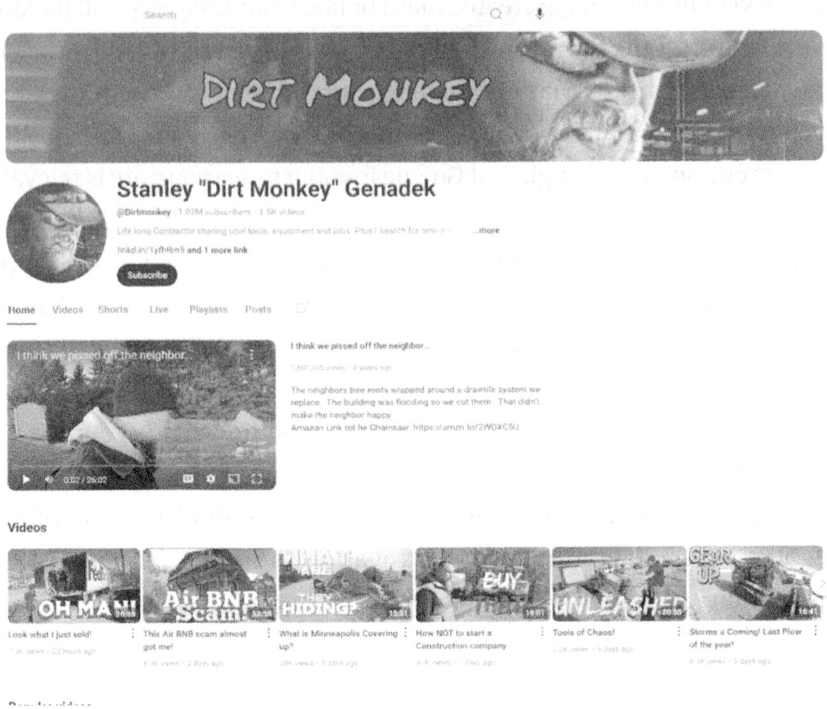

In the description area of his videos, he always includes links to his website and social media, creating valuable backlinks. Notice how each video includes his business information and service areas. This strategy doesn't just build his authority as an expert but creates a constant stream of links back to his main business site.

Above the Fold

Keeping a video above the fold means that you don't have to scroll down to see the most important information. Notice that as soon as this page is pulled up you immediately see the video. You will want to do the same, providing an intro video about who you are and what you do. That video, placed correctly above the fold, will improve on-page site time and reduce your bounce rate.

I've mentioned the fact that video gives you more placement in search. It's going to give you better search engine optimization because you get the links from the video sites, you're improving your time on site, and reducing your bounce rate. But the benefit of video that is probably even more powerful than anything, is that it's going to improve conversion. You can have the best SEO strategy in the world and drive hundreds of people that are looking for your services to your home page or to your subpage daily. But, if it's not converting and people aren't picking up the phone and calling to hire you for your services after they visit your site, you're missing a major opportunity.

Improving Conversion with Video

Improving conversion is one of the main things having intelligent video on your site will do for you. The fact is that video clips resonate with people. They like video because it gives them the chance to get to know and trust you before they call you, especially if you follow my strategy rather than creating a super corporate video. If you create authentic video of your team, the owner or your crew supervisor talking directly to the camera, connecting with you on an emotional level, answering questions and giving a strong call to action, your conversion rate will improve.

Video also gives you the ability to connect with different people. Everybody thinks in a different way. Some people are readers and will read all the content on a page. Some people are listeners, so if there's the opportunity to listen to something rather than read, they'll choose to listen. Other people like something visual. Motion grabs their eye. By having video on your website, combined with text (I'm not saying to abandon text), you have the opportunity to connect with every type of person. Some people will watch the video and only connect with that, because they wouldn't take the time to read a plain text web page.

Types of Videos for Paving Companies

There are several video formats that work particularly well for paving contractors:

1. **Before and After Transformations** Before and after videos create powerful visual evidence of your capabilities. These can be as simple as a short clip showing the condition of a driveway or parking lot before work begins, followed by the completed project. The visual impact of seeing cracked, deteriorated asphalt transformed into a smooth, clean surface is incredibly persuasive. These videos should be 30-90 seconds long and focus on showing dramatic improvements and quality of work. The side-by-side or transition shots showing deteriorated pavement transformed into smooth, fresh surfaces create an immediate impact that text or still photos simply cannot match.

2. **Project Time-Lapse Videos** Time-lapse videos compress hours or days of work into a minute or two, showcasing your team's efficiency and the entire process. These videos help potential customers understand what to expect during their project while highlighting your professional approach and equipment capabilities. These videos typically run 1-2 minutes and show condensed footage of an entire paving project from start to finish. They're particularly effective for demonstrating your crew's efficiency and the care taken throughout the process.

3. **Educational Content** Educational videos position you as an industry expert. Topics might include "How to Determine if Your Asphalt Needs Replacing or Repair," "The Difference Between Asphalt and Concrete Driveways," "5 Ways to Extend the Life of Your Commercial Parking Lot," or "What to Expect During Your Paving Project." These videos should be 2-5 minutes long and focus on explanations of paving processes, material differences, and maintenance tips. They attract viewers actively researching paving services and help address common questions or

concerns before they become objections.

4. Customer Testimonial Videos Testimonial videos featuring real customers speaking about their positive experiences are incredibly persuasive. These can be simple interviews where customers discuss why they chose your company, their experience during the project, their satisfaction with the results, and what they'd tell someone considering your services. These videos typically run 1-3 minutes and build trust through social proof. Nothing sells your services better than a satisfied customer explaining why they chose you and how happy they are with the results.

5. Company Overview/Introduction An introduction video helps potential customers get to know your company on a personal level. This might include your company history and founding story, introduction to key team members, your service philosophy and values, overview of equipment and capabilities, and service area and specializations. These videos should be 1-3 minutes long and focus on humanizing your business and building connection. They're perfect for your homepage and "About Us" section.

6. Service-Specific Videos Create dedicated videos for each of your core services, such as Residential Driveway Installation, Commercial Parking Lot Paving, Asphalt Repair and Patching, Sealcoating Services, and Concrete Work. These 1-2 minute videos highlight specific offerings and expertise. They allow you to target specific customer needs and appear in more relevant searches. Each video should include detailed information about the particular service and can be embedded on the corresponding service page of your website.

Leveraging Video

How can we leverage video? We understand that it's powerful, it's going to improve your SEO, it's going to help us get better placement on the search engines, and it could potentially help with conversion. How can we expand upon this?

What we want to do is create simple videos about your company, your services, and the most frequently asked questions. You are then going to upload those videos to YouTube and other video-sharing sites, and syndicate them to your website and social media profiles.

What type of video should you create? Like I keep saying, "People resonate with people." Keep it simple, be real and be personable. Put your real face on the camera, or the face of someone that represents your company. Be frank and to the point. It doesn't have to be a 20-minute video. An appropriate length would be 30 seconds to three minutes long, enough to get the message across.

Don't Overthink It!

Don't feel like you have to go all out and hire a high-end production crew or go out and buy an HD camera in order to make this happen. The reality is, you can create video clips using technology that you already have. If you've got a 4g smartphone or a webcam, you have the ability to create video content that will work for your website.

You don't need high-end editing software either. YouTube gives you the ability to upload regular video and edit it right within the system. By edit, I mean cropping and tailoring the video to begin and end where you wish. You can put your phone number down in the bottom area of the video as well as a link to your website. Or you can use a simple editing software like iMovie (free with Macintosh computers) and Movie Maker (free with the PC).

Using the technology that you already have, stand in front of a company sign with your logo or in your office, and talk to the camera; talk with the people that are visiting your website, because that's going to stick with them.

Equipment and Production Basics

Creating effective videos doesn't require expensive equipment or professional production. Here are the essentials for producing quality paving videos:

Essential Equipment

- **Cameras**: Modern **smartphones** (iPhone 12+ or equivalent Android) are capable of excellent video quality and are often all you need for basic videos. For higher quality, a **mid-range camera** ($500-900) offers better low-light performance and lens options. **Action cameras** like GoPro are excellent for mounting on equipment to capture dynamic footage during operations, and **drones** can provide impressive aerial footage of larger commercial projects for $400-600.
- **Audio**: Audio is critical – the built-in microphone on cameras/phones is rarely sufficient. Consider a **lavalier (clip-on) microphone** for interviews ($20-80) or a **shotgun microphone** for better directional audio ($50-200). A **wind shield** is essential for outdoor recording to prevent wind noise.
- **Stabilization**: A **tripod** is essential for static shots and professional appearance. A **gimbal** can be used for smooth movement shots, especially useful for walking tours of projects. **Vehicle/equipment mounts** can capture footage during the paving process.
- **Lighting**: Schedule filming during **optimal daylight hours** when possible. **Portable LED light panels** ($50-150) can be used for interviews or detail shots.

Basic Production Process

- **Planning**: Script or outline key points to cover, plan essential shots (before condition, process highlights, finished result), check weather forecasts for outdoor filming, and prepare interview questions for testimonials.
- **Filming**: Capture more footage than you think you'll need, get multiple angles of the same process, film in landscape (horizontal) orientation, keep the camera steady, ensure proper lighting (avoid backlighting), and for before/after shots, use consistent angles and lighting conditions.
- **Editing Software Options**:
- **Entry Level (Free)**: iMovie (Mac), Windows Video Editor (PC)
- **Mid-Range**: Adobe Premiere Elements ($99), Filmora ($69.99/year)
- **Professional**: Adobe Premiere Pro ($20.99/month), Final Cut Pro ($299)
- **Mobile**: LumaFusion (iOS, $29.99), KineMaster (Android/iOS, subscription)
- **Editing Best Practices**: Keep videos concise and focused, add text overlays to highlight key points, include your company logo/contact information, use transitions sparingly, add background music (use royalty-free sources like Epidemic Sound or YouTube's Audio Library), and consider adding captions for accessibility.
- **Branding**: Always include branding elements such as consistent intro and outro segments, lower-third graphics with names and titles, a watermarked logo in corner, and an end screen with call-to-action and contact information.

Cost-Effective Approaches

You don't need to invest thousands in equipment to create effective videos.

- **Smartphone Setup ($100-300)**: Smartphone you own, tripod mount

adapter ($15-25), basic tripod ($30-50), lavalier microphone ($20-80), simple editing app ($0-30).
- **Leverage Existing Work**: Make video documentation part of your regular project process. Assign a team member to capture "before" conditions when providing estimates, take regular progress photos/videos, and capture final results for every project.
- **Batch Production**: Film multiple videos in one day, create templates for recurring video types, and develop a consistent editing style that speeds up post-production.

What Kind of Videos Should You Create?

You can create just about anything you want. But the ones that are going to be most relevant are the ones that pertain to your services.

The **first video** that I recommend you make is an introduction for your website. This can be as simple as, "Thank you so much for visiting the Joe's Paving Company website. We specialize in providing paving services to the Dallas area. These are the things that make us unique and why people tend to choose us. We'd love the opportunity to serve you. Give us a call right away at the number below, and we can send somebody to your house to resolve your asphalt issue right away." A simple video along those lines should be the first step of your plan. It's a necessity.

The other videos that you want to create should be about your **primary services**. This ties in well with the SEO strategy discussed previously. You want to make sure you have a page on your website for each one of the services that you provide.

The other very powerful piece of content that you should incorporate, but should be phase two, would be your **frequently asked questions (FAQ)**. Make a list of the questions that people tend to ask and create a little video about it. A few examples include: What to do in the event of a pothole; what to do about cracks in your driveway; Why restripe your parking lot. Get creative! This is common information to you, but the average consumer doesn't know. Creating a little video providing answers to these frequently asked questions makes for great video content for your YouTube channel, to be syndicated on your social media profiles, and/or uploaded to your blog on your website.

Sharing Your Message

Now that we know what types of videos we want to create and how to create them, what should we say? Should we have a script? Should we wing it? You want to be natural, you want to be authentic, and you want to be real. Some people must have a script because they don't feel comfortable doing video outside of a scripted methodology. But, if there is any way you can get in front of a camera and speak naturally like you would to a customer in person about your services, that's going to work best.

What to Say

Here is a simple script you can follow: "At Joe's Paving Company, we provide a full range of paving services (to the specific area, whatever area you're in, or whatever service this video is about)." Have a brief description of what you do in that area, and then, "If you're in need of this service in your area, we can help. Call our office today at 555-5555."

Let's do an example from another industry. Say you are an auto repair shop owner specializing in general repair or 4x4 services, your page might say:

"From Standard Interval Maintenance, to extensive repair, XYZ has you covered. Don't pay high dealership pricing for the same service XYZ can provide for a fraction of the cost, using the same OEM parts and Manufacturer suggested procedures to keep your vehicle running at its best! You don't want to sit around. You don't want to have to call 10 different companies. You just want to feel confident that who you call is going to get to you within a reasonable period of time. We are going to resolve the issue and we are not going to overcharge you. We can help you build an off-road machine capable of finding the road less traveled and exploring roads the average 4-wheel drive vehicle isn't capable of reaching. You can reach us at 555-5555. As a matter of fact, if you reference this coupon code "Auto Repair Video" we'll knock $20.00 off your repair."

A simple video like that for each one of your services should always include a call to action telling them what to do. Also, if you feel comfortable with it, referencing a discount could go a long way. Don't over think this. Think about the core services that you offer. Shoot a quick 30-second to one-and-a-half-minute video about each and you're ready to roll.

YouTube Optimization

Creating videos is just the first step. To ensure your content reaches potential customers, proper optimization is essential:

YouTube Channel Setup

- **Channel Art**: Professional banner with logo and contact info
- **"About" Section**: Complete company details, service areas, keywords
- **Custom URL**: Claim once eligible (100+ subscribers)
- **Playlists**: Organize videos by service type or project category

Channel Optimization:

- **Channel Description**: Include business name, location, primary services, website, phone number, service area. Use relevant keywords.
- **Channel Trailer**: Create a video introducing your company.

Video Optimization Techniques

- **Title**: Include primary keyword + location (e.g., "Asphalt Driveway Installation in Dallas, TX"). Keep under 60 characters. Be compelling and specific.
- **Description**: Place website URL at the beginning (with http://). Include keywords, video summary, timestamps (for longer videos), NAP info, and relevant hashtags (3-5 max).
- **Tags**: Use brand terms, primary keywords, location terms, related terms. Research competitor tags. Use tools like TubeBuddy or vidIQ.
- **Thumbnail**: Create custom thumbnails. Use high-contrast images, text overlay, consistent branding. Show dramatic before/after images.
- **End Screens/Cards**: Promote related videos, link to website, include contact info.

What to Do with Your Video Content

Once you've created your videos, you need to set up a YouTube channel. Go to YouTube.com and upload your video, naming it correctly and intelligently using terms people will use when searching. For example, if somebody is looking for auto repair services, they are going to type in "your city auto repair services." You want to name the video using your keywords.

When you upload it to YouTube, title it with something like "Denver Auto Repair specialists" or "Denver Hail Damage Repair services" and then put a description with a link to your site. Include something like "Visit us online at yourcompany.com/haildamagerepair" and then include a description about what you do, briefly outlining what was said in your video.

YouTube Best Practices

- **Channel Title**: Use "City + Service + Company Name" (e.g., "Dallas Paving Contractor - ABC Paving").
- **Tags**: Add relevant keywords to your channel settings.
- **Description**: Include services, city, phone number, and consistent NAP.
- **Avatar**: Use your company logo or a professional team photo.

Log into YouTube, create your channel, and confirm your email. Go to "My Channel" settings to make updates:

- Change logo/avatar.
- Update channel name to include keywords and location.
- Add channel keywords (tags).
- Write a detailed "About" section including description, city, phone, and full NAP (consistent with other listings).

Video Tagging Best Practices

When tagging your videos:

- **Title**: City Service - Company (mix up slightly)
- **Description**: Start with http://url.com, describe service using keywords, add NAP info at bottom.
- **Tags**: Use keywords (city + service), company name.
- **Thumbnail**: Choose the most compelling screenshot.
- **Advanced Settings**: Add address to video location.

The first thing you want to do is have your primary keywords in the title of the video as well as a description that includes the http:// before your web address. In the description area, you can put in "We're a full service XYZ company. We serve this area. This is our name, address and phone number," but at the very top, you should have your website address, including the http://. If you just put www.yourcompany.com, YouTube won't understand the link and it will show that it isn't clickable. If you put http:// the link will be clickable, and visitors will go straight to your page, and they also get the link authority from having that link back to your website.

Choose the screenshot and add video. Whenever you upload your video you are able to control your title and your description, as well as the ability to add tags.

Titles Matter

Again, don't call your videos "your company name." Don't call it "teeth cleaning." Don't call it "auto repair." Call it **"Your city + that service,"** and then your company name. Title your videos the same way that somebody would search. If it's your intro video, you might want to call it "your city + your primary service" Example: you're a local "Lakeland cosmetic dentistry – XYZ Dentistry." If it's the teeth cleaning page, "your city teeth cleaning services – XYZ Dentistry". It is really critical that you have the right titles on your video. This is what is going to make it so Google can locate it and include it in search results.

The next thing you want to do in your **description** is to put the link at the very top. The first thing you want to do is include a link back to the home page or to the specific page that you're discussing in the video. If it's the teeth cleaning page, don't put a link to your home page. Put a link to that teeth cleaning page, and again http://yourcompany.com — make sure you've got that http://.

Below, you add your **tags**. Within those tags you can put in your city dentist, your city auto repairing, your city teeth cleaning, and everything in between.

SEO Strategies for YouTube

- **Keyword Research**: Use Google Keyword Planner, research common paving questions, check autocomplete, analyze competitors.
- **Video Schema Markup**: Implement on website embeds. Include upload date, description, thumbnail.
- **Engagement Signals**: Respond to comments, ask questions, request engagement, share across platforms.
- **YouTube Analytics**: Monitor traffic drivers, audience retention, traffic sources, use insights for future content.

Video Integration on Website and Social Media

Your videos should be leveraged across all your marketing channels for maximum impact.

Website Integration

- **Homepage**: Feature short company overview/highlight reel above the fold. Consider autoplay (muted). Include CTA.
- **Service Pages**: Embed relevant service-specific videos. Pair with written content. Demonstrate complex processes.
- **Video Gallery**: Create project showcase or testimonial section. Organize by type/service. Include descriptions.
- **Landing Pages**: Add videos to increase conversions (up to 80%). Keep short (30-90s) and focused on offer.
- **Technical Implementation**: Optimize for fast loading (compression, lazy loading), responsive embedding, include transcripts.

What Else Can You Do with Your Videos?

Now that you've updated your video and you've properly optimized it, your title is correct, and your description is posted, how can we use these videos? Where are we going to leverage them? Well, to really get the benefits of that conversion component, we need those videos to be posted on our website and social profiles as well.

The best way to do this is to copy the "embed code" and post the videos right on your site. The intro video should be embedded on the home page and the service-specific videos should be posted on the appropriate subpages.

The way we do this is right within our YouTube channel or YouTube account. Go to the video manager and find the list of all the videos that you have. Choose the video that you want to post on your website and choose the share and embed option. You will then be provided with a little piece of code.

It goes from <iframe> to </iframe>. This is the specific code for that video. If you are updating your website on your own, copy and paste the code right into your website's HTML. If you have a detached web manager, send the code off to them with details on where you want it posted. Once the code is embedded in your HTML, it will show up on the page itself. That's what we really want to do with these videos.

And, of course we don't have to limit ourselves to YouTube. There are a lot of very well known video sharing sites out there.

Social Media Distribution

- **Platform Optimization**: Upload natively to Facebook. Create short versions (30-60s) for Instagram feed/Reels, longer for IGTV. Focus on commercial projects for LinkedIn. Use quick transitions for TikTok.
- **Content Repurposing**: Create multiple short clips from longer videos. Add captions (85% FB videos watched silently). Optimize aspect ratio. Extract moments for GIFs.
- **Scheduling**: Share when audience is most active. Plan regular video content. Boost effective videos.
- **Cross-Promotion**: Promote YouTube videos elsewhere. Use email to share new videos. Encourage sharing ("tag someone...").

Using Project Videos as Testimonials

Project videos can serve as powerful testimonials even without customer interviews.

- **Show Transformation**: Problem to solution. Text overlays on issues addressed. End with satisfied customer if possible.
- **Add Customer Voice**: Overlay text quotes. Include brief audio testimonials. Show customer reactions.
- **Focus on Results**: Highlight challenges overcome. Show measurement tools (slope, thickness). Demonstrate quality testing.
- **Context**: Include project details (size, time). Note unique challenges. Mention project longevity (if applicable).

Video is a critical platform in the modern marketing environment. As AI content becomes increasingly pervasive - it is your "real" and personal content that will make you stand out.

III

Part Three

Now we turn our attention to "offline" marketing channels, like direct mail. These have stood the test of time, and should be an integral part of your marketing strategy.

11

Introduction To Offline Marketing Channels

While digital marketing has transformed how paving companies find customers, traditional offline marketing channels remain powerful tools for generating high-quality leads. In many cases, these "old-school" tactics outperform their digital counterparts, particularly when targeting specific neighborhoods or commercial properties.

In Part 3, we'll explore the most effective offline marketing strategies for paving companies. We'll begin with direct mail—a method that, despite predictions of its demise, continues to deliver impressive results for contractors. We'll then cover local newspaper and magazine advertising, door-to-door marketing, yard signs and vehicle branding, local broadcast advertising, billboard advertising, referral marketing, and community networking.

Each of these channels has unique strengths and applications. By incorporating them strategically into your overall marketing plan, you can create multiple touchpoints with potential customers and reach audiences who might not find you through digital channels alone.

Let's start by exploring one of the most consistently effective offline marketing channels for paving contractors: direct mail.

12

Direct Mail Marketing

Direct mail marketing—sending physical marketing materials to prospective customers via postal mail—remains one of the most effective ways for paving companies to target specific neighborhoods or commercial property owners. Despite the growth of digital marketing, direct mail delivers tangible advantages that make it a valuable component of any paving contractor's marketing strategy.

Why Direct Mail Works for Paving Companies

The effectiveness of direct mail for paving contractors comes down to several key factors:

- **Geographically Targeted**: You can select specific neighborhoods or streets to target, focusing on areas with older homes, recent construction, or characteristics that indicate potential need for your services.
- **Tangible Impact**: Unlike digital ads that can be easily scrolled past, physical mail pieces must be handled by the recipient. This creates a different type of engagement than digital marketing.
- **Less Competition**: While email inboxes overflow with marketing messages, physical mailboxes receive far fewer pieces. Your direct

mail piece has a better chance of being noticed.

- **High-Value Services**: Paving services typically involve significant investments, making the higher cost-per-lead of direct mail justified by the large contract values.
- **Visual Medium**: Direct mail allows you to showcase before/after photos of your work, which is particularly effective for demonstrating paving transformations.

Research Findings on Direct Mail Effectiveness

According to research data, direct mail produces solid results for home service businesses:

- The average cost per lead for direct mail in the home services context is around **$51**, according to the Data & Marketing Association (DMA).
- Response rates of **1-2% are typical for prospect lists**, while mailings to existing customers can generate **5% or higher** response rates.
- Direct mail recipients spend **25% more** than non-direct mail recipients.
- The median ROI for direct mail is **29%**, putting it on par with social media marketing.

For a paving company, these numbers translate to practical outcomes. If you mail 1,000 postcards at a cost of approximately $500 (including design, printing, and postage), a 1.5% response rate would generate 15 leads at a cost of about $33 per lead. If one-third of those leads convert to jobs with an average value of $3,500, the campaign would generate $17,500 in revenue from a $500 investment—a substantial return.

Postcard Design Principles for Paving Services

The design of your direct mail piece significantly impacts response rates. For paving companies, the following design principles have proven effective:

Visual Elements

- **Before/After Photography**: The most powerful visual for paving companies is the dramatic transformation from old, cracked pavement to smooth, fresh asphalt. Use high-quality before/after photos of your actual work—avoid stock photography that recipients will recognize as inauthentic.
- **Company Branding**: Maintain consistent branding including your logo, colors, and fonts that match your website and other marketing materials. This builds recognition across all customer touchpoints.
- **Clear Contact Information**: Make your phone number and website prominent and easy to read. Consider including a QR code that leads directly to a landing page with a special offer.
- **Professional Design**: Invest in professional design services or use quality templates from your direct mail provider. Amateur-looking materials signal amateur work quality to potential customers.

Content Elements

- **Compelling Headline**: Lead with a strong headline addressing a pain point: "Is Your Driveway an Embarrassment?" or "Transform Your Property's First Impression in Just One Day."
- **Clear Value Proposition**: Explain why the recipient should choose your company. Focus on benefits like increased property value, curb appeal, and safety.
- **Special Offer**: Include a time-limited offer or discount to create urgency: "Spring Special: 15% Off Driveways" or "Book by June 15

and Save $300."

- **Social Proof**: Add a short testimonial from a satisfied customer, ideally from the same neighborhood you're targeting.
- **Call to Action**: Tell recipients exactly what to do next: "Call Today for Your Free Estimate" or "Visit our website to schedule your free property assessment."

Format Options

Different formats work for different purposes:

- **Standard Postcards (4.25" x 6")**: These are the most cost-effective option and work well for simple messages and seasonal reminders.
- **Oversized Postcards (6" x 9" or larger)**: These stand out in the mail stack and provide more room for before/after photos and detailed information.
- **Self-Mailers**: These folded pieces can include more content and multiple photos without an envelope. They work well for explaining more complex services or showcasing multiple projects.
- **Letters**: For higher-end commercial prospects, a professional letter on company letterhead can be more appropriate than a postcard.
- **Lumpy Mail**: Including a small 3D object creates curiosity and virtually guarantees the mail will be opened. For example, a small sample of asphalt with a message like "We can make your whole driveway this smooth."

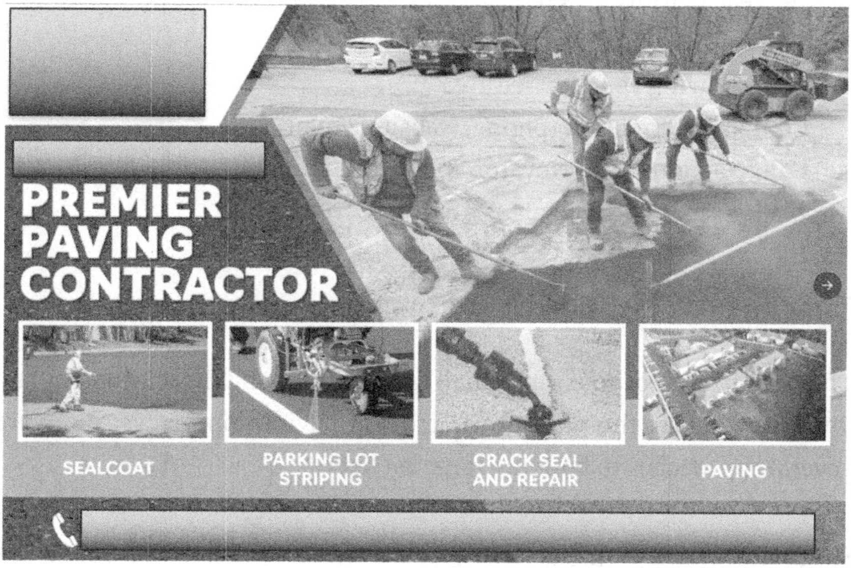

Here's an example of an effective layout for a 6" x 9" postcard:

Front Side:

- Large, attention-grabbing headline: "Transform Your Cracked Driveway in Just ONE Day!"
- Dramatic before/after photos taking up most of the space
- Your logo and contact information
- A burst with your special offer: "Spring Special: 15% Off Through May 31st"

Back Side:

- Company name and logo at the top
- Brief paragraph explaining your expertise and quality materials
- 3-4 bullet points highlighting benefits ("Increases Property Value,"

"5-Year Warranty," etc.)

- Testimonial from a local customer
- Map showing your service area
- Contact information (phone, website, email)
- Call to action: "Call Now for Your Free Estimate!"
- Mailing area with recipient's address

Targeting and List Building

The effectiveness of your direct mail campaign depends heavily on sending your materials to the right prospects. For paving companies, there are several approaches to building targeted lists:

Geographic Targeting Focus on specific neighborhoods or areas based on:

- **Home Age**: Target subdivisions where homes are 15-20 years old, as this is typically when driveways need replacement. County property records can provide construction dates.
- **Home Value**: Higher-value homes typically have longer driveways and owners with more disposable income for property improvements.
- **Recent Construction**: New developments where homes have just been completed but still need driveways installed.
- **Local Climate Factors**: Areas with severe freeze-thaw cycles or particularly harsh weather conditions that accelerate pavement deterioration.
- **Previous Project Proximity**: Target homes within a 1-mile radius of your completed projects. Neighbors often notice quality paving work.

List Sources Several sources can provide targeted mailing lists:

- **Current Customer Database**: Your existing customers are your best source for repeat business and referrals. Keep their contact information updated and organized.

- **Public Records**: County assessor records provide property information including age, size, and ownership details. These can be accessed directly or through data services.
- **List Brokers**: Companies like InfoUSA, Experian, and Exact Data sell targeted lists based on numerous demographic and property criteria. Expect to pay $0.10-$0.25 per name depending on specificity.
- **New Homeowner Lists**: Services like Welcomemat or MoversTech provide lists of recent home buyers who often have immediate driveway needs.
- **Commercial Property Directories**: For commercial paving, directories like CoStar or services like D&B Hoovers can help identify property management companies and commercial property owners.
- **Post Office EDDM (Every Door Direct Mail)**: This service allows you to mail to every address on selected postal routes without needing specific addresses. It's cost-effective for saturating target neighborhoods.

List Segmentation for Paving Companies Divide your list into segments to create more relevant messaging:

- **Residential vs. Commercial**: These customers have different needs, concerns, and decision processes.
- **Previous Customers**: Segment by service type and time since last service (for maintenance offers).
- **Property Type**: Homeowners, multi-family property managers, commercial property owners, industrial facilities, etc.
- **Service Need**: New installation vs. repair/resurfacing vs. maintenanc e/sealcoating.
- **Geographic Area**: Create neighborhood-specific messaging mentioning local landmarks or recent projects in the area.

By segmenting your list, you can create more personalized messages that speak directly to each prospect's specific situation, significantly improving response rates.

Multi-Touch Campaigns

Single mailers rarely achieve maximum impact. Multi-touch campaigns—sending a sequence of coordinated pieces over time—dramatically improve response rates:

Sample Multi-Touch Campaign for Spring Season

- **Touch 1 (Early March)**: Oversized postcard introducing your company and spring specials, focusing on winter damage repair.
- **Touch 2 (Late March, to non-responders)**: Standard postcard with more urgent messaging about scheduling before the summer rush.
- **Touch 3 (Early April, to non-responders)**: Self-mailer with more detailed information about your process and materials, plus testimonials from satisfied customers.
- **Touch 4 (Late April, to non-responders)**: Final "last chance" postcard emphasizing that the special offer expires soon and your schedule is filling up.

This approach typically generates 30-50% more responses than a single mailing, as each subsequent touch reinforces your message and catches prospects at different stages of readiness.

Cross-Channel Integration

Direct mail works best when integrated with other marketing channels:

- **Direct Mail + Digital**: Include a unique URL or QR code on your mailer that leads to a dedicated landing page. This allows you to track responses and retarget visitors with online ads.
- **Direct Mail + Phone**: Follow up high-value mailings with a phone

call: "I'm just calling to make sure you received our information about driveway paving services..."

- **Direct Mail + Email**: If you have email addresses for recipients, send a coordinating email shortly after the mail piece should have arrived.
- **Direct Mail + Door-to-Door**: Have your sales team canvass neighborhoods shortly after mail pieces arrive, referencing the mailer when they knock.

This integrated approach creates multiple touchpoints and gives prospects different ways to respond based on their preferences.

Tracking Response Rates

To maximize ROI, you need to know which campaigns and elements are working:

Response Tracking Methods

- **Dedicated Phone Numbers**: Use different phone numbers for different campaigns to track which one generated the call.
- **Campaign-Specific Promo Codes**: Include a unique code that customers mention when they call.
- **Personalized URLs (PURLs)**: Create personalized web addresses for recipients to visit (e.g., yourpavingcompany.com/johnsmith).
- **QR Codes**: Include QR codes that direct to specific landing pages with tracking parameters.
- **Ask Customers**: Train your staff to always ask new leads, "How did you hear about us?"
- **Revenue Commander Integration**: Our Revenue Commander platform can track and attribute leads from your direct mail campaigns, connecting them to your overall marketing analytics.

Response Rate Calculation To calculate response rate, use this simple formula: Response Rate = (Number of Responses ÷ Number of Pieces Mailed) × 100 For example, if you mail 1,000 postcards and receive 15 calls, your response rate is 1.5%.

But what really matters is ROI, not just response rate. To calculate this: ROI = [(Revenue Generated - Campaign Cost) ÷ Campaign Cost] × 100 For example, if your $500 campaign generated $17,500 in revenue: ROI = [($17,500 - $500) ÷ $500] × 100 = 3,400%

These metrics help you determine which campaigns and list segments are most profitable and deserve continued investment.

Seasonal Campaign Planning

Paving is inherently seasonal in most regions, and your direct mail strategy should align with these seasonal patterns:

Spring (March-May)

- **Theme**: "Repair Winter Damage" / "Boost Your Curb Appeal"
- **Targeting**: Focus on areas with visible winter damage. Target homeowners preparing for spring real estate listings.
- **Offers**: Early-bird specials, spring clean-up packages combining paving with other services.
- **Timing**: Begin mailings as soon as weather allows work to begin. Emphasize scheduling before the summer rush.

Summer (June-August)

- **Theme**: "Summer Transformation" / "Finish Your Outdoor Space"
- **Targeting**: New homeowners, commercial properties planning maintenance during good weather.
- **Offers**: Package deals (driveway + walkway), weekend scheduling for

residential customers.
- **Timing**: Focus on early summer as schedules often fill by mid-season.

Fall (September-November)

- **Theme**: "Prepare for Winter" / "Last Chance Before Winter"
- **Targeting**: Properties with minor damage that could worsen during winter, commercial properties preparing for end-of-year budgets.
- **Offers**: Fall maintenance packages, pre-winter sealcoating, "use it or lose it" budget offers for commercial customers.
- **Timing**: Create urgency around beating the winter weather.

Winter (December-February)

- **Theme**: "Plan Now for Spring" / "Lock in Last Year's Pricing"
- **Targeting**: Commercial property planning, homeowners in planning phase.
- **Offers**: Early booking discounts for spring projects, winter planning consultations.
- **Timing**: Focus on budget planning periods. In warmer regions, promote off-season discount work.

Each of these seasonal campaigns should be designed with appropriate imagery and messaging. For example, spring campaigns might show melting snow revealing damaged pavement, while fall campaigns could emphasize protection from upcoming winter conditions.

Direct Mail Success Story: Neighborhood Domination Strategy

Here's a real-world example of an effective direct mail strategy for a paving company:

A mid-sized paving contractor in the Midwest implemented what they called a "Neighborhood Domination Strategy." They would identify a neighborhood with homes 15-20 years old, then:

1. Send an initial oversized postcard to every home in the neighborhood with a special offer.
2. When they secured their first project in the neighborhood, they placed yard signs during the work.
3. After completing the first driveway, they took professional photos and created a second, neighborhood-specific postcard showing the actual work in the recipient's neighborhood: "We just completed this beautiful driveway for your neighbor on Elm Street!"
4. To create additional urgency, they offered a neighborhood discount: "Book while our crews are already in your neighborhood and save 15% on mobilization costs."
5. They followed up with door hangers in a 2-block radius of each completed project.

The results were impressive. Their typical response rate for standard postcards was 1.2%, but this neighborhood-focused approach increased response to 3.8%. The company regularly secured 5-8 jobs from a single neighborhood of 200 homes, creating efficient routing and higher profit margins due to reduced travel time and setup costs. The strategy effectively turned one job into multiple projects through strategic direct mail follow-up.

Implementation Checklist

Use this checklist to implement an effective direct mail campaign for your paving company:

Planning and Strategy

- Define campaign objectives and target audience

- Set budget and expected ROI goals
- Determine optimal timing based on seasonality
- Select appropriate mail format for your message
- Develop compelling offer and call to action

List Development

- Identify target neighborhoods or commercial properties
- Source or build appropriate mailing lists
- Clean and verify addresses
- Segment list for personalized messaging
- Prepare list in required format for mailing service

Design and Production

- Create compelling headline and copy
- Select powerful before/after imagery
- Include all necessary elements (offer, contact info, CTA)
- Design for visual impact and readability
- Proofread all content carefully
- Print sample for final approval

Mailing and Tracking

- Set up tracking mechanisms (unique phone numbers, codes, URLs)
- Integrate with Revenue Commander for response tracking
- Schedule mailings for optimal delivery timing
- Prepare follow-up touches for non-responders
- Brief staff on handling and tracking responses

Analysis and Optimization

- Record all responses by source and campaign

- Calculate response rates and ROI
- Identify highest-performing segments and offers
- Document lessons learned for future campaigns
- Plan follow-up campaigns based on results

Conclusion: Direct Mail as Part of Your Marketing Mix

Direct mail should be viewed as one component of an integrated marketing strategy. It works particularly well for paving companies because of the visual nature of your work, the geographic targeting possibilities, and the high value of each converted lead. When combined with digital marketing, yard signs, vehicle branding, and other channels we'll discuss in upcoming chapters, direct mail creates multiple touchpoints with potential customers. This multi-channel approach significantly increases the likelihood that when a property owner decides to invest in paving, your company will be top-of-mind.

In the next chapter, we'll explore local newspaper and magazine advertising—another traditional channel that continues to deliver results for paving companies targeting specific communities.

13

Local Newspaper And Magazine Advertising

Despite declining readership, local newspapers and magazines remain valuable advertising channels for paving companies. These publications reach engaged local audiences, including decision-makers who may not be as active online. Understanding when and how to effectively utilize print advertising can provide a valuable supplement to your digital and direct mail efforts.

The Current State of Print Advertising

The landscape of print advertising has changed significantly over the past decade:

- **Declining Overall Readership**: Print circulation has decreased as readers shift to digital sources. However, this decline varies significantly by market and publication type.
- **Demographic Shifts**: Print readers now skew older, more affluent, and more established in their communities—demographics that align well with paving service needs.
- **Reduced Ad Clutter**: With fewer advertisers using print, your ad has

less competition for attention.

- **Greater Negotiating Power**: Many publications now offer more flexible rates and value-added services to attract advertisers.
- **Community Focus**: Local publications have doubled down on hyper-local content that cannot be found elsewhere, maintaining relevance with their core audience.

Research Findings on Print Advertising

Our research on local print advertising reveals important insights:

- A small ad in a local weekly newspaper might cost around **$225 per week for a 2.5"x4" ad reaching about 10,000 households**. This works out to roughly a $22 CPM (cost per thousand impressions).
- Larger metropolitan newspapers can charge several hundred to thousands of dollars for bigger ads.
- According to Fit Small Business, the average cost for a one-column-inch black and white ad in print is about **$756**, though this average skews higher due to major publications.
- **Fewer than half of people find print ads (newspaper/magazine) to be credible**—people know ads are biased, so they may view them skeptically.
- Print advertising typically generates response rates of **0.5-2%**—lower than direct mail but still significant when targeting the right audience.

These statistics highlight both the challenges and opportunities of print advertising. While overall trust and response rates may be lower than some channels, the targeted reach and demographic alignment can make it worthwhile for paving contractors in specific markets.

Types of Print Publications for Paving Advertising

Different types of publications offer various advantages for paving contractors:

Community Newspapers These smaller, locally-focused papers often serve specific towns, neighborhoods, or suburbs. They typically feature:

- High Local Relevance: Content focused exclusively on local news, events, and businesses.
- Loyal Readership: Often read cover-to-cover by engaged community members.
- Affordable Rates: Much lower cost than metropolitan publications.
- Targeted Distribution: Circulation limited to your precise service area.

These publications are ideal for paving companies with a specific geographic focus. Readers often turn to these papers specifically to connect with local businesses.

Metro/Regional Newspapers Larger newspapers covering cities or regions offer:

- Broader Reach: Access to a larger audience across multiple communities.
- Zoned Editions: Many offer neighborhood-specific inserts where you can target just your service areas.
- Digital + Print Packages: Often include online components with your print ad.
- Special Sections: Home improvement or "Spring Fix-Up" sections that align perfectly with paving services.

While more expensive, these publications can help establish broader market presence and brand recognition.

Community Magazines Monthly or quarterly magazines focused on local areas provide:

- High Production Quality: Glossy format showcases project photos effectively.
- Longer Shelf Life: Magazines stay in homes for weeks or months, creating multiple exposure opportunities.
- Targeted Demographics: Many focus on affluent neighborhoods and homeowners.
- Contextual Placement: Place your ad near relevant home improvement articles.

These publications often work well for higher-end residential paving services.

Industry-Specific Publications Publications targeting relevant industries or interests include:

- Real Estate Guides: Reach property owners interested in improving value.
- Home & Garden Magazines: Target homeowners actively investing in property improvements.
- Chamber of Commerce Directories: Connect with local businesses who may need commercial paving.
- HOA Newsletters: Direct access to neighborhoods with potential for multiple projects.

These specialized publications provide highly targeted access to prospect groups with specific needs.

Creating Effective Print Ads for Paving Companies

The limited space in print advertising requires strategic design and content decisions:

Print Ad Elements An effective paving company print ad should include:

- **Attention-Grabbing Headline**: Direct benefit statement like "Transform Your Property in Just One Day" or problem-focused approach like "Is Your Cracked Driveway Hurting Your Property Value?"
- **Compelling Visual**: Before/after photos work exceptionally well for paving companies. Show dramatic transformations relevant to your target audience.
- **Clear Offer**: Specific, time-limited promotion that creates urgency.
- **Credibility Elements**: Years in business, certifications, or a brief testimonial.
- **Contact Information**: Phone number, website, and physical location if relevant.
- **Call to Action**: Explicit instruction like "Call today for your free estimate" or "Visit our website to see more project photos."
- **Logo and Branding**: Consistent with your other marketing materials.

Ad Sizes and Formats Common newspaper ad sizes include:

- **Classified Ads**: Inexpensive text-only listings in the classified section. These have limited impact but can work as supplementary placements.
- **Display Ads**: Ranging from 1/8 page to full-page, these allow for visuals and more comprehensive messaging. For most paving companies, 1/4 page ads represent a good balance of visibility and cost.
- **Inserts/Flyers**: Pre-printed materials inserted into the newspaper, allowing for larger format and better print quality. These typically require higher volume commitments.

The most cost-effective size often depends on the publication. Request a media kit from each publication you're considering to compare options.

Design Best Practices Professional design significantly impacts response rates:

- **Simplicity**: Focus on one clear message rather than cramming too much information.
- **High Contrast**: Ensure text is easily readable with strong contrast between text and background.
- **Quality Images**: Use high-resolution photos that will reproduce well in print.
- **White Space**: Include enough blank space to make your ad stand out and prevent a cluttered appearance.
- **Consistent Branding**: Maintain visual consistency with your other marketing materials.
- **Borders**: Consider adding a border to set your ad apart on crowded pages.

Remember that newspaper print quality is generally lower than magazines, so avoid very small text or detailed images that might not reproduce clearly.

Strategic Placement for Maximum Impact

Where and when your ad appears significantly affects its performance:

Section Placement Different sections reach different audiences:

- **Home & Garden**: Perfect alignment with paving services.
- **Real Estate**: Targets people actively buying or selling homes who may need driveway improvements.
- **Local News**: Highest readership section in most publications.

- **Business**: Good for targeting commercial property owners.

Premium placement (such as back page, inside front cover, or above the fold on a prominent page) costs more but can dramatically increase visibility.

Frequency and Timing Consistency is crucial for print advertising:

- **Consistent Presence**: Regular ads build recognition and trust. A single ad rarely produces significant results.
- **Seasonal Timing**: Align with spring home improvement, fall maintenance, or other seasonal triggers.
- **Special Issues**: Target "Home Improvement" issues or annual "Service Provider Guides."
- **Day of Week**: For newspapers, some days have higher readership or reach different audiences. For example, Sunday editions typically have the highest readership, while Wednesday real estate sections might reach active property buyers.

Most print advertising professionals recommend a minimum three-month commitment to properly evaluate effectiveness.

Cost Considerations and Negotiation Strategies

Print advertising costs vary widely, but there are ways to maximize your budget:

Typical Pricing Structures Publications generally offer several pricing options:

- **One-Time Rate**: The highest cost per insertion, for single ad placements.
- **Short-Term Contract**: Reduced rates for commitments of 3-6

months.

- **Annual Contract**: The lowest rates, often 30-50% below one-time rates, for 12-month commitments.
- **Column Inch Pricing**: Many newspapers price by column inch (one column wide by one inch high), with discounts for larger sizes.
- **CPM-Based Pricing**: Some publications offer rates based on cost per thousand readers reached.

Negotiation Tactics The printed rate card is rarely the final price. Consider these negotiation strategies:

- **Request Remnant Space**: Last-minute unsold space is often available at steep discounts.
- **Frequency Discounts**: Commit to multiple insertions for lower per-ad rates.
- **Combo Deals**: Ask about packages that include their digital edition or website.
- **Seasonal Specials**: Many publications offer discounted rates during slower advertising periods.
- **Barter Arrangements**: In smaller markets, sometimes publications will trade advertising space for services.
- **Added Value**: Request complementary editorial coverage, social media mentions, or bonus insertions.

Always ask for the publication's media kit, which includes readership demographics, distribution information, and rate card. This helps you compare value between different publications.

Measuring Print Advertising Results

Unlike digital marketing, print doesn't provide automatic analytics, but you can still track performance:

Tracking Methods Implement these strategies to measure response:

- **Dedicated Phone Numbers**: Use a unique tracked number in each publication.
- **Special Offer Codes**: Include publication-specific promotion codes that customers must mention.
- **Custom URLs**: Create unique website addresses for each publication (e.g., yourcompany.com/tribune).
- **QR Codes**: Include scannable codes linking to tracking-enabled landing pages.
- **Customer Surveys**: Always ask new customers how they heard about you.
- **Revenue Commander Integration**: Our platform can incorporate print advertising data into your overall marketing analytics by tracking these response mechanisms.

Performance Metrics Key metrics to evaluate print advertising success include:

- **Cost Per Lead (CPL)**: Total ad cost divided by number of responses.
- **Cost Per Acquisition (CPA)**: Total ad cost divided by number of new customers acquired.
- **Return on Investment (ROI)**: Revenue generated compared to ad spend.
- **Lifetime Customer Value**: Consider the long-term value of customers acquired, not just the initial job.

Keep in mind that print advertising often has a longer response cycle than digital channels. Some readers might save your ad and contact you weeks or months later.

Case Study: Targeted Magazine Advertising Success

Here's a real-world example of effective print advertising for a paving company:

A mid-sized paving contractor in a suburban area was struggling to break into the higher-end residential market. They identified an upscale community magazine that was distributed exclusively to homes valued at $500,000 and above in their target area.

Instead of running a standard ad, they worked with the publication to create a half-page "advertorial" format that looked like an article titled "5 Signs Your Luxury Driveway Needs Attention." The piece included expert advice along with subtle promotion of their services and a small portfolio of high-end projects they had completed.

They committed to a six-month run with the monthly publication, rotating between the educational advertorial and a more traditional ad featuring dramatic before/after photos of upscale properties.

The results:

- The campaign generated 27 direct inquiries over six months
- 14 of those inquiries converted to jobs
- The average project value was $9,200 (compared to their typical $4,500 average)
- Total campaign cost: $3,600
- Revenue generated: $128,800
- ROI: 3,478%

The key to success was precise targeting of affluent homeowners through a publication they trusted, combined with educational content that positioned the company as experts in high-end paving work.

Print Advertising Integration with Other Channels

Print advertising works best as part of an integrated marketing approach:

Cross-Channel Reinforcement Coordinate print with other marketing efforts:

- **Consistent Messaging**: Use similar headlines and offers across all channels for reinforcement.
- **Digital Follow-Up**: Retarget online visitors who came from print ad URLs.
- **Direct Mail Enhancement**: Send direct mail to the same zip codes where your print ads appear for frequency and recognition.
- **Local SEO Alignment**: Ensure your Google Business Profile highlights the same offers and services featured in print ads.

This consistent, multi-channel approach creates multiple touchpoints with potential customers, increasing the effectiveness of each individual channel.

Creative Cross-Promotion Ideas Use print to promote other marketing channels:

- Social Media Call-Outs: "See more project photos on our Facebook page"
- Review Highlights: Feature snippets from your Google or Yelp reviews in print ads
- QR Codes: Link to video testimonials or project galleries
- Contest Promotion: "See our ad in the Tribune and enter code PAVE2023 on our website to win a free driveway sealcoating"

These cross-promotions help move prospects from print to digital channels where you can engage them more thoroughly.

Implementation Checklist

Use this checklist to implement effective print advertising:

Research and Planning

- Identify publications reaching your target audience
- Request media kits and readership demographics
- Compare cost per thousand readers (CPM) across options
- Determine optimal ad size and frequency
- Set clear goals and tracking mechanisms

Creative Development

- Create compelling headline and core message
- Select high-impact photography
- Design ad to stand out from surrounding content
- Include all essential elements (offer, contact info, CTA)
- Ensure design reproduces well in publication's print quality
- Develop tracking mechanism (code, custom URL, etc.)

Implementation

- Negotiate best possible rates and placement
- Submit artwork according to publication specifications
- Verify correct appearance in first issue
- Brief staff on handling and tracking responses
- Integrate tracking with Revenue Commander

Evaluation and Optimization

- Monitor response by publication and ad version
- Calculate cost per lead and ROI

- Test different headlines, offers, or designs
- Adjust placement or frequency based on results
- Decide whether to continue, modify, or discontinue based on performance

Conclusion: Print's Place in Modern Paving Marketing

While print advertising may not dominate marketing budgets as it once did, it remains a valuable channel for paving companies, particularly when targeting specific geographic areas or demographic groups. The key is viewing print as a complementary channel rather than a standalone strategy.

Print advertising works best when it's:

- Highly targeted to specific publications reaching your ideal customers
- Consistently maintained rather than run as one-off insertions
- Integrated with your digital, direct mail, and other marketing efforts
- Properly tracked to measure true ROI
- Regularly evaluated and optimized based on performance

When implemented strategically, print advertising can help establish your local presence, build credibility, and reach potential customers who might not find you through digital channels alone.

In the next chapter, we'll explore door-to-door marketing—a direct, high-impact approach that can be particularly effective for paving companies looking to capitalize on neighborhood momentum.

14

Door-To-Door Marketing

Door-to-door marketing—directly engaging potential customers at their homes or businesses—is a time-tested approach that remains remarkably effective for paving contractors. Despite the digital transformation of marketing, this grassroots method delivers exceptional results when implemented correctly, particularly for services with high visual impact like paving.

Why Door-to-Door Works for Paving Companies

The effectiveness of door-to-door marketing for paving contractors stems from several factors:

- **Demonstration Effect**: When potential customers can physically see your work on a neighbor's property, the quality speaks for itself. Door-to-door allows you to leverage completed projects by immediately contacting nearby properties.
- **Geographic Efficiency**: By canvassing neighborhoods where you're already working, you can cluster jobs in the same area, reducing travel time and equipment transportation costs.
- **High-Impact Visuals**: You can show physical samples, project photos, or even point to nearby completed work—far more powerful than

digital images.

- **Personal Connection**: Face-to-face interaction builds trust more quickly than any other marketing method. Potential customers can assess your professionalism and ask questions directly.
- **Immediate Feedback**: You gain valuable insights about what matters to homeowners in a specific area, allowing you to refine your pitch on the spot.
- **Difficult to Ignore**: Unlike digital ads that can be scrolled past or direct mail that might be discarded unopened, a person at the door typically receives at least a moment of attention.
- **Competitive Advantage**: As fewer companies engage in door-to-door marketing, those who do it well can stand out in the marketplace.

For paving contractors specifically, the visual nature of your work makes this approach particularly effective. When a potential customer can see a freshly paved driveway across the street, the contrast with their own aging pavement becomes immediately apparent.

Strategic Approaches to Door-to-Door Marketing

Not all door-to-door strategies are created equal. For paving companies, these approaches have proven most effective:

Project-Based Canvassing This approach involves canvassing nearby properties when you're already working in a neighborhood:

How It Works:

While your crew is paving one property, a sales representative canvasses nearby homes to leverage the visual impact of your work in progress. The representative can invite neighbors to watch the project unfold and see the quality firsthand.

Advantages:

- Creates immediacy—prospects can see your work quality right there in their neighborhood
- Offers potential for "group discounts" when multiple neighbors sign up
- Reduces travel costs for estimates and work
- Allows your sales team to point directly to the project as an example

Implementation:

- Identify 15-20 homes surrounding each job site with similar driveways/needs
- Canvass while your crew is working or just after completion when the transformation is most visible
- Bring before/after photos of the project you're completing or just completed
- Offer a "neighborhood discount" for booking while you're already in the area
- Leave door hangers for residents who aren't home

This approach converts at significantly higher rates than cold canvassing because prospects can immediately verify your work quality.

Targeted Neighborhood Sweeps This strategy involves systematically canvassing entire neighborhoods selected for specific characteristics:

How It Works:

Identify neighborhoods with favorable characteristics (home age, value, visible need for paving services) and systematically visit every home that appears to need your services.

Advantages:

- Allows for high-efficiency routing of your sales team
- Creates neighborhood awareness and word-of-mouth
- Enables you to become the "go-to" paver in specific areas
- Provides opportunity to distribute branded materials throughout a community

Implementation:

- Research neighborhoods built 15-20 years ago (when many driveways reach end of life)
- Focus on mid-to-high value homes where owners can afford quality paving
- Create a systematic approach to cover every relevant home
- Track which homes you've visited and any feedback received
- Return to promising prospects who weren't ready at first contact

While conversion rates are typically lower than project-based canvassing, the volume of contacts can make this approach worthwhile, particularly in well-selected neighborhoods.

Commercial Property Canvassing For commercial paving contractors, a different approach is required:

How It Works:

Identify commercial districts with aging parking lots or industrial areas with deteriorating pavement, then make in-person visits to discuss maintenance or replacement needs.

Advantages:

- Targets higher-value projects
- Reaches decision-makers who might ignore other marketing channels
- Allows for immediate property assessment and discussion
- Creates opportunity to build business relationships

Implementation:

- Research commercial properties in your service area
- Identify the property manager or owner before visiting if possible
- Bring commercial-focused materials and references
- Offer a free inspection and assessment
- Be prepared to discuss financing options for larger projects
- Follow up formally with a professional proposal

Commercial canvassing typically requires more preparation and professionalism than residential approaches, but the higher project values justify the additional effort.

Canvassing Materials and Tools

Equipping your canvassing team with the right materials dramatically improves results:

Essential Materials

Door Hangers: These remain one of the most effective leave-behind items. Design them with:

- Bold before/after photos
- Clear contact information
- Special offer with expiration date

- QR code linking to a neighborhood-specific landing page

Company Brochure: A professional, full-color brochure that details:

- Your services and process
- Materials used and their benefits
- Warranty information
- Insurance and licensing details
- Customer testimonials from nearby projects

Project Portfolio Book: A binder or tablet showing:

- Professional photos of completed projects
- Projects similar to the prospect's needs
- Local work that prospects might recognize
- Testimonials from satisfied customers

Business Cards: Professional cards with:

- Representative's direct number
- Company website and social media
- QR code to your Google reviews

Estimate Forms: Professional forms for immediate estimates:

- Carbon copy or digital format
- Space for project details and measurements
- Clear pricing and terms
- Signature line for immediate approval

Physical Samples: Small samples showing:

- Asphalt or concrete quality

- Different finishes available
- Sealcoating options
- Material cross-sections showing proper installation depth

Technology Tools Modern technology can enhance traditional door-to-door efforts:

CRM Mobile Apps: Allow representatives to:

- Look up property information before knocking
- Take notes on each interaction
- Schedule follow-ups immediately
- Track which homes have been visited

Mapping Software: Helps plan efficient routes and track coverage:

- Plan logical routes to minimize walking time
- Mark completed contacts and interested prospects
- Share territory coverage between team members
- Identify homes to revisit based on interest level

Measurement Apps: Enable quick, professional estimates:

- Calculate square footage using smartphone cameras
- Provide accurate measurements for estimates
- Create professional-looking property diagrams
- Email estimates to customers on the spot

Digital Portfolios: Tablets showing:

- High-resolution project galleries
- Before/after sliders
- Video testimonials
- Time-lapse project videos

These technological tools not only improve efficiency but also enhance your professional image compared to competitors using outdated methods.

Training Your Canvassing Team

The success of door-to-door marketing ultimately depends on the effectiveness of your representatives:

Key Skills Development

First Impression Techniques:

- Professional appearance aligned with your brand (uniform or business casual)
- Confident, friendly greeting that quickly identifies who you are and why you're there
- Respect for the customer's time ("I'll only take a minute of your time")
- Body language that appears open and trustworthy (appropriate distance, good posture)

Neighborhood Knowledge:

- Familiarity with local property values and home styles
- Awareness of recent projects in the area
- Understanding of common issues in that neighborhood
- Knowledge of local regulations affecting paving

Qualification Questions:

- When the driveway or parking area was last paved
- Current maintenance concerns
- Timeline for potential projects
- Budget considerations
- Decision-making process

Objection Handling:

- Responding to "I'm not interested" (acknowledge, then provide a quick value statement)
- Addressing price concerns (focus on value and quality)
- Handling "I need to think about it" (offer information leave-behind)
- Responding to "I need to talk to my spouse" (schedule a time when both are available)

Closing Techniques:

- Asking for a specific next step (appointment for detailed estimate)
- Creating urgency through limited-time offers
- Using assumptive closes ("Would Tuesday or Wednesday be better for your estimate?")
- Following up appropriately without pressuring

Safety Protocols:

- Working in teams when possible
- Respecting "No Soliciting" signs
- Maintaining appropriate hours (typically 10am-7pm)
- Carrying proper identification and company credentials
- Awareness of neighborhood safety considerations

Role-Playing Scenarios Regular practice through role-playing significantly improves performance:

Typical Scenarios to Practice:

- The busy homeowner who has only 30 seconds
- The skeptical property owner with bad contractor experiences
- The interested prospect with detailed technical questions
- The price-focused customer looking for the lowest bid
- The homeowner who needs to consult with their spouse

Role-playing should include both the initial contact and follow-up situations, with team members taking turns playing different roles.

Canvassing Scripts While representatives should never sound robotic, having a proven script framework improves consistency:

Sample Residential Introduction Script:

"Good afternoon! My name is [Name] with [Company]. We're currently paving your neighbor's driveway at [Address/Description], and I noticed your driveway might be due for some attention as well. [Pause for response] We're offering a special discount for neighbors while our equipment is already in the area. Could I ask how old your current driveway is? [Engagement question] [Based on response]: We specialize in [relevant service based on their needs], and we're booking projects for next month. Would you be interested in a free, no-obligation estimate while we're in the neighborhood? It only takes about 15 minutes, and I can show you exactly what we're doing at your neighbor's property."

Sample Commercial Introduction Script:

"Good morning! I'm [Name] with [Company]. We specialize in commercial parking lot maintenance and restoration, and I noticed your lot may be showing signs of aging. Is the property manager available for a quick conversation? [Pause] [When speaking with decision-maker]: We've recently completed several projects in this area, including [mention nearby commercial property if applicable]. I'd like to offer you a complimentary pavement assessment that identifies potential issues before they become costly repairs. We can schedule this at your convenience, and there's absolutely no obligation. Would you be interested in learning what preventative measures could save you money in the long run?"

These scripts should be adapted to your specific services and market, but the structure—introduction, observation, engagement question, and value proposition—remains effective across contexts.

Legal and Ethical Considerations

Door-to-door marketing carries specific legal requirements and ethical considerations:

Local Regulations Before beginning any canvassing campaign, research local ordinances:

Common Regulations:

- Permits or licenses required for door-to-door solicitation
- Restricted hours (typically no soliciting after dark)
- Required identification or company credentials
- Registration with local police department
- Restrictions in certain neighborhoods or HOAs
- Cooling-off periods for contracts signed during home solicitation

These regulations vary significantly by municipality, so check requirements for each area where you plan to canvass.

Professional Ethics Ethical practices not only protect your reputation but also improve results:

Best Practices:

- Honor "No Soliciting" signs without exception
- Never use high-pressure tactics or fear-based selling
- Be completely honest about pricing and timelines
- Respect the prospect's time and privacy
- Provide written information about cooling-off periods
- Never disparage competitors with false claims
- Always follow through on promises made during canvassing

Building Trust Trust is essential for door-to-door success:

Trust-Building Elements:

- Clearly branded vehicles parked visibly nearby

- Professional uniforms or attire with company logo
- Proper identification badges with photos
- Leave-behind materials with full company information
- References to local projects and testimonials
- Offering to connect prospects with previous customers
- Membership in Better Business Bureau or industry associations

These elements help overcome the natural skepticism many people feel toward door-to-door salespeople.

Tracking and Measuring Results

Accountability and performance tracking are essential for optimizing your canvassing efforts:

Key Performance Indicators Monitor these metrics to evaluate effectiveness:

Contact Rate: Percentage of homes where you make contact with a resident

- Formula: (Number of contacts ÷ Number of doors approached) × 100
- Benchmark: 30-40% for residential neighborhoods during standard hours

Appointment Rate: Percentage of contacts that result in scheduled estimates

- Formula: (Number of appointments ÷ Number of contacts) × 100
- Benchmark: 10-20% for well-targeted neighborhoods

Conversion Rate: Percentage of appointments that become customers

- Formula: (Number of sales ÷ Number of appointments) × 100

- Benchmark: 25-35% for properly qualified appointments

Cost Per Acquisition: Total canvassing cost divided by number of new customers

- Formula: Total cost (labor, materials, etc.) ÷ Number of sales
- Benchmark: Should be significantly lower than your average profit per job

Return on Investment: Revenue generated compared to canvassing investment

- Formula: (Revenue from canvassing sales - Total canvassing cost) ÷ Total canvassing cost
- Benchmark: 300%+ for effective campaigns

Tracking Tools Several tools can help track canvassing performance:

CRM Integration: Connect canvassing activities with your customer database:

- Log all contacts in your CRM system
- Track the source of each lead specifically to door-to-door efforts
- Record all follow-up activities and results
- Calculate lifetime value of customers acquired through canvassing

Revenue Commander Integration: Our platform can:

- Provide mobile data entry for field representatives
- Track canvassing results alongside other marketing channels
- Generate performance reports by representative, neighborhood, and time period
- Calculate true ROI by connecting sales data with canvassing costs

Representative Accountability:

- Daily activity reports showing doors knocked, contacts made, and appointments set
- GPS tracking of canvassing routes to ensure coverage
- Recording of key objections and feedback for training purposes
- Comparison of individual performance against team averages

These tracking methods not only measure effectiveness but also identify opportunities for improvement in both territory selection and sales techniques.

Success Story: Multi-Channel Integration Approach

Here's how one paving company successfully integrated door-to-door marketing with other channels:

A medium-sized paving contractor in the Northeast developed what they called their "Concentric Circle Strategy." When they secured a project in a new neighborhood, they:

1. First, conducted immediate door-to-door canvassing of the 20 closest homes to the project, offering a "neighborhood discount" for scheduling while crews were already on-site.
2. Next, they distributed door hangers to the next 50 homes in the surrounding area, featuring photos of the project they were completing in the neighborhood.
3. Then, they sent direct mail postcards to the next 200 homes in the wider neighborhood, with messaging that referenced their work in the area.
4. Finally, they targeted Facebook ads to the entire zip code, mentioning the number of projects they had completed in that specific neighborhood.

The results from this integrated approach were impressive:

- 30% of the immediate door-to-door contacts resulted in estimates
- 40% of those estimates converted to jobs
- Door hangers generated a 5% response rate
- Direct mail brought in a 2% response rate
- The overall campaign regularly turned one initial project into 8-12 total jobs in the same neighborhood

The key to success was the tight integration between channels, with consistent messaging emphasizing their presence in the neighborhood and the social proof of multiple local projects.

Implementation Checklist

Use this checklist to implement an effective door-to-door marketing campaign:

Planning and Preparation

- Research local solicitation regulations and obtain permits if needed
- Select target neighborhoods based on age, home value, and visual need
- Prepare professional canvassing materials (door hangers, brochures, etc.)
- Develop scripts and train representatives thoroughly
- Set specific goals for contacts, appointments, and conversions

Execution

- Create efficient routing for representatives
- Ensure proper identification and professional appearance
- Document all contacts and follow-up needs

- Coordinate with project schedules for neighborhood canvassing
- Respect local regulations and solicitation hours

Follow-Up Process

- Schedule next-day callbacks for interested prospects
- Send personalized emails or texts to contacts made
- Deliver promised estimates or information promptly
- Add contacts to your email list (with permission)
- Record all interactions in your CRM system

Analysis and Optimization

- Track performance metrics by representative and neighborhood
- Calculate cost per lead and customer acquisition cost
- Identify most responsive neighborhood profiles
- Refine scripts based on common objections and feedback
- Adjust team training based on performance data

Conclusion: The Personal Touch in a Digital World

In an era dominated by digital marketing, door-to-door canvassing provides something increasingly rare: personal, face-to-face interaction. For paving contractors, this approach leverages the visual impact of your work and creates opportunities to cluster projects efficiently in specific neighborhoods.

When implemented professionally and ethically, door-to-door marketing can deliver not only high conversion rates but also build stronger customer relationships than those initiated through digital channels. The personal connection established during canvassing often leads to higher satisfaction, more referrals, and better customer retention.

Rather than viewing door-to-door as an outdated approach, successful paving contractors see it as a competitive advantage—a high-touch complement to their digital marketing efforts. In an industry where quality workmanship and trust are paramount, the value of in-person connection should not be underestimated.

In the next chapter, we'll explore yard signs and vehicle branding—passive marketing tools that create continuous visibility in your service area and reinforce the impacts of your active marketing efforts.

15

Yard Signs And Vehicle Branding

While many marketing channels require ongoing investment to maintain visibility, yard signs and vehicle branding turn your everyday operations into continuous marketing opportunities. These highly visible assets build awareness, establish credibility, and generate leads at a remarkably low cost per impression. For paving companies, whose work is inherently visible and mobile, these tools are especially effective.

The Power of Yard Signs

Yard signs placed at job sites create immediate local awareness and credibility for your paving company. They transform every project into a neighborhood marketing opportunity.

Research Findings on Yard Sign Effectiveness Our research has yielded important insights about the impact of job site signage:

- Yard signs cost approximately **$5-$20 each** to produce, depending on size, material quality, and quantity ordered.
- Signs are essentially a one-time investment that can generate leads for months or years.
- Properties in visible locations (corner lots, busy streets) can generate

hundreds of impressions daily from a single sign.
- Signs create a "halo effect" of awareness in neighborhoods where you work, leading to clusters of jobs in specific areas.
- They leverage the powerful demonstration effect of showing potential customers your work quality through a completed project.

The cost-effectiveness of yard signs is exceptional. If a $20 sign displayed for two weeks generates even one job, the return on investment is extraordinary. Many paving contractors report that yard signs account for 10-15% of their new customer inquiries with minimal ongoing cost.

Strategic Placement of Yard Signs Not all sign placements are equally effective. Consider these strategic approaches:

Project-Based Placement:

- Secure permission from customers to place signs during and after project completion
- Offer small discounts to customers who allow extended sign placement (2-4 weeks)
- Position signs to be visible from the highest traffic direction
- Use larger signs for highly visible properties
- Move signs to different positions during the project for maximum exposure

High-Visibility Locations:

- Focus on corner lots with exposure to cross-traffic
- Prioritize projects near traffic signals where drivers stop
- Highlight projects near schools, shopping centers, or other community hubs
- Place signs at entrances to subdivisions where you're working
- Consider nearby walking paths where pedestrians will notice details

Permanent and Semi-Permanent Placements:

- Commercial properties often allow longer-term sign placement
- Negotiate with business clients to maintain signs after project completion
- Consider sponsorship signs at local parks, sports fields, or community centers
- Explore partnerships with complementary businesses (landscapers, builders, etc.)

The key is maximizing visibility while maintaining professional standards. Signs should enhance, not detract from, the appearance of the completed project.

Effective Yard Sign Design The design of your yard sign significantly impacts its effectiveness:

Size and Format Options:

- Standard sizes: 18" x 24" and 24" x 36" are most common for paving projects
- Corrugated plastic (coroplast) provides durability and weather resistance
- Metal signs offer greater longevity for long-term placements
- A-frame signs provide visibility from multiple directions
- Consider adding smaller "riders" for special offers or awards

Design Elements:

- Company name and logo with high visibility from a distance
- Phone number in large, bold font (readable from a passing car)
- Website URL that is short and memorable
- Brief service list highlighting your specialties

- Optional QR code linking to project gallery or reviews
- Professional credentials or years in business

Visual Impact:

- High-contrast colors that stand out without looking garish
- Simple, clean layout without clutter
- Consistent branding with all your other marketing materials
- Weather-resistant printing to maintain appearance
- Properly secured installation to prevent tilting or falling

Content Strategy:

- Clear identification of the service provided ("Driveway Paving" or "Commercial Asphalt")
- Benefit-focused messaging ("Increasing Property Values Since 1995")
- Calls to action ("Call for Your Free Estimate")
- Territory identification ("Serving [Your Service Area]")

Remember that yard signs serve both branding and direct response purposes. While they should generate calls, they also build name recognition that supports all your other marketing efforts.

Implementation Tips for Yard Signs To maximize the impact of your yard sign strategy:

Customer Agreements:

- Include sign placement permission in your standard contracts
- Specify duration (typically 2-4 weeks post-completion)
- Offer incentives for extended placement
- Be respectful of HOA restrictions or customer concerns

Tracking Effectiveness:

- Ask new customers how they heard about you
- Track leads that specifically mention seeing your signs
- Note which projects generate the most sign-related inquiries
- Calculate cost per lead from sign investments

Maintenance Program:

- Regularly inspect signs for damage or fading
- Clean signs when retrieving them from completed projects
- Replace weather-damaged signs promptly
- Update designs periodically to maintain fresh appearance

Inventory Management:

- Maintain sufficient inventory for all active projects
- Track sign locations and retrieval dates
- Assign responsibility for placement and retrieval
- Create a sign check-out/check-in system for crews

By systematizing your yard sign strategy, you transform every project into a marketing opportunity that continues generating leads long after your crews have moved on.

Vehicle Branding: Mobile Billboards

Your company vehicles travel throughout your service area every day. With proper branding, each one becomes a moving billboard that generates continuous awareness and leads.

Research Findings on Vehicle Branding Impact Vehicle wraps and branding show remarkable return on investment:

- Vehicle wraps have one of the **lowest costs per impression of any ad-**

vertising medium at approximately $0.48 per thousand impressions (CPM).

- A fully wrapped vehicle in an urban area can generate between **30,000 to 70,000 impressions daily**.
- Vehicle ads produce **97% message recall** among viewers (compared to 19% for stationary billboards).
- **92% of business owners** who use vehicle wraps consider them the most effective form of local advertising.
- Wrapped vehicles generate nearly **four times more online brand activations per dollar** compared to TV or print advertising.

These statistics demonstrate why vehicle branding is considered one of the highest-ROI marketing investments available to local service businesses.

Vehicle Branding Options and Costs Several options exist for vehicle branding, with varying costs and impact:

Full Vehicle Wraps:

- Cost: $2,000-$4,000 per vehicle depending on size
- Coverage: Entire vehicle surface transformed into advertising
- Lifespan: 5-7 years with proper care
- Impact: Maximum visibility and professional appearance
- Best for: Primary vehicles seen regularly in public (estimator vehicles, crew trucks)

Partial Wraps:

- Cost: $1,000-$2,500 depending on coverage area
- Coverage: 25-75% of vehicle surface
- Lifespan: 5-7 years with proper care
- Impact: Strong visibility while reducing cost
- Best for: Secondary vehicles or when full wraps exceed budget

Vinyl Lettering and Logos:

- Cost: $300–$800 per vehicle
- Coverage: Company name, logo, contact info on doors, sides, rear
- Lifespan: 5–7 years
- Impact: Professional identification without full graphic treatment
- Best for: Supporting vehicles or companies with limited marketing budgets

Magnetic Signs:

- Cost: $50–$150 per pair
- Coverage: Removable door signs with basic information
- Lifespan: 1–3 years with proper care
- Impact: Limited visibility but still professional
- Best for: Personal vehicles used occasionally for business or temporary fleet additions

Equipment Branding:

- Cost: Varies by equipment type ($100–$1,000)
- Coverage: Logos and information on pavers, rollers, and other visible equipment
- Lifespan: Depends on equipment usage and conditions
- Impact: Creates professional appearance on job sites
- Best for: Equipment visible from street during operations

The best approach often combines these options based on vehicle type and usage. Primary vehicles that frequently travel in high-visibility areas justify full wraps, while support vehicles might use more basic branding.

Effective Vehicle Design Strategies Maximize the impact of your vehicle branding with these design principles:

Essential Content Elements:

- Company name and logo (highly visible from a distance)
- Primary services offered ("Asphalt Paving · Driveways · Parking Lots")
- Phone number in large, readable font
- Website URL (simple and memorable)
- Service area identification
- Professional credentials or certifications

Design Considerations:

- High contrast colors that stand out in traffic
- Large, bold text readable from at least 50 feet away

- Strategic placement of key information (sides, rear, hood)
- Consistent branding with all other marketing materials
- Balance between eye-catching design and professional appearance
- Consideration of vehicle colors and contours in the design

Visual Impact Strategies:

- Before/after photos of dramatic paving transformations
- Action images showing your equipment or crew at work
- Benefits-focused messaging ("Increase Your Property Value")
- Coverage area map if regionally focused
- QR codes linking to your website or reviews (place on rear for stopped traffic)

Remember that vehicles blend advertising and professional image. The design should attract attention without appearing unprofessional or excessive.

Fleet Implementation Strategy Develop a systematic approach to vehicle branding across your fleet:

Vehicle Prioritization:

- Primary customer-facing vehicles (sales/estimator cars or trucks)
- Trucks that transport crews to job sites
- Equipment transport vehicles with high road visibility
- Support vehicles based on public exposure
- Heavy equipment based on job site visibility from streets

Phased Implementation:

- Start with highest-visibility vehicles if budget is limited
- Create a multi-year plan to brand all vehicles systematically

- Consider wrapping new vehicles immediately upon purchase
- Coordinate with vehicle maintenance schedules for minimal downtime
- Update older vehicle branding on a rotating schedule

Maintenance and Care:

- Train drivers on proper care of wrapped vehicles
- Establish cleaning protocols that protect graphics
- Inspect wraps regularly for damage or peeling
- Budget for repairs or touch-ups as needed
- Plan for replacement on a 5-7 year cycle

Driver Guidelines:

- Establish driving behavior expectations for branded vehicles
- Create parking policies that maximize visibility
- Implement cleanliness standards for all branded vehicles
- Develop protocols for accident or damage reporting
- Train staff on how to leverage vehicle branding in customer interactions

Remember that branded vehicles represent your company everywhere they go. A comprehensive implementation strategy ensures they create a consistently positive impression.

Integration of Yard Signs and Vehicle Branding

While effective individually, yard signs and vehicle branding create synergistic benefits when strategically integrated:

Coordinated Visual Branding Ensure visual consistency across all materials:

Design Alignment:

- Use identical logos, fonts, and colors on all materials
- Maintain consistent messaging and positioning
- Ensure phone numbers and websites match exactly
- Create a recognizable visual system across all touchpoints
- Coordinate updates across all materials simultaneously

Brand Recognition Building:

- Repetition of visual elements builds faster recognition
- Multiple exposures across different formats reinforce memory
- Consistent branding creates impression of larger company presence
- Professional coordination signals attention to detail
- System reinforces each individual marketing piece

Tactical Integration Leverage the synergistic opportunities of combined branding:

Project Visibility Maximization:

- Place yard signs at active projects where branded vehicles are visible
- Position vehicles strategically when parked at job sites
- Schedule equipment delivery to maximize street visibility
- Create "mini billboard" effect when multiple branded elements are present
- Take photos of branded vehicles at job sites for social media content

Territory Domination Strategy:

- Concentrate yard signs and vehicle presence in target neighborhoods
- Create impression of market leadership through multiple touchpoints
- Leverage completed projects with signs to validate vehicle branding

promises
- Develop neighborhood-focused campaigns with coordinated presence
- Track combined impact on lead generation by area

Cross-Promotion Opportunities:

- Include images of branded vehicles on yard signs
- Show yard signs in vehicle wrap designs
- Reference both in other marketing materials
- Create unified visual story across all touchpoints
- Develop campaign themes that work across all formats

When properly integrated, yard signs and vehicle branding create a powerful territorial presence that makes your company appear omnipresent in your service area.

Case Study: Comprehensive Signage Strategy

Here's a real-world example of effective integration of yard signs and vehicle branding:

A mid-sized paving contractor serving both residential and commercial clients implemented what they called their "Visibility Everywhere" strategy:

- They invested in professional vehicle wraps for their entire fleet of 12 vehicles, including estimator trucks, crew transport, and equipment trailers. Each wrap featured dramatic before/after photos relevant to the type of work that vehicle typically supported.
- They developed a three-tiered yard sign system:
- Standard 18" x 24" signs for all residential projects
- Larger 4' x 4' signs for commercial projects
- Premium 4' x 8' signs for high-visibility locations

- They negotiated permission to leave signs at completed projects for extended periods by offering a maintenance discount program—15% off sealcoating for customers who allowed signs to remain for 60+ days.
- They implemented strict vehicle appearance standards, requiring daily cleaning and strategic parking at job sites for maximum street visibility.
- They created a tracking system where customers were asked specifically if they had seen the company's vehicles or yard signs before contacting them.

The results were impressive:

- 23% of new customers mentioned seeing their vehicles before calling
- 18% specifically cited seeing yard signs at other projects
- Lead generation costs dropped by 34% compared to the previous year
- They dominated certain neighborhoods with multiple signs from past projects
- Competitors reported having trouble breaking into the company's core territories

The key to success was consistency, quality, and strategic integration of all branded elements to create an impression of market leadership.

Implementation Checklist

Use this checklist to implement effective signage and vehicle branding:

Yard Sign Strategy

- Design professional yard signs with clear company information
- Establish quantity needs based on projected project volume
- Include sign permission clauses in all customer contracts

- Create placement and retrieval protocols for job sites
- Train crews on proper sign installation and positioning
- Implement tracking system for sign-generated leads
- Develop incentives for extended sign placement
- Create maintenance schedule for sign inventory

Vehicle Branding Plan

- Prioritize vehicles based on visibility and customer contact
- Select appropriate branding level for each vehicle
- Develop consistent design system across fleet
- Research and select qualified vehicle wrap provider
- Create phased implementation schedule if needed
- Establish vehicle care and maintenance protocols
- Train drivers on representing the brand while driving
- Implement strategic parking policies for maximum visibility

Integration Elements

- Ensure consistent visual identity across all materials
- Create coordination between job site signage and vehicles
- Develop measurement system for combined impact
- Integrate imagery across all marketing channels
- Train all staff on leveraging branding in customer interactions
- Create neighborhood targeting strategies using both elements
- Review and update all branded materials annually

Conclusion: Continuous Visibility for Paving Companies

Yard signs and vehicle branding represent some of the most cost-effective marketing investments available to paving contractors. They transform your everyday operations into continuous advertising, building awareness and generating leads long after the initial investment.

Unlike many marketing channels that require ongoing spending to maintain visibility, properly implemented signage and vehicle branding create thousands of impressions daily for years with minimal additional cost. They also reinforce your other marketing efforts by creating multiple touchpoints with potential customers.

For paving companies, whose work is inherently visible and whose vehicles traverse their service areas daily, these tools should be core components of any marketing strategy. When implemented with attention to quality, consistency, and strategic placement, they create a powerful presence that builds credibility and generates a steady stream of leads.

In the next chapter, we'll explore local broadcast advertising—radio and television strategies that can help establish your paving company as a recognized name in your market.

16

Local Broadcast Advertising

Despite the digital revolution, traditional broadcast advertising remains a powerful channel for paving companies to reach local audiences. Radio and television offer unique advantages—they can reach people during their daily commutes or in their homes, building brand awareness and trust through audio and visual storytelling.

Radio Advertising

Radio continues to be a surprisingly resilient and effective medium for local businesses, including paving contractors. Many business owners overlook radio, assuming it's been completely displaced by digital platforms, but the data tells a different story.

The Enduring Power of Radio In 2024, AM/FM radio retains remarkable reach despite the proliferation of streaming services and podcasts. Research findings show that radio reaches approximately **84% of adults 18+ each week**, surpassing even social media or television in reach. People spend significant time with radio, especially while driving, and importantly, radio dominates in-car listening with about **86% share of ad-supported audio in vehicles**.

This dominance of in-car listening is particularly valuable for paving companies. Think about it: when is a property owner most likely to notice the condition of their driveway or parking lot? Often, it's when they're pulling in or out of that surface. A driver hearing a paving ad while experiencing a bumpy ride on deteriorated pavement creates a perfect context for your message to resonate.

Radio Advertising Costs Radio advertising is generally more affordable than many business owners realize, especially compared to television. According to industry data, costs typically range from **$10 to $20 per spot per 1,000 listeners** (which is a $10-$20 CPM). To put this in practical terms, if a station has 50,000 listeners during a particular time slot, a single 30-second ad might cost between $500-$1,000. However, buying remnant inventory or targeting less busy times can significantly reduce these costs.

The actual costs you'll pay depend on several factors:

- **Market Size**: Small local stations in rural areas might charge as little as $50-$200 per week for a package of spots, while prime drive-time slots in large metropolitan areas can cost $5,000+ per week.
- **Daypart**: Morning and evening drive times (typically 6-10 AM and 3-7 PM) are the most expensive because they have the largest audiences. Midday, evening, overnight, and weekend slots cost considerably less.
- **Frequency**: Most stations offer significant discounts for volume and longer-term commitments. A 13-week package will cost less per spot than a one-week flight.
- **Station Popularity**: A top-rated station commands higher rates than one with lower ratings.

In addition to airtime costs, you'll need to factor in production expenses. Creating a professional radio ad might cost a few hundred dollars, though many stations will help produce your spot as part of your advertising package, especially for new advertisers.

A typical small-market budget might look like this:

- $1,500 monthly for 3-4 spots per day during weekdays
- Production costs: $200-$300 (often waived with larger packages)
- Total monthly investment: $1,500-$1,800

In mid-sized markets, this same schedule might cost $2,500-$4,000 monthly.

Effective Radio Ad Strategies Creating memorable radio ads requires a different approach than print or visual advertising. You're working with audio only, so your message needs to capture attention quickly and create a mental image for listeners.

- **Script Development** The foundation of any radio ad is the script. While a typical 30-second ad contains about 75-85 words, every word must count:
- **Grab Attention in the First 3-5 Seconds**: Start with a compelling question, sound effect, or statement that identifies a problem your prospect is experiencing.
- *"That cracking sound you hear every time you pull into your driveway? That's money being wasted on temporary fixes."*
- **Address a Specific Pain Point**: Focus on the problems your customers experience rather than just listing your services.
- *"Tired of patching that crumbling driveway year after year? A properly installed asphalt surface can last 15-20 years with minimal maintenance."*
- **Include Your Unique Selling Proposition**: Clearly state what makes your paving company different from competitors.
- *"At Smith Paving, we don't just resurface your asphalt—we rebuild from the base up, providing a transferable 10-year warranty that no other*

paving company in the area offers."

- **Create Mental Imagery**: Use descriptive language that helps listeners visualize their property with your solution.
- *"Imagine pulling up to your home on a smooth, pristine driveway that enhances your property's value and curb appeal..."*
- **Include a Clear Call-to-Action**: Tell listeners exactly what to do next, and make it easy to remember.
- *"Call 555-PAVE now for your free estimate, or visit SmithPaving.com."*
- **Repeat Key Information**: Research shows that repetition increases retention. Mention your company name at least twice and repeat the call-to-action.
- **Sample Script for a 30-Second Ad:**

SFX: Car driving over bumpy pavement ANNOUNCER: That bumpy ride into your driveway isn't just annoying—it's damaging your vehicle and lowering your property value. At Smith Paving, we've transformed over 3,000 driveways in the Springfield area with professional asphalt installations that last. Unlike other contractors, we offer a written 10-year warranty on all our residential work, backed by our 35 years in business. Summer special: Get 15% off when you schedule your free estimate this month. Smith Paving—where quality meets the road. Call 555-PAVE today. That's 555-PAVE.

- **Voice and Production Quality** The voice and production quality of your radio ad significantly impact its effectiveness:
- **Voice Selection**: Choose a voice that matches your brand personality. A deep, authoritative voice might work well for emphasizing quality and durability, while a friendly, conversational tone might be better for building trust.
- **Music and Sound Effects**: Strategic use of sound effects (like the sound of cracking asphalt or a smooth car drive) can help listeners visualize the problem and solution. Background music should complement your message without overwhelming it.

- **Professional Production**: While many stations offer free production, consider investing in professional recording and mixing if you plan to use the ad across multiple stations or for an extended period. The quality difference is often noticeable and reflects on your brand.
- **Consistency Across Campaigns**: Develop audio branding elements like a distinctive voice, music bed, or sound effect that remains consistent across all radio ads. This creates recognition even when listeners aren't giving their full attention.
- **Campaign Strategy and Placement** The strategy behind when and where your ad runs is just as important as the content of the ad itself:
- **Station Selection**: Research stations that reach your target demographic. For paving services, news/talk radio, classic rock, and country formats often reach property owners and decision-makers. Most stations can provide detailed demographic information about their listeners.
- **Frequency Over Reach**: It's better to advertise frequently on one or two stations than occasionally across many. The advertising principle of effective frequency suggests that listeners need to hear your message at least 3-7 times before it sinks in.
- **Flight Scheduling**: Instead of spreading your budget thinly across the year, consider running concentrated "flights" during peak seasons for paving work. For example, you might run heavier schedules in spring and early summer when property owners are thinking about improvement projects.
- **Daypart Strategy**: While drive times reach the most listeners, they're also the most expensive. Consider a mix of prime and non-prime times to maximize your frequency within budget.
- **Sponsorship Opportunities**: Many stations offer weather, traffic, or home improvement segment sponsorships. These can create stronger associations between your brand and relevant content, often at a better value than straight spot buys.

Tracking Radio Advertising Response One challenge with radio advertising is measuring its direct impact. Unlike digital ads, there's no immediate click to track. However, there are several effective approaches to measure radio ROI:

- **Dedicated Phone Numbers**: Use a unique phone number in your radio ads that forwards to your main line. This allows you to track exactly how many calls came from radio.
- **Unique Website URLs**: Create a simple, memorable landing page specifically for radio (e.g., SmithPaving.com/radio) and only promote it on-air.
- **Special Offers**: Include a radio-exclusive offer or discount code that customers must mention to receive.
- **Customer Surveys**: Simply ask new customers, "How did you hear about us?" and track responses over time.
- **Call Tracking Software**: Services like CallRail can provide detailed analytics on where calls originate, even with a single tracking number.

When measuring results, remember that radio often has a cumulative effect. Someone might hear your ad multiple times before taking action, or they might search for your company online after hearing your ad rather than calling the number directly.

Radio Success Story: Johnson Paving Let me share a real example of how radio worked for a medium-sized paving company. Johnson Paving in a mid-sized Midwestern market had historically relied on yard signs and referrals but wanted to grow their residential business. They invested $2,500 monthly in a local news/talk station, running a mixture of drive-time and midday spots. Their approach included:

- A memorable tagline: "Paving the way to a better driveway"
- A vanity phone number: 555-PAVE
- Seasonal messaging that changed quarterly
- Sponsorship of the afternoon traffic report

After six months, they tracked:

- 42 direct calls from their tracking number
- 28 conversions to actual jobs
- Average job value of $4,200
- Total revenue of $117,600 from a $15,000 investment

Additionally, when surveying all new customers, they found that many who discovered them through other means mentioned hearing their radio ads, indicating a "halo effect" that strengthened their other marketing channels. The most surprising outcome was the commercial leads they received—several business owners heard the ads during their commutes and called for commercial lot quotes, which had significantly higher values than residential jobs.

Is Radio Right for Your Paving Company? Radio advertising might be particularly effective for your paving business if:

- You operate in a market where commute times are long and local radio listenership is strong
- You want to build brand awareness and name recognition in your community
- You have a unique selling proposition that can be clearly communicated verbally
- You're looking to complement your digital marketing with a traditional channel that reaches people while they're literally looking at roads and driveways
- You have sufficient budget to maintain consistent presence (usually $1,500+ monthly in smaller markets)

Radio might not be the best choice if:

- Your service area is extremely limited (just a few zip codes)

- You lack the budget for consistent frequency
- Your target audience is highly specific in a way that radio's broader reach doesn't efficiently address

For most established paving companies looking to grow, radio can be an effective component of a multi-channel marketing strategy, especially during peak seasons when demand is highest.

Local TV Advertising

Television advertising has traditionally been viewed as the domain of large national brands with massive budgets. However, local TV advertising can be surprisingly accessible for mid-sized paving companies and provides unique advantages that other media cannot match.

The Visual Impact of Television The greatest strength of television advertising is its unmatched ability to demonstrate transformation—the core of what paving companies deliver. A 30-second TV spot can show the dramatic before-and-after of a deteriorated driveway or parking lot being transformed into a smooth, attractive surface. This visual demonstration creates desire in a way that radio, print, or even digital ads cannot match.

Television also carries an inherent credibility. When potential customers see your company on TV, they often perceive you as more established, successful, and trustworthy than competitors who don't advertise on television. This perception alone can justify the investment for paving contractors aiming to position themselves as market leaders.

Television Advertising Costs Television advertising costs vary significantly based on market size, programming, and time of day. Research findings indicate that for local TV ads, the CPM (cost per thousand impressions) typically ranges from **$5 to $35**, with an average around $20 CPM. To put this in concrete terms, a local cable ad that reaches 100,000 viewers might cost approximately $2,000. This might sound expensive compared to some digital options, but the impact per impression is often significantly higher.

The cost structure for TV advertising includes several components:

Airtime Costs:

- Broadcast TV (local affiliates of ABC, CBS, NBC, FOX): Higher reach but higher cost, typically $200-$1,500+ per 30-second spot depending on program and time
- Cable TV (local insertions on channels like HGTV, CNN, History): More targeted but lower reach, typically $25-$300 per 30-second spot
- OTT/Connected TV (streaming services): Growing option with targeting capabilities, often sold on a CPM basis ($20-$40 CPM)

Daypart Pricing:

- Prime Time (8-11 PM): Most expensive but highest viewership
- Early Fringe (4-8 PM): Good balance of cost and viewership
- Daytime (9 AM-4 PM): Lower cost, reaches those at home during day
- Late Night (11 PM-2 AM): Least expensive, limited audience
- Weekend: Variable pricing, often good value for sports programming

Production Costs:

- Professional commercial production typically ranges from **$1,000 to $5,000** for a basic 30-second spot
- Higher-end productions with multiple filming locations, professional talent, or special effects can cost $5,000-$25,000+
- Many cable providers offer simple production packages for $500-$1,500
- These costs can be amortized over the life of the campaign

A typical small-market TV campaign for a paving company might involve:

- $3,000-$5,000 for commercial production (one-time cost)
- $3,000-$8,000 monthly for a mix of cable spots during programs relevant to homeowners
- Total first-month investment: $6,000-$13,000, with ongoing monthly costs of $3,000-$8,000

This represents a significant investment, which is why television is typically employed by established paving companies rather than new businesses.

Strategic Approaches to TV Advertising To maximize return on investment, paving companies should employ these strategic approaches:

- **Commercial Production Strategies** The production quality of your commercial directly impacts its effectiveness:
- **Focus on Transformation**: The most compelling paving commercials show clear before-and-after sequences. Capture the same property from identical angles to highlight the dramatic improvement.
- **Establish Credibility**: Include brief shots of your professional crew and equipment in action. This demonstrates capability and scale of operations.
- **Feature Real Customers**: Testimonials from satisfied customers add authenticity. Even a simple statement like "We couldn't be happier with our new driveway" can be powerful.
- **Demonstrate Expertise**: Have the owner or manager explain a technical aspect of quality paving in layman's terms. This positions your company as knowledgeable experts.
- **Create Emotional Appeal**: Connect the improved pavement to lifestyle benefits—children playing safely, increased property value, or pride in home appearance.
- **Clear Call-to-Action**: End with a specific instruction ("Call now for

your free estimate") and ensure your phone number remains on screen long enough to be remembered or written down.

- **Sample Commercial Concept:**

OPEN: Shot of severely cracked, deteriorated driveway VO: "This isn't just an eyesore—it's decreasing your property value and could damage your vehicles." TRANSITION: Time-lapse of Smith Paving crew installing new asphalt VO: "At Smith Paving, we don't just cover problems—we solve them from the ground up." CUT TO: Same property with beautiful new driveway VO: "Our professional installation includes proper base preparation and premium materials that last." CUT TO: Satisfied homeowner in front of new driveway HOMEOWNER: "Smith Paving transformed our property. The crew was professional, and the results speak for themselves." CUT TO: Owner in company shirt with equipment in background OWNER: "We've been serving this community for 25 years. Call today for your free estimate." CLOSING: Logo, phone number, and website displayed prominently VO: "Smith Paving—Quality that stands the test of time. Call 555-PAVE today."

- **Media Buying Strategies** How you purchase TV time can significantly impact your campaign's effectiveness:
- **Target Programming, Not Just Time Slots**: Identify shows that index highly with property owners—local news, home improvement programs, sports, and weather segments often reach your ideal audience.
- **Consider Seasonal Timing**: Allocate more of your budget during prime paving seasons (typically spring and summer). You might increase spending in April-May to capture early-season planning, then reduce during winter months.
- **Leverage Local News**: Local news programs often have the highest viewership among decision-makers and property owners. The news adjacency (right before or after) can be a good value.
- **Test Cable vs. Broadcast**: Cable offers more targeted placement (like

running on HGTV or DIY Network) but reaches smaller audiences. Broadcast offers greater reach but at higher cost. Test both approaches to see what works best for your market.

- **Bundle Digital Extensions**: Many TV stations offer digital components—banner ads on their websites, OTT/streaming placements, or social media promotion—as part of larger packages. These can extend your reach to cord-cutters.
- **Negotiate Added Value**: Stations often include bonus spots, interviews on morning shows, or website features as incentives for advertisers. Always ask what added value they can provide.

Measuring Television Ad Performance Television has traditionally been challenging to measure precisely, but several approaches can help track effectiveness:

- **Dedicated Phone Numbers**: Use unique tracking numbers that appear only in your TV ads.
- **Specific Landing Pages**: Create a simple URL used only in your television advertising (e.g., SmithPaving.com/tv).
- **Code Words or Special Offers**: Include a TV-only discount code or promotional offer that customers must mention.
- **Website Traffic Correlation**: Monitor spikes in website traffic during and immediately after your ads air.
- **Call Timing Analysis**: Track when calls come in relative to when your ads are running.
- **Brand Lift Studies**: Measure awareness before and after a campaign to gauge the impact on your market presence.
- **Post-Purchase Surveys**: Simply ask new customers where they heard about you.

When evaluating TV advertising ROI, consider both direct and indirect benefits. While you want to track direct leads, television also creates a "halo effect" that enhances other marketing channels. Someone might see your TV ad, later search for you online, and then convert through your website—television deserves partial credit for that conversion.

Local TV Success Story: Capital Paving To illustrate the potential of local TV advertising, consider Capital Paving, a mid-sized commercial and residential paving company in a market of approximately 500,000 people. They had been established for 12 years and wanted to position themselves as the premium provider in their region. Their television strategy included:

- A $4,500 investment in commercial production featuring dramatic before/after transformations
- $6,000 monthly spent on a mix of local news adjacencies and targeted cable placements
- Consistent airing over a 6-month peak season (April-September)
- A unique phone number and landing page for tracking

The results after six months:

- 64 directly attributed leads from the dedicated phone number
- 38 conversions to completed jobs (59% conversion rate)
- Average job value of $7,800
- Total attributed revenue of $296,400 from a $40,500 investment

Beyond these direct metrics, Capital Paving reported several indirect benefits:

- Increased leverage in negotiations with commercial clients
- Higher close rates on all estimates (TV had established credibility)
- Ability to command premium pricing due to perceived market position
- Recruitment benefits—job applicants mentioned seeing the commercials

This example demonstrates that while television requires a significant investment, the returns can justify the expense for established paving companies looking to elevate their market position.

Is TV Right for Your Paving Company? Local TV advertising is most appropriate for paving companies that:

- Are established in their market with stable operations and capacity
- Have sufficient budget ($5,000+ monthly during campaign periods)
- Seek to position themselves as market leaders
- Want to expand into higher-value commercial projects
- Have visually impressive transformation examples to showcase
- Can handle a significant increase in lead volume

Television advertising might not be suitable if:

- Your company is new or operates on a very tight budget
- You focus exclusively on smaller residential jobs
- You lack the capacity to handle significant growth
- Your service area is extremely limited

For many medium to large paving companies, television can be the channel that elevates them from "just another contractor" to the recognized leader in their market—a position that often justifies the higher cost per lead compared to other channels.

Strategic Integration of Radio and TV For paving companies with sufficient budget, combining radio and television creates powerful synergy. Research shows that multi-channel exposure significantly increases brand recall and response rates. When a prospect hears your message on radio during their morning commute, then sees your commercial that evening, the reinforcement builds familiarity and trust.

Consider a coordinated approach where:

- Radio builds frequency and awareness with multiple weekly exposures
- Television creates impact and demonstration of your capabilities
- Both channels use consistent messaging, offers, and branding elements
- Broadcast schedules are staggered to maximize reach throughout the day

This integrated approach can establish your paving company as the dominant player in your market, often creating a competitive advantage that's difficult for others to overcome.

17

Billboard Advertising

Billboards represent one of the oldest forms of advertising, yet they remain remarkably effective for local service businesses like paving companies. The physical presence of a large, visible advertisement along routes your prospects travel daily creates repetitive exposure that builds brand awareness and recognition.

The Strategic Value of Billboard Advertising

Unlike most advertising, billboards work 24/7, delivering your message to thousands of passersby each day. For paving contractors, billboards offer several unique advantages:

- **Location Relevance**: Billboards can be strategically placed near commercial districts, affluent residential areas, or along commuter routes where decision-makers regularly travel.
- **Continuous Exposure**: Unlike a TV commercial that airs occasionally or a digital ad that appears briefly, billboards provide constant visibility.
- **Visual Demonstration**: Large-format images can showcase dramatic before/after transformations of your paving projects.
- **Implied Permanence**: The physical presence of a billboard subcon-

sciously suggests your company is established and stable—you're "here to stay."

- **Competitor Disruption**: A well-placed billboard can intercept potential customers before they reach your competitors' locations.

Billboard Advertising Costs

Billboard advertising costs vary significantly based on location, format, and market size. According to industry research, monthly billboard rental in small to mid-sized cities typically ranges from **$1,500 to $5,000**, while prime locations in major metropolitan areas can exceed $10,000 monthly.

The cost is primarily determined by the number of impressions (viewers) the billboard receives. This is measured in CPM (cost per thousand impressions), which typically ranges from **$3 to $6** for traditional billboards. For example, a billboard that's seen by approximately 100,000 people monthly with a $5 CPM would cost around $500 per thousand views, or $5,000 total.

Several factors influence billboard pricing:

- **Location**: Billboards on busy highways or main thoroughfares command premium prices compared to those on secondary roads.
- **Format and Size**: Standard bulletins (14' x 48') cost more than smaller posters (10' x 22') or junior posters (6' x 12').
- **Illumination**: Lighted billboards that remain visible at night typically cost 20-30% more than non-illuminated ones.
- **Digital vs. Static**: Digital billboards (rotating electronic displays) generally cost more per exposure but allow for shorter commitment periods and time-of-day targeting.
- **Contract Length**: Most billboard companies offer significant discounts for longer-term commitments (6-12 months versus month-to-month).

In addition to monthly rental costs, you'll need to budget for production:

- Static Billboard Production: $500-$1,000 for design and printing of vinyl
- Digital Billboard Production: $200-$500 for design of digital files
- Installation Costs: $0-$500 depending on contract terms

For perspective, here's a cost breakdown for different markets:

Small Market (Population under 100,000):

- Secondary Road Poster: $800-$1,500/month
- Main Road Bulletin: $1,500-$3,000/month
- Digital Rotation (8 spots): $600-$1,200/month

Mid-Sized Market (Population 100,000-500,000):

- Secondary Road Poster: $1,200-$2,500/month
- Main Road Bulletin: $2,500-$5,000/month
- Digital Rotation (8 spots): $800-$2,000/month

Large Market (Population 500,000+):

- Secondary Road Poster: $2,000-$4,000/month
- Main Road Bulletin: $4,000-$10,000+/month
- Digital Rotation (8 spots): $1,500-$3,500/month

For most paving companies, a billboard represents a significant marketing investment that should be carefully considered as part of a broader strategy.

Designing Effective Billboard Messages

Billboard design requires a fundamentally different approach than other advertising media. Viewers typically have only **5-7 seconds** to absorb your message while driving past. This constraint demands extreme simplicity and clarity:

Content Best Practices

- **Limit Text to 7 Words or Less**: The most effective billboards communicate their entire message in 7 words or fewer. Every additional word reduces comprehension and recall.
- **Focus on a Single Message**: Attempt to communicate just one idea, offer, or brand statement. Billboards trying to convey multiple messages typically fail to communicate any of them effectively.
- **Use Contrasting Colors**: High contrast between text and background dramatically improves readability at a distance. Dark text on light backgrounds or vice versa works best.
- **Employ Large, Simple Typography**: Use bold, sans-serif fonts that can be read from hundreds of feet away. Avoid decorative or script fonts entirely.
- **Include Location Context When Relevant**: If your billboard is near your business or a specific area you serve, reference that: "Next Exit" or "Serving [Area Name]" helps localize your message.

Visual Design Strategies

- **Before/After Imagery**: For paving companies, dramatic before/after photos can instantly communicate your value proposition without words.
- **Use White Space Effectively**: Resist the urge to fill the entire billboard. Empty space around your key elements improves focus and readability.
- **Incorporate Your Vehicle/Equipment**: Showing your recognizable

trucks or equipment helps viewers connect the billboard to vehicles they see on the road.

- **Consider Dimensional Elements**: Adding 3D extensions that project beyond the billboard frame significantly increases attention and recall.
- **Ensure Night Visibility**: If your billboard is illuminated, ensure text and imagery remain clear and legible at night. Test colors for how they appear under lighting.

Contact Information Essentials

- **Prioritize Phone Number**: Make your phone number large and prominent—it's often the most important element for direct response.
- **Simple Web Address**: If including a website, keep it short and memorable. Consider a dedicated landing page (e.g., ABCPaving.com/billboard) to track effectiveness.
- **Company Name Prominence**: Your company name should be instantly identifiable, ideally through both text and logo.
- **Avoid Social Media Handles**: Unless your campaign specifically drives social engagement, leave social media icons/handles off billboards—they're too small to read at speed.

Effective Billboard Examples for Paving Companies Here are three concept examples that follow these principles:

Example 1: Direct Response Focus

- Visual: Clear before/after driveway transformation
- Headline: "FROM EYESORE TO IMPRESSIVE"
- Contact: "555-PAVE" (extremely large)
- Branding: Company logo and "Since 1986"

Example 2: Memorable Branding Play

- Visual: 3D extension showing asphalt "pouring" over billboard edge
- Headline: "WE'VE GOT YOU COVERED"
- Contact: Phone number and simple website
- Branding: Large company logo

Example 3: Location-Specific Approach

- Visual: Map showing service area with your location marked
- Headline: "YOUR LOCAL PAVING EXPERTS"
- Contact: Phone number
- Branding: Company logo and trucks

Each of these examples communicates a single, clear message while maintaining the simplicity required for billboard effectiveness.

Strategic Billboard Placement

The location of your billboard is often more important than its design. Consider these strategic approaches to placement:

- **Geographic Targeting**: Place billboards in areas where your ideal customers live or work. For residential paving, target affluent neighborhoods with aging homes. For commercial paving, focus near business districts or industrial parks.
- **Commuter Routes**: Identify major commuter routes where decision-makers travel daily. The repetitive exposure builds familiarity over time.
- **Proximity to Completed Projects**: When possible, position billboards near neighborhoods or commercial areas where you've recently completed impressive projects. This creates immediate relevance.
- **Competitor Intercepts**: Strategic placement near competitors' locations or along routes to reach them can intercept potential customers before they make contact with rivals.
- **Seasonal Considerations**: Some locations may be more valuable during certain seasons. A billboard near a beach area might have higher visibility during summer months when traffic increases.

Working with an experienced outdoor advertising representative can help identify the optimal locations based on traffic counts, demographics, and your specific business goals.

Measuring Billboard ROI and Effectiveness

Billboards have traditionally been challenging to measure precisely, but several approaches can help track their impact:

- **Dedicated Phone Numbers**: Use a unique tracking number that appears only on your billboard. This allows you to count direct response calls.
- **Custom URLs**: Create a simple, memorable URL used exclusively on your billboard (e.g., ABCPaving.com/drive).
- **Promotional Codes**: Include a billboard-specific discount code that customers must mention to receive a special offer.
- **Geographic Analysis**: Monitor increases in calls, website visits, or leads from the zip codes surrounding your billboard location.
- **Brand Lift Surveys**: Conduct awareness surveys before and after billboard placement to measure changes in recognition.
- **Before/After Sales Analysis**: Compare business volume in the targeted area before and after billboard installation.
- **Call Inquiry Tracking**: Simply ask new callers, "How did you hear about us?" and track billboard mentions over time.

When evaluating billboard performance, it's important to consider both direct and indirect effects. While direct response is valuable, billboards primarily build awareness, credibility, and recognition that may result in future business or enhance the effectiveness of your other marketing channels.

Billboard Success Story: Metro Paving

To illustrate the potential of billboard advertising, consider Metro Paving, a mid-sized paving contractor serving both residential and commercial clients in a metropolitan area of approximately 400,000 people. After years of primarily generating business through referrals and some digital marketing, Metro invested in a strategically placed billboard on a major commuter route that connected affluent suburbs with the downtown business district. Their investment included:

- $3,600 monthly for a premium illuminated bulletin location
- $900 for vinyl production and installation
- 12-month contract with first right of renewal

The billboard featured:

- A striking before/after image of a commercial parking lot transformation
- Their tagline: "PAVING PERFECTION"
- Phone number and website
- Company logo and "Family-owned since 1992"

After tracking results for one year, Metro attributed the following outcomes to the billboard:

- 76 direct calls to their tracking number
- 42 projects completed from those calls
- Average project value of $8,500
- Total revenue of $357,000 from a $44,100 investment
- 810% ROI

Beyond these measurable results, Metro reported significant secondary benefits:

- Increased recognition in sales meetings with commercial prospects
- Higher close rates on all estimates (the billboard had established credibility)
- Easier recruitment of quality employees
- Enhanced perception as a market leader

This example demonstrates that while billboards require substantial investment, the long-term value can significantly exceed the costs for established paving companies.

When Billboards Make Sense for Paving Companies

Billboard advertising isn't right for every paving business. Consider these factors when deciding if billboards should be part of your marketing mix:

Favorable Conditions for Billboard Advertising Billboards are likely to be effective when:

- **You Have Established Operations**: Billboards work best for companies that have been in business several years and have the capacity to handle increased lead volume.
- **Your Target Area Is Geographically Defined**: If your service area centers around specific communities or commercial districts that can be reached with strategic placement.
- **You Offer Both Residential and Commercial Services**: Billboards reach diverse audiences, making them efficient when you serve multiple segments.
- **You Have Sufficient Budget**: You can afford $1,500+ monthly for at least 6-12 months without straining finances.
- **You Seek Market Leadership Position**: You're trying to establish your company as the dominant provider in your area.
- **You Have Other Marketing Working**: Billboards complement existing marketing rather than standing alone.

Situations Where Billboards May Not Be Ideal Billboards might not be the best investment when:

- **You're a New Business**: Without established operations and reputation, the impact may be limited.
- **Your Service Area Is Very Limited or Widespread**: If you only serve a few neighborhoods or, conversely, cover multiple counties, billboard efficiency decreases.
- **Your Budget Is Constrained**: Limited marketing funds might be better allocated to more targeted channels initially.
- **You Need Immediate Lead Generation**: Billboards build awareness over time rather than driving immediate response.
- **You Have Very Specific Target Criteria**: If you only focus on certain types of paving projects or very specific client profiles, billboards' broad reach may be inefficient.
- **You Lack Tracking Capabilities**: Without proper systems to measure impact, it's difficult to assess billboard ROI.

Integration with Other Marketing Channels

Billboards work best as part of an integrated marketing strategy. Consider how they complement other channels:

- **With Digital Marketing**: Billboards create awareness that can lead to branded searches online. Ensure your digital presence (website, SEO, Google Business Profile) is strong to capture this traffic.
- **With Direct Mail**: Target neighborhoods near your billboard with direct mail to reinforce your message and provide more detailed information.
- **With Radio/TV**: Use consistent messaging and branding across all broadcast media to create a surround-sound effect.
- **With Vehicle Graphics**: Ensure your service vehicles feature branding that matches your billboard, creating recognition when prospects see

your crews working.

- **With Social Media**: Incorporate your billboard in social content—share photos of it being installed or people posing with it to extend its reach.

The most effective billboard campaigns don't exist in isolation but reinforce and amplify your other marketing efforts.

Billboard Alternatives for Smaller Budgets

If traditional billboards exceed your budget, consider these alternatives that provide similar visibility at lower cost:

- **Mobile Billboards**: Truck-mounted billboards that can be driven through targeted neighborhoods cost approximately $500-$1,500 per day, allowing for short-term, targeted exposure.
- **Bus Bench Advertising**: Benches at bus stops in strategic locations offer billboard-like visibility at $200-$500 monthly per location.
- **Transit Shelter Ads**: Bus stop shelters provide excellent visibility to both vehicle traffic and pedestrians at $300-$700 monthly.
- **Wrapped Vehicles**: Converting your own service vehicles into moving billboards through professional wraps creates thousands of daily impressions at a one-time cost of $2,000-$4,000 per vehicle.
- **Yard Signs**: Strategic placement of lawn signs at completed job sites costs just $5-$20 each and builds neighborhood awareness.

Each of these alternatives follows the same design principles as billboards—simple messaging, bold visuals, and clear contact information—while fitting smaller marketing budgets.

Planning Your Billboard Campaign

If you decide billboards make sense for your paving company, follow these steps to maximize effectiveness:

- Set Clear Objectives: Define what you want to achieve—increased brand awareness, more residential leads, commercial expansion, etc.
- Determine Budget Parameters: Establish your monthly budget and commitment duration (minimum 3-6 months for measurable results).
- Research Locations: Work with an outdoor advertising representative to identify high-value locations that reach your target audience.
- Develop Simple, Bold Creative: Create a design that communicates your core message in 5-7 words with striking visuals.
- Implement Tracking Mechanisms: Set up dedicated phone numbers, URLs, or offer codes to measure direct response.
- Establish Baseline Metrics: Document awareness, call volume, and inquiry sources before your billboard launches for comparison.
- Plan for Consistent Exposure: Billboards work through repetition; commit to at least 3-6 months in one location rather than moving frequently.
- Create Seasonal Variations: If using digital billboards or planning a long-term campaign, develop seasonal variations of your message.
- Coordinate with Other Marketing: Align billboard messaging with your other marketing channels for consistent branding.
- Conduct Regular Performance Reviews: Evaluate results quarterly, adjusting your approach based on measurable outcomes.

A well-planned billboard campaign can establish your paving company as a recognized industry leader in your market, creating a valuable brand asset that delivers returns for years to come.

18

Strategic Integration of Traditional and Digital Marketing

While we've examined radio, television, and billboard advertising individually, their true power emerges when strategically integrated with your digital marketing efforts. For paving companies, this integrated approach creates multiple touchpoints with potential customers throughout their decision journey.

The Multi-Channel Advantage

Research consistently shows that consumers encounter a brand multiple times before taking action. According to marketing research, it takes an average of **8-12 touchpoints** across different channels before the typical customer converts. By strategically combining traditional and digital channels, you create a surround-sound effect that builds familiarity, trust, and urgency.

Consider this typical customer journey for someone needing driveway paving:

- **Awareness Stage**: Notices deteriorating condition of driveway

- *Traditional Touchpoint*: Sees your billboard during commute
- *Digital Touchpoint*: Searches "driveway repair" and sees your Google Ad
- **Consideration Stage**: Researches options and companies
- *Traditional Touchpoint*: Hears your radio ad during morning drive
- *Digital Touchpoint*: Visits your website to learn about services and view project photos
- **Decision Stage**: Ready to request quotes
- *Traditional Touchpoint*: Notices your truck working in neighborhood
- *Digital Touchpoint*: Checks your Google reviews and submits quote request

At each stage, the combination of traditional and digital touchpoints reinforces your message and builds confidence in your company.

Creating Cross-Channel Consistency

For this integrated approach to work effectively, consistency is essential across all channels:

- **Visual Brand Consistency**: Use the same logo, color scheme, and typography across all media. A prospect should immediately recognize your billboard design elements in your website header or truck graphics.
- **Message Alignment**: While you'll adjust content for each channel's strengths, maintain consistent core messaging about your unique selling propositions and key benefits.
- **Voice and Tone**: Develop a distinctive brand voice that carries through all communications, whether it's a radio script, billboard headline, or social media post.
- **Call-to-Action Clarity**: Direct prospects to your primary response channel consistently—whether that's calling a specific number, visiting your website, or requesting a quote online.

- **Promotional Coordination**: When running special offers or seasonal promotions, ensure the same offer appears across all channels simultaneously.

This consistency creates a multiplier effect—each channel reinforces the others, building stronger brand recognition than any single channel could achieve alone.

Channel Allocation Strategy

To effectively allocate your marketing budget across traditional and digital channels, consider these strategic approaches:

Foundation First: Ensure your digital foundation (website, SEO, Google Business Profile) is solid before investing significantly in traditional media. Without this foundation, traditional advertising will drive prospects to competitors with stronger online presence.

Seasonality Shifts: Adjust your channel mix seasonally. During peak paving season, invest more in immediate response channels like Google Ads and radio. During off-seasons, shift toward awareness building through billboards and social media.

Geographic Layering: In your primary service areas, implement multiple channels simultaneously for maximum impact. In secondary markets, use more targeted and cost-efficient approaches.

Budget Proportions: For a mid-sized paving company, a balanced allocation might look like:

- 40-50% Digital (Website, SEO, PPC, Social Media)
- 30-40% Traditional Broadcast (Radio, TV if budget allows)
- 10-20% Outdoor/Print (Billboards, Vehicle Wraps, Strategic Print)

- 5-10% Experimental (Testing new channels or approaches)

Track and Adjust: Continuously measure performance across channels and shift resources toward those delivering the best returns for your specific business.

Remember that the optimal channel mix varies based on your company's size, growth goals, competitive landscape, and local market conditions.

Measurement and Attribution

One of the most challenging aspects of integrated marketing is accurately attributing results to specific channels. When a prospect encounters your company through multiple touchpoints, which one deserves credit for the conversion?

To address this challenge:

- **Implement Multi-Touch Attribution**: Move beyond simplistic "last-click" attribution to understand how different channels contribute throughout the customer journey.
- **Use Tracking Codes**: Assign unique phone numbers, URLs, or offer codes to each channel for direct attribution.
- **Conduct Regular Surveys**: Ask new customers how they first heard about you and what other touchpoints influenced their decision.
- **Track Lift Metrics**: Measure the performance lift in one channel when adding another (e.g., does direct website traffic increase in areas where you add billboards?).
- **Create Control Groups**: Test multi-channel campaigns in specific geographic areas while maintaining baseline marketing in others to isolate the impact.

Revenue Commander provides comprehensive tracking capabilities that can help connect these touchpoints, offering a clearer picture of how your traditional and digital marketing efforts work together to drive results.

Success Example: Integrated Marketing for Summit Paving

To illustrate the power of strategic integration, consider Summit Paving, a mid-sized company serving both residential and commercial clients in a competitive metropolitan area. After years of relying primarily on referrals and basic digital marketing, Summit implemented an integrated approach with a $20,000 monthly marketing budget allocated as follows:

- **Digital Marketing: $8,000**
- SEO & Content: $2,500
- Google Ads: $3,500
- Social Media: $1,500
- Email Marketing: $500
- **Traditional Marketing: $12,000**
- Radio Campaign: $4,500
- Billboard (1 premium location): $3,500
- Vehicle Wraps & Job Site Signage: $1,000 (amortized cost)
- Local TV (seasonal): $3,000

Key to their approach was thematic consistency. Their "Built to Last" campaign featured:

- Radio ads emphasizing their 7-year warranty
- Billboard showing dramatic before/after with "BUILT TO LAST" headline
- TV spots demonstrating their thorough base preparation process
- Google ads with "Built to Last" in the headlines
- Social content featuring project durability and longevity
- Wrapped vehicles reinforcing the same messaging

After 12 months of this integrated approach, Summit achieved:

- 112% increase in total lead volume
- 68% increase in average project value
- 143% increase in revenue
- 73% increase in name recognition (measured via local survey)

Most importantly, their analysis showed that customers exposed to multiple marketing channels:

- Converted at 2.3x the rate of single-channel exposure
- Had 40% higher average project value
- Were 65% more likely to refer others
- Had 70% lower price sensitivity during negotiations

This example demonstrates how traditional and digital channels can work synergistically to deliver results far greater than either approach could achieve independently.

Conclusion: Finding Your Optimal Mix

There is no one-size-fits-all approach to marketing for paving companies. The optimal mix of traditional and digital channels depends on your specific business goals, target market, competitive landscape, and budget constraints.

However, the evidence clearly shows that integrated, multi-channel marketing delivers superior results to single-channel approaches. While digital marketing provides the targeting precision and measurability modern businesses need, traditional channels like radio, television, and billboards offer reach, impact, and credibility that digital alone cannot match.

For most established paving companies seeking growth, the question isn't whether to use traditional marketing, but rather how to strategically integrate it with digital efforts for maximum impact. By approaching marketing as an ecosystem rather than isolated channels, you can create a presence that dominates your market and drives sustainable business growth.

The most successful paving contractors view their marketing investments not as expenses but as assets that build equity in their brand—equity that pays dividends through higher-value projects, increased referrals, and the ability to command premium pricing in their market.

As you develop your marketing strategy, remember that consistency across channels and patience with building awareness are essential. Traditional media typically requires longer commitment periods to show results, but when properly integrated with digital efforts, creates a marketing foundation that competitors find difficult to match.

19

Referral Marketing

Of all marketing channels available to paving companies, referrals consistently produce the highest-quality leads with the lowest acquisition cost. Word-of-mouth recommendations from satisfied customers, business partners, and community members create pre-sold prospects who already trust your company before you ever speak with them.

The Unmatched Power of Referrals

Research consistently shows that referrals outperform all other lead sources in terms of trust, conversion rates, and lifetime value. According to our research findings:

92% of consumers trust recommendations from friends and family over any form of advertising. This statistic highlights why building a systematic referral process is critical.

- Word-of-mouth has a substantial influence on approximately **$6 trillion in annual consumer spending**.
- Referred customers typically have a **16% higher lifetime value** compared to non-referred customers.
- Referral leads convert at **30% higher rates** than leads from other

marketing channels.

- The cost per acquisition for referral leads is typically **50-70% lower** than other channels.

For paving contractors, these statistics translate into tangible business outcomes. A single successful referral can generate thousands of dollars in revenue with virtually no marketing cost. Furthermore, referred customers tend to be more trusting, less price-sensitive, and more likely to refer others, creating a compounding effect over time.

Why Referrals Work So Well for Paving Companies

Paving services involve significant investment and trust in the contractor's capability. Several factors make referrals particularly effective in this industry:

- **Trust Transfer**: When a satisfied customer recommends your company, they're transferring their trust to the prospect, essentially vouching for your reliability and quality.
- **Tangible Results**: Paving projects create visible results that neighbors, friends, and business associates notice. A beautifully paved driveway or parking lot serves as a permanent advertisement for your work.
- **Infrequent Purchase**: Most property owners only need paving services occasionally, making personal recommendations particularly valuable when they do.
- **High-Stakes Decision**: Given the investment and permanence of paving work, prospects are eager to reduce risk by following trusted recommendations.
- **Community Visibility**: Local service businesses benefit from community connections and relationships that naturally facilitate referrals.

As one paving contractor noted in our interviews, "A customer who comes to us through a referral is already 80% sold before we even provide an estimate. They're less focused on price comparison and more interested in confirming their friend's positive experience."

Building a Structured Referral Program

While some referrals happen organically, a systematic approach dramatically increases their frequency and quality. Here's how to build an effective referral program for your paving company:

Program Structure Elements

Clear Incentives:

- Determine what you'll offer in exchange for referrals. This could include:
- Cash rewards ($50-$200 is typical for residential referrals, more for commercial)
- Discount on future services (10-20% off their next maintenance service)
- Gift cards to popular local restaurants or retailers
- Charitable donations in the customer's name
- Service upgrades or complimentary maintenance

Referral Tiers:

- Consider creating multiple reward levels based on:
- Number of referrals provided
- Size of referred projects
- Type of customer (residential vs. commercial)
- Example tiered structure:
- First successful referral: $100 gift card
- Second referral: $150 gift card

- Third and subsequent referrals: $200 gift card plus 15% off their next service

Qualifying Criteria:

- Define clearly what constitutes a "successful" referral:
- Must be a new customer (not existing in your database)
- Must schedule and receive an estimate
- Must convert to a paid project over a minimum value
- Referrer must be identified at the inquiry stage
- Transparent criteria prevent misunderstandings and disputes.

Reward Timing:

- Determine when referral rewards are delivered:
- After estimate (encourages more referrals regardless of close rate)
- After project booking (ensures qualified projects only)
- After project completion and payment (safest financially but creates delay)
- Split rewards (partial at estimate, remainder at completion)
- Earlier payment encourages continued referral activity but may require budget for non-converting referrals.

Program Terms and Conditions:

- Create clear documentation outlining:
- Eligibility requirements (past customers, current customers, partners)
- Referral qualification process
- Reward structure and payment timing
- Any limitations or restrictions (maximum annual rewards, etc.)
- Tax implications if applicable
- Having these terms documented prevents misunderstandings and

keeps the program legally compliant.

Implementation Process

Once you've designed your program structure, implement it systematically:

Program Launch Communication:

- Announce your referral program through:
- Email announcement to past customers
- Direct mail to your customer database
- In-person explanation at project completion
- Mention in all invoices and follow-up communications
- Information on your website and social media
- Clearly explain the benefits and simple process for participation.

Staff Training:

- Ensure all team members understand:
- Program details and benefits
- How to explain the program to customers
- Process for capturing referral information
- Handling of common questions
- Role-play conversations to build confidence in discussing referrals.

Tracking System:

- Implement a system to track:
- Who made each referral
- Referral contact information and status
- Stage in the sales process
- Completion status and reward eligibility

- Reward delivery confirmation
- Revenue Commander provides specialized referral tracking capabilities that integrate with your broader marketing data.

Marketing Materials:

- Create supporting materials like:
- Printed referral cards customers can give to friends
- Digital referral links for email or social sharing
- Referral section on your website
- "Refer and Earn" reminders on invoices
- Simple one-page explanation of the program
- Professional materials signal the importance you place on referrals.

Referral Celebration:

- Acknowledge and celebrate referrals:
- Personal thank-you notes to referrers
- Public recognition (with permission) on social media
- Annual "Top Referrer" awards for most active customers
- Feature successful referral stories in your newsletter
- Celebration reinforces the behavior and encourages others to participate.

Incentives That Drive Referral Behavior

The right incentives can dramatically increase referral frequency. Different incentives motivate different customer segments:

Cash Rewards

- Direct cash payments are highly motivating for many customers:
- Typical range: $50-$200 for residential referrals, $250-$1,000 for

commercial projects
- Pros: Universal appeal, clear value
- Cons: Can appear transactional, may attract referrals focused on the reward rather than good match
- Implementation: Send check or electronic payment promptly after qualification criteria are met

Future Service Discounts

- Offering discounts on future services encourages both referrals and repeat business:
- Typical offer: 10-20% off next service, or free maintenance service (like crack sealing)
- Pros: Promotes customer retention, can have higher perceived value than cash
- Cons: Value only realized when customer needs service again
- Implementation: Issue dated discount certificate valid for 12-24 months

Gift Cards

- Popular local restaurants or retailers provide an alternative to cash that feels more like a gift:
- Typical value: $50-$200 to popular local establishments or national chains
- Pros: Feels more like a gift than a payment, creates positive association
- Cons: Less flexible than cash, requires maintaining inventory of cards
- Implementation: Hand-deliver with a thank-you note for maximum impact

Charitable Donations

- For some customers, a donation to a charity in their name is more meaningful than personal rewards:
- Typical structure: Customer chooses from 3-4 local charities for donation in their name
- Pros: Appeals to community-minded customers, enhances company reputation
- Cons: Less directly motivating for some customer segments
- Implementation: Provide donation certificate and acknowledgment from the charity

Dual-Sided Incentives

- Offering benefits to both referrer and the new customer can be particularly effective:
- Example structure: Referrer gets $100, new customer gets 10% off first project
- Pros: Easier for customers to make referrals when friends also benefit
- Cons: Higher cost per acquisition
- Implementation: Clearly communicate both aspects of the reward program

The most successful programs often offer choices among these incentives, allowing customers to select what motivates them most. One paving contractor reported doubling their referral rate by simply switching from a one-size-fits-all approach to offering a choice of three different rewards.

Asking for Referrals Effectively

How and when you ask for referrals significantly impacts success rates. Follow these best practices:

Optimal Timing

The most effective times to request referrals include:

Immediately After Project Completion: When satisfaction is highest and your work is fresh and visible:

- During the final walkthrough when the customer is admiring the finished result
- As part of the project completion paperwork
- In your follow-up "satisfaction check" call (1-3 days after completion)

Following Positive Feedback: When a customer expresses satisfaction:

- After receiving a compliment about your work
- When a customer sends a thank-you note
- After they post a positive online review

During Regular Maintenance Visits: When you're maintaining previous work:

- During annual sealcoating or maintenance visits
- When performing warranty work (showing your commitment to quality)

Anniversary Touchpoints: When reaching out about project anniversaries:

- On the one-year anniversary of project completion
- During seasonal check-in communications

Value-Delivery Moments: When providing additional value:

- When sharing helpful maintenance tips
- After resolving a concern promptly and effectively

The key principle is to ask when the customer is experiencing positive feelings about your company, not when they're focused on payments or any project challenges.

Effective Asking Methods

How you phrase your referral request dramatically impacts response rates:

Direct 1-to-1 Request: The most effective approach is a personal, specific ask:

- "John, I'm wondering if you might know one or two neighbors who might also need their driveway repaved this season? We've got the equipment in the area for the next month and could offer them the same quality work we did for you."
- This personalized, specific approach yields 2-3× higher response rates than generic requests.

The Compliment-Based Ask: Frame your request as a result of their discernment:

- "We really appreciate working with knowledgeable customers like you who recognize quality work. Do you know others who might value the same level of craftsmanship?"

The Help-Based Ask: Position referrals as helping others, not just your business:

- "If you know anyone else struggling with driveway drainage issues like you were, we'd be happy to help them the same way we helped you."

The Social Proof Ask: Leverage the power of community:

- "We've done several driveways in this neighborhood now. If any of your neighbors have asked about your new driveway, we'd love to talk with them."

The Value-Add Ask: Offer something for the prospect, not just the referrer:

- "If any of your friends or colleagues mention needing paving work, I'd be happy to offer them a free assessment and the same preferred pricing we extended to you."

The common element in effective asks is making them specific, personal, and value-focused rather than generic or self-serving.

Multi-Channel Referral Requests

Implement a systematic approach to requesting referrals across multiple channels:

In-Person Requests:

- Train all customer-facing staff to ask for referrals at appropriate moments
- Provide referral cards they can leave with customers
- Create a simple script for consistent messaging

Email Campaigns:

- Send dedicated referral request emails to satisfied customers

- Include referral reminders in regular newsletters
- Follow up specifically after positive reviews or feedback

Direct Mail:

- Include referral program brochures with invoices
- Send periodic postcards highlighting the referral rewards
- Create "Share with a friend" cards customers can pass along

Website Integration:

- Add a prominent "Refer a Friend" section to your website
- Create an easy online referral form
- Feature testimonials from customers who've received referral rewards

Social Media:

- Create shareable content about your referral program
- Acknowledge and thank referrers (with permission)
- Run special referral promotions tied to seasonal events

By implementing requests across multiple channels, you create multiple opportunities for customers to participate in your referral program.

Partner Referral Networks

Beyond customer referrals, strategic partnerships with complementary businesses can create a steady stream of qualified leads:

Identifying Strategic Partners

The best referral partners typically include:

Complementary Service Providers: Businesses that serve the same customers but don't compete directly:

- Landscaping companies
- General contractors
- Concrete contractors
- Excavation companies
- Home builders and remodelers
- Property management companies
- Real estate agents
- Home inspectors

Upstream Service Providers: Businesses customers interact with before needing paving:

- Real estate agents working with new homebuyers
- Home builders during new construction
- Property inspectors identifying pavement issues
- Mortgage lenders financing property improvements

Downstream Service Providers: Businesses customers engage after paving:

- Landscapers enhancing property surroundings
- Line striping companies for parking lots
- Fencing companies for property boundaries
- Outdoor lighting installers

Supply Chain Partners: Businesses in your supply network:

- Material suppliers who hear customer needs
- Equipment rental companies serving DIY customers
- Local building supply retailers

The ideal partner has these characteristics:

- Serves a similar customer demographic
- Has complementary rather than competing services
- Maintains high quality standards and reputation
- Has regular customer contact
- Values long-term relationships

Structuring Partner Referral Arrangements

Partner referrals can be organized in several ways:

Reciprocal Referrals: The simplest arrangement where both parties agree to refer business to each other when appropriate:

- Requires mutual trust and similar quality standards
- Works best with comparable service frequency and client base
- Example: Paving contractor and landscaper referring clients to each other

Financial Referral Fees: More formal arrangements with defined compensation:

- Typical fees range from 5-10% of project value
- Usually capped at a maximum amount
- May require invoicing and 1099 reporting
- Example: Paying a property manager 7% of projects they refer (up to $500)

Service Exchange: Trading services instead of financial payment:

- Provide paving services to partner in exchange for referrals
- Value services at retail rates for fair exchange
- Document agreement clearly
- Example: Providing free sealcoating to a general contractor's office parking lot

Co-Marketing Partnerships: Jointly marketing your complementary services:

- Shared direct mail campaigns
- Joint workshops or events
- Combined service packages
- Example: Partnering with a landscaper on a "Complete Property Makeover" package

Formalized Contractor Networks: Membership in organized referral groups:

- Local contractor alliances
- BNI (Business Network International) chapters
- Industry association referral programs
- Example: Joining a home service contractor network where each member represents a different specialty

Partner Referral Implementation

To create effective partner referral relationships:

Identify and Qualify Potential Partners:

- Research reputation and customer satisfaction

- Ensure quality standards align with yours
- Verify financial stability and business longevity
- Assess cultural fit and business ethics

Initial Partnership Discussion:

- Schedule a dedicated meeting to discuss collaboration
- Present clear value proposition for partnership
- Discuss expectations for referral quality and volume
- Explore compensation models that benefit both parties

Create Formal Agreement:

- Document referral terms and conditions
- Specify compensation structure and timing
- Define what constitutes a qualified referral
- Include termination provisions if needed
- Consider having the agreement reviewed by an attorney

Establish Communication Channels:

- Create a simple process for sharing leads
- Determine preferred contact methods
- Set expectations for response timing
- Implement regular check-ins to maintain relationship

Educate Their Team:

- Provide information about your services and ideal clients
- Create simple, shareable materials they can use
- Offer to conduct a brief training session for their staff
- Make it easy for them to explain your services accurately

Track and Report Results:

- Document all referrals received and their outcomes
- Share success stories with the referring partner
- Provide regular activity reports
- Celebrate mutual wins and milestones

Show Appreciation:

- Send thank-you notes for quality referrals
- Consider special appreciation events or gifts
- Acknowledge partners publicly when appropriate
- Make referring you a positive experience

A well-managed partner network can become one of your most reliable lead sources. One paving contractor we worked with generated 35% of their annual revenue through a network of just seven strategic partners, with property management companies being particularly valuable sources.

Revenue Commander Referral Tracking

Managing a robust referral program requires systematic tracking and analytics. Revenue Commander provides specialized tools for complete referral management:

Referral Source Tracking

Revenue Commander allows you to:

- Record the specific source of each referral (customer, partner, staff, etc.)
- Document referral date and initial contact information
- Track which marketing efforts prompted the referral

- Maintain a complete history of all referrals from each source
- Calculate the lifetime referral value of each customer or partner

Referral Journey Monitoring

The platform enables tracking of each referral through the sales process:

- Document initial contact date and method
- Record estimate appointment and outcome
- Track conversion to sale with project details
- Monitor project completion and payment
- Calculate the precise value of each converted referral

Reward Management

Efficiently manage your referral incentive program:

- Track reward eligibility status for each referral
- Document reward selection when options are offered
- Record reward distribution dates and methods
- Calculate total reward program expenditures
- Analyze reward effectiveness by type and amount

Performance Analytics

Gain valuable insights into your referral program's effectiveness:

- Calculate referral conversion rates by source
- Compare referral quality across different channels
- Analyze the time from referral to completed project
- Measure average project value by referral source
- Track program ROI over time with complete financial analytics

Customer Lifetime Value Analysis

Understand the true value of referring customers:

- Compare the lifetime value of referred vs. non-referred customers
- Track how often referring customers make additional referrals
- Calculate the compound value of "referral chains"
- Identify your most valuable referral sources
- Predict future referral potential in your customer base

These comprehensive tracking capabilities transform your referral program from a passive opportunity into an actively managed, high-performance lead generation system.

Following Up With Referrals

The way you handle incoming referrals significantly impacts their conversion rate. Referrals are your highest-quality leads and deserve specialized treatment:

Rapid Response Protocol

Speed is critical when responding to referrals:

Immediate Acknowledgment:

- Respond to referral introductions within 1 hour during business hours
- Send an initial acknowledgment even if detailed follow-up must wait
- Thank both the referrer and the prospect in your first communication
- Example: "Thank you for the introduction, John. Susan, I appreciate you considering us and would love to discuss your project. When would be a convenient time to connect?"

Prioritized Scheduling:

- Offer expedited appointment options to referred prospects
- Create scheduling flexibility for high-value referrals
- Consider dedicated referral response staff during peak seasons
- Example: "As a referred customer, we'd be happy to accommodate your schedule, including evening or weekend appointments if that's more convenient."

Personalized Communication:

- Reference the referrer appropriately in communications
- Acknowledge any specific needs or concerns mentioned by the referrer
- Tailor your messaging to the relationship between referrer and prospect
- Example: "Mike mentioned you're concerned about proper drainage on your sloped driveway. That's actually one of our specialties, and we've solved similar challenges for many properties in your area."

Preparation and Research:

- Research the prospect before initial contact when possible
- Review similar projects you've completed in their area
- Understand the specific needs that prompted the referral
- Example: "I noticed you're in the Highland Park neighborhood where we've done several projects. The soil conditions there require specific base preparation that we're very familiar with."

The combination of speed, personalization, and preparation signals to the prospect that you value the referral relationship and their business.

The Referral Sales Process

Referred leads require a somewhat different sales approach than cold leads:

Acknowledge the Relationship:

- Begin by thanking them for considering you based on the referral
- Share a positive comment about your experience with the referrer (when appropriate)
- Use the established trust as a foundation for the relationship
- Example: "John has been a great customer for years. We just completed his third project last month, and I'm glad he connected us."

Leverage Shared Information:

- Reference relevant details the referrer may have shared
- Confirm understanding of their specific needs
- Adapt your presentation based on what they likely already know about you
- Example: "Sarah mentioned you're concerned about the lifespan of asphalt in your climate. Let me share how we specifically address those concerns..."

Balance Education and Expertise:

- Even with referrals, establish your expertise through education
- Avoid assuming they understand technical aspects of paving
- Provide value through information while respecting their knowledge
- Example: "Even though you're familiar with our work through Mike, I'd like to explain our three-stage installation process so you understand what makes our approach different."

Customize the Estimate Experience:

- Provide more detailed options than you might for non-referred leads
- Offer insights specific to their property's unique conditions
- Consider bringing portfolio materials showcasing similar projects
- Example: "Based on what I'm seeing at your property, I've prepared three options that vary in terms of materials and longevity."

Respect the Existing Trust:

- Be transparent about pricing and process
- Avoid high-pressure sales tactics that could damage trust
- Provide honest, straightforward recommendations
- Example: "Given what you've shared about your budget constraints, I actually think our mid-range option would be the most cost-effective for your situation."

Extend the Referral Chain:

- Once relationship is established, introduce your referral program
- Explain how they can benefit from referring others
- Plant the seed for future referrals early in the relationship
- Example: "Once your project is complete and you're satisfied with our work, we'd love to offer you the same referral benefit that John received for connecting us."

This referral-specific approach respects the existing trust while still providing the education and expertise needed to close the sale effectively.

Maintaining Communication Loop

One critical aspect of referral management is keeping the original referrer informed:

Initial Update:

- Thank the referrer again after initial contact with the prospect
- Provide appropriate feedback about the interaction
- Respect privacy while acknowledging progress
- Example: "Just wanted to let you know I connected with Susan yesterday. Thank you again for the introduction! We're meeting next Tuesday to look at her driveway."

Milestone Communication:

- Share appropriate updates at key points in the sales process
- Inform referrer when their reward eligibility changes
- Respect confidentiality regarding specific project details
- Example: "Good news! Susan's project is now scheduled for next month. Your referral reward will be processed once we begin work."

Completion Acknowledgment:

- Formally thank referrer once project is complete
- Process and deliver any promised rewards promptly
- Share appropriate positive outcomes (with prospect's permission)
- Example: "Susan's driveway is now complete, and she's very pleased with the results. Your $100 referral bonus has been processed and should arrive within the week. Thank you again for your confidence in us!"

Ongoing Appreciation:

- Periodically acknowledge valuable referrers
- Consider special recognition for multiple referrals
- Include top referrers in special events or appreciation programs
- Example: "You've referred three customers to us this year, making you one of our top referral partners. We'd like to invite you to our annual client appreciation dinner next month."

This communication loop reinforces the value you place on referrals and encourages continued referral activity from satisfied customers.

Measuring Word-of-Mouth Effectiveness

Implementing systematic measurement transforms referral marketing from a passive, hopeful approach into a strategically managed program with predictable results:

Key Performance Indicators

Track these essential metrics to evaluate your referral program:

Referral Rate: The percentage of customers who provide at least one referral:

- Formula: (Number of referring customers ÷ Total customer base) × 100
- Benchmark: 10–15% for passive programs, 25–35% for active programs
- Improvement goal: Increase by 5 percentage points annually

Referral Conversion Rate: The percentage of referrals that become customers:

- Formula: (Number of referrals converted ÷ Total referrals received) ×

100

- Benchmark: 40-60% (significantly higher than other lead sources)
- Improvement goal: Optimize sales process for referred leads

Cost Per Referral Acquisition (CPRA): The average cost to acquire a referral:

- Formula: (Total referral program costs ÷ Number of referrals received)
- Benchmark: Varies by reward structure, typically $50-$200
- Improvement goal: Maintain or reduce while increasing volume

Referral Revenue Percentage: Portion of total revenue from referred customers:

- Formula: (Revenue from referral customers ÷ Total revenue) × 100
- Benchmark: 20-30% for established programs
- Improvement goal: Increase by 2-3 percentage points annually

Referral Customer Value: Average project value from referred customers:

- Formula: Total referral revenue ÷ Number of referral customers
- Benchmark: Typically 10-25% higher than non-referred customers
- Improvement goal: Maintain premium value compared to other channels

Referral ROI: Return on investment from referral program:

- Formula: (Profit from referral projects - Referral program costs) ÷ Referral program costs
- Benchmark: 5:1 or higher (500%+)
- Improvement goal: Maintain high ROI while scaling program

Referral Cycle Time: Average time from referral receipt to project completion:

- Formula: Sum of all referral cycle days ÷ Number of completed referral projects
- Benchmark: Varies by season and project type
- Improvement goal: Reduce by streamlining referral response process

These metrics provide a comprehensive view of your referral program's performance and highlight specific areas for improvement.

Referral Program Analytics

Beyond basic metrics, deeper analytics reveal important insights:

Source Analysis:

- Track which customer segments generate the most referrals
- Identify characteristics of your best referrers
- Determine which partners produce the highest-converting referrals
- Example insight: "Customers with project values over $10,000 are 3× more likely to refer others."

Timing Patterns:

- Analyze when referrals most commonly occur in the customer relationship
- Identify seasonal patterns in referral behavior
- Determine optimal timing for referral requests
- Example insight: "78% of referrals occur within 30 days of project completion."

Incentive Effectiveness:

- Compare response rates for different reward structures
- Analyze which incentives produce the highest-quality referrals
- Calculate ROI by incentive type
- Example insight: "Cash rewards generate 40% more referrals, but service discounts produce 25% higher average project values."

Geographic Distribution:

- Map referral patterns across your service area
- Identify neighborhood clusters and opportunities
- Target marketing efforts to capitalize on referral momentum
- Example insight: "The Lakeside neighborhood has generated 15 referrals from just 3 initial customers."

Lifetime Value Comparison:

- Compare long-term value of referred vs. non-referred customers
- Track repeat business patterns for referral customers
- Analyze upsell and cross-sell success with referred customers
- Example insight: "Referred customers are 35% more likely to purchase maintenance services within two years."

These analytical insights allow you to continuously refine your referral program for maximum impact.

Revenue Commander Analytics Features

Revenue Commander provides specialized analytics for comprehensive referral program management:

Referral Source Dashboard:

- Visual representation of your most productive referral sources

- Filtering by time period, project type, and geographic area
- Comparative performance across different referrer categories
- Trend analysis showing program growth over time

Customer Referral Potential Scoring:

- Predictive algorithms identifying customers most likely to refer
- Automated flagging of high-potential referrers for targeted outreach
- Identification of satisfied customers who haven't yet referred
- Prioritization of referral requests based on likelihood scores

Referral Program ROI Calculator:

- Comprehensive cost tracking across all program elements
- Revenue attribution for direct and indirect referral impacts
- Automated calculation of key financial metrics
- Comparison of referral program ROI against other marketing channels

Referral Journey Visualization:

- Tracking of referral progression through each sales stage
- Identification of conversion bottlenecks in the referral process
- Comparison of sales cycle efficiency for referrals vs. other leads
- Time-based analytics for process optimization

Referral Network Mapping:

- Visual representation of referral relationships and chains
- Identification of "super-referrers" and their extended influence
- Mapping of multi-generational referral patterns
- Strategic planning tools for network expansion

These advanced analytics transform your referral program from a passive collection of individual recommendations into a strategically managed system for predictable growth.

Case Study: Systematic Referral Marketing

To illustrate the impact of a well-structured referral program, consider the experience of Premier Paving, a mid-sized contractor serving both residential and commercial clients in a competitive suburban market:

Initial Situation

- Approximately 10% of new business came from passive referrals
- No formal tracking or incentive program in place
- Inconsistent asking for referrals by team members
- Limited follow-up with referral prospects
- No integration with other marketing channels

Implemented Solution Premier Paving developed a comprehensive referral program with these elements:

Structured Incentives:

- Tiered rewards based on project value
- Choice of cash payment, future service discount, or charity donation
- Special "neighborhood bonus" for referring adjacent properties

Systematic Processes:

- Referral request at multiple touchpoints in customer journey
- Dedicated team member for referral program management
- Automated tracking through Revenue Commander
- Regular referral source analysis and optimization

Multi-Channel Promotion:

- Referral program featured on website and social media
- Email campaigns to past customers highlighting success stories
- Branded leave-behind materials for every customer
- Regular staff training on referral conversions

Partner Network Development:

- Strategic partnerships with 12 complementary businesses
- Formal agreements with top-performing real estate agents
- Quarterly partner appreciation events
- Co-marketing opportunities with select partners

Referral-Specific Sales Process:

- Priority scheduling for referral appointments
- Enhanced proposal presentation for referred prospects
- Specialized follow-up sequences
- Closed-loop communication with referrers

Results After 12 Months The impact of this systematic approach was transformative:

- Referral rate increased from 10% to 37% of customers
- Referral lead conversion rate reached 64% (compared to 23% for other leads)
- Referral sources expanded to include 15+ regular partner businesses
- Average referred project value was 28% higher than non-referred projects
- Referral revenue grew to represent 42% of total company revenue
- Program ROI calculated at 843% (over $8 return for every $1 invested)
- Customer acquisition cost decreased 34% company-wide due to

referral efficiency

Most importantly, the systematic nature of the program created predictability. Premier Paving could now forecast referral volume and factor it into their growth plans with confidence.

Implementation Checklist

Use this comprehensive checklist to implement an effective referral marketing program:

Program Design

- Define referral program objectives and success metrics
- Determine reward structure and incentive options
- Establish qualification criteria and verification process
- Create terms and conditions documentation
- Design tracking and reporting systems
- Set initial 90-day goals for the program

Team Preparation

- Train all team members on program details
- Develop scripts for requesting referrals at different touchpoints
- Create role-specific responsibilities for program implementation
- Establish performance expectations for referral generation
- Implement regular referral program updates in team meetings
- Create recognition system for team members who generate referrals
- Develop documentation for training new team members
- Set up referral handling protocols for front-line staff

Customer Communication

- Create program announcement for existing customers
- Develop referral request emails and templates
- Design printed referral cards and materials
- Prepare website content explaining the program
- Create social media posts promoting referral benefits
- Draft thank-you communications for both referrers and new customers

Partner Network Development

- Identify initial partner targets based on complementary services
- Create partner program value proposition
- Develop formal agreement templates
- Prepare partner education materials about your services
- Design co-marketing opportunities and materials
- Establish communication protocols for referral sharing

Tracking and Measurement

- Set up referral source tracking in CRM or Revenue Commander
- Implement referral status and stage monitoring
- Create reward fulfillment tracking system
- Develop regular reporting schedule and format
- Establish baseline metrics for future comparison
- Configure ROI calculation methodology

Program Launch and Optimization

- Execute soft launch with select customers
- Gather feedback and adjust processes as needed
- Implement full program launch
- Schedule regular program review and optimization sessions
- Create testing plan for different incentives and messaging

- Develop expansion strategy for increasing program reach

Conclusion: The Referral Marketing Advantage

In a world of increasingly expensive and competitive marketing channels, referral marketing stands out as the most cost-effective, highest-converting lead source available to paving contractors. The 92% of consumers who trust recommendations from friends and family represent an enormous opportunity for companies willing to implement systematic referral processes.

Unlike many marketing investments that depreciate over time, a well-structured referral program appreciates as your customer base grows and your referral culture strengthens. Each new customer becomes not just a revenue source but a potential ambassador for your business.

The most successful paving contractors recognize that referrals aren't just a passive, occasional benefit but a strategic asset that can be systematically cultivated. By implementing proper incentives, consistent processes, effective tracking, and regular optimization, you can transform word-of-mouth from a welcome surprise into a predictable, scalable growth engine.

In the next chapter, we'll explore how to extend your referral success through strategic networking and community marketing—building relationships with local organizations, associations, and complementary businesses to further expand your presence and profitability.

20

Networking and Community Marketing

While direct customer referrals form the foundation of word-of-mouth marketing, strategic networking and community involvement create additional pathways to reach potential customers. For paving contractors, being actively engaged in local business communities, industry associations, and neighborhood events establishes your company as a trusted, integral part of the areas you serve.

The Strategic Value of Business Networking

Unlike most other marketing channels, business networking creates multi-dimensional benefits for paving companies:

- **Lead Generation**: Connections with other business owners, property managers, and community leaders directly produce project opportunities.
- **Reputation Enhancement**: Active participation in business communities builds credibility and positions your company as an established local leader.
- **Strategic Partnerships**: Networking creates opportunities for collaborative relationships with complementary businesses that extend your reach.

- **Competitive Intelligence**: Regular interaction with peers and associated industries provides valuable market insights and trends.
- **Professional Development**: Industry connections facilitate knowledge exchange and best practice sharing that improves your operations.

For paving contractors, these benefits are particularly valuable. The substantial investment and long-term nature of paving projects make trust and reputation critical factors in customer decision-making. Networking creates visibility and relationships that build this trust foundation.

Industry Associations

Membership and participation in industry-specific associations provide unique benefits for paving contractors:

Key Paving Industry Associations

Several organizations serve the paving and asphalt industries, each offering different benefits:

National Asphalt Pavement Association (NAPA)

- National-level organization focused on asphalt paving advocacy and education
- Provides technical resources, market data, and best practices
- Offers certification programs and quality initiatives
- Hosts annual conventions and regional meetings
- Publishes industry research and standards
- Membership typically costs $1,000-$3,000 annually depending on company size

State Asphalt Pavement Associations

- State-specific organizations addressing local regulations and markets
- Provide localized technical assistance and resources
- Offer networking with regional contractors and suppliers
- Advocate for industry interests with state lawmakers
- Typically more affordable than national associations ($500-$1,500 annually)

American Public Works Association (APWA)

- Focuses on infrastructure and public works projects
- Connects contractors with municipal decision-makers
- Provides education on government contracting procedures
- Offers certification programs relevant to public projects
- Membership ranges from $219-$970 depending on category

Associated General Contractors of America (AGC)

- Broad construction industry association with specialized paving divisions
- Provides business management resources and legal guidance
- Offers networking with larger general contractors who may need subcontractors
- Provides safety training and compliance assistance
- Membership typically costs $1,000-$5,000 based on annual revenue

Local Contractor Associations

- Community-based organizations focused on specific geographic markets
- Provide highly targeted networking with local decision-makers
- Often more affordable than national associations
- May offer group purchasing or insurance programs
- Membership typically ranges from $250-$1,000 annually

Maximizing Association Benefits

Many paving contractors join associations but fail to extract full value from their membership. Strategic engagement maximizes return on your investment:

Committee Participation

- Volunteer for committees aligned with your expertise and interests

Benefits include:

- Higher visibility among peers and industry leaders
- Input on standards and practices affecting your business
- Early access to industry trends and developments
- Relationship building with key industry figures
- Start with: Membership, Education, or Events committees which typically welcome new volunteers

Educational Programs

- Take advantage of technical and business management training

Benefits include:

- Competitive advantage through enhanced knowledge
- Certification credentials that differentiate your company
- Reduced liability through improved processes
- Staff development and retention
- Focus on: Technical certifications, safety programs, and business management courses

Convention and Meeting Attendance

- Prioritize participation in annual conventions and regional meetings

Benefits include:

- Concentrated networking opportunities
- Access to multiple suppliers and partners at one location
- Latest product and technology demonstrations
- Educational sessions on emerging trends
- Maximize value by: Setting specific networking goals, scheduling key meetings in advance, and bringing multiple team members when appropriate

Thought Leadership Opportunities

- Seek opportunities to contribute expertise to association publications and events

Benefits include:

- Enhanced reputation as an industry expert
- Increased visibility to potential customers
- Differentiation from competitors
- Marketing content that can be repurposed across channels
- Start with: Offering to participate in panel discussions, submitting case studies, or contributing to association publications

Government Affairs Participation

- Engage with legislative and regulatory initiatives affecting the industry

Benefits include:

- Influence on policies impacting your business
- Relationships with government officials and agencies
- Early awareness of regulatory changes
- Visibility as an industry advocate
- Approach by: Attending legislative days, participating in regulatory committees, and supporting industry advocacy campaigns

One mid-sized paving contractor attributed over $450,000 in annual revenue directly to relationships developed through active association participation. "Anyone can join and put the logo on their website," the owner noted. "The real value comes from becoming a recognized participant in the community."

Strategic Association Selection

With limited time and resources, strategic selection of associations is essential:

Match Business Goals: Choose associations aligned with your specific business objectives:

- Seeking commercial work? Prioritize organizations where commercial property managers participate
- Pursuing municipal contracts? Focus on public works associations
- Expanding residential business? Select organizations with residential contractor involvement
- Improving technical capabilities? Join associations with strong educational programs

Evaluate Membership Composition: Research who belongs to each organization:

- Request membership directories before joining
- Attend events as a guest to assess attendee quality
- Ask for introductions to current members
- Identify whether competitors or potential partners participate

Consider Time Commitment: Assess realistic participation capacity:

- Meeting frequency and locations
- Committee expectations
- Event attendance requirements
- Leadership path opportunities
- Start with 1-2 associations where you can participate meaningfully rather than joining many with minimal involvement

Calculate ROI Potential: Estimate potential return compared to investment:

- Annual dues and fee structures
- Event and education costs
- Time commitment valuation
- Potential project opportunities through connections
- Compare to other marketing channel costs (cost per lead/acquisition)

Review Track Record: Research association effectiveness:

- Membership growth or decline trends
- Event attendance patterns
- Legislative or regulatory achievements
- Educational program quality
- Member satisfaction and retention

This strategic selection process ensures your association investments align with business objectives and provide meaningful returns.

Chamber of Commerce Participation

Local Chambers of Commerce represent one of the most accessible networking opportunities for paving contractors. While their effectiveness varies significantly by location, strategically selected and utilized Chamber memberships can deliver substantial business development benefits.

Chamber Selection Criteria

Not all Chambers offer equal value. Evaluate potential Chamber memberships based on:

Membership Demographics: Assess whether the Chamber includes your target customers:

- Business size distribution (small, medium, large enterprises)
- Industry representation (commercial property owners, developers, etc.)
- Geographic focus aligned with your service area
- Decision-maker vs. employee participation

Activity Level: Determine how actively engaged members are:

- Meeting and event attendance statistics
- Committee participation rates
- Member retention percentages
- Social media and communication engagement

Programming Relevance: Evaluate whether offerings match your needs:

- Networking event formats and frequency
- Educational content quality and topics
- Business development resources and support

- Advocacy focus and effectiveness

Organizational Stability: Assess the Chamber's foundation:

- Leadership quality and continuity
- Financial sustainability
- Membership growth trends
- Community reputation and influence

Many communities have multiple Chamber options, including:

- Regional/Metropolitan Chambers (larger, broader business focus)
- Community/Suburban Chambers (smaller, locally focused)
- Minority or Diversity-Focused Chambers (Black, Hispanic, Women's Business, etc.)
- Industry-Specific Chambers (Construction, Real Estate, etc.)

Consider membership in 1-2 strategically selected Chambers rather than distributing limited resources across many organizations.

Maximizing Chamber Membership Value

Active participation dramatically increases Chamber membership ROI:

Strategic Event Selection

- Choose events based on attendee quality rather than quantity
- Focus on formats conducive to meaningful conversation:
- Small-group roundtables outperform large receptions for relationship building
- Industry-specific forums attract more qualified prospects than general mixers
- Educational sessions provide opportunity to demonstrate expertise

- Maintain consistent presence rather than occasional attendance
- *Example strategy:* Commit to monthly attendance at one high-value event rather than sporadic participation in many

Committee Involvement

- Select committees matching your expertise or target markets:
- Building/Facilities committees need insights from paving contractors
- Economic Development committees connect with commercial growth
- Government Affairs committees influence infrastructure priorities
- Membership committees provide exposure to all new businesses
- Progress to leadership roles in committees aligned with your strengths
- *Example approach:* Join the Building Committee to advise on parking lot maintenance best practices, positioning yourself as the expert in this area

Thought Leadership Opportunities

- Volunteer as a speaker for relevant topics:
- "Property Maintenance Strategies for Business Owners"
- "Infrastructure Planning for Commercial Developments"
- "Sustainable Paving Options for Modern Businesses"
- Contribute articles to Chamber publications and newsletters
- Host educational events at your facility or completed project sites
- *Example content:* Develop a "Commercial Property Maintenance Calendar" as a valuable resource for business owners

Strategic Relationship Cultivation

- Identify high-potential connections within membership:
- Property management companies
- Commercial real estate professionals
- Facilities managers

- General contractors and developers
- Develop systematic approach to relationship building:
- Create target list of 10-15 key prospects
- Research their business before interaction
- Prepare relevant value-focused conversation points
- Establish follow-up system after initial meetings
- Build relationships with Chamber staff who can facilitate introductions
- *Example tactic:* Research three target members before each event and prepare specific questions relevant to their business needs

Sponsorship Evaluation

- Assess sponsorship opportunities based on strategic value:
- Alignment with target customer participation
- Speaking or presentation opportunities included
- Exclusivity in your service category
- Ongoing visibility vs. one-time exposure
- Focus on quality over quantity of impressions
- *Example approach:* Rather than sponsoring the annual gala, sponsor the quarterly property managers' roundtable for more targeted exposure

One paving contractor attributed over $125,000 in commercial projects directly to Chamber connections in their first year of active involvement. Their approach focused on becoming a resource for property maintenance information rather than directly selling services.

Chamber Marketing Integration

Maximize Chamber benefits by integrating with your broader marketing strategy:

Digital Connection

- Link Chamber directory listings to specific landing pages
- Feature Chamber membership prominently on your website
- Connect with members on LinkedIn after in-person meetings
- Share Chamber event participation on social media

Content Development

- Repurpose Chamber presentations for blog content
- Create case studies featuring Chamber member projects
- Develop special offers exclusively for fellow members
- Feature testimonials from Chamber-sourced customers

Database Integration

- Import Chamber directory into your CRM
- Tag contacts with specific Chamber affiliation
- Track engagement and conversion metrics by Chamber source
- Develop Chamber-specific nurture campaigns

Co-Marketing Opportunities

- Identify complementary businesses for joint marketing
- Organize collaborative educational events
- Share booth space at Chamber expos and trade shows
- Create service packages with synergistic members

Referral Program Promotion

- Highlight your referral program specifically to Chamber members
- Offer Chamber-exclusive referral incentives
- Acknowledge Chamber-sourced referrals in organization communi-

cations

- Recognize top Chamber referrers at events

This integrated approach ensures your Chamber investment supports your broader marketing objectives while leveraging the unique relationship attributes of Chamber membership.

Community Events and Sponsorships

Strategic participation in community events creates visibility, goodwill, and relationship opportunities that drive business growth. For paving contractors, whose work literally forms the foundation of community infrastructure, this connection is particularly valuable.

Event Selection Strategy

Not all community events offer equal business development value. Consider these factors when evaluating opportunities:

Audience Alignment

- Assess attendee demographics against your target customer profiles
- Consider decision-maker representation vs. general public
- Evaluate geographic reach relative to your service area
- *Example alignment:* Home shows attract property owners actively considering improvements

Engagement Quality

- Identify events allowing meaningful interaction vs. passive visibility
- Consider duration and format of potential customer conversations
- Evaluate competitor presence and differentiation opportunities
- *Example quality:* Interactive workshops provide deeper engagement

than parade sponsorships

Brand Consistency

- Ensure event aligns with your company values and positioning
- Consider whether audience perceptions match your quality standards
- Evaluate organizer reputation and event production quality
- *Example consistency:* Premium home shows align with high-quality paving contractors

Value Metrics

- Calculate potential reach relative to investment
- Compare cost-per-impression to other marketing channels
- Consider long-term relationship value beyond immediate leads
- *Example metrics:* \$1,500 sponsorship reaching 500 qualified prospects = \$3 per impression

Competitive Positioning

- Identify whether key competitors participate
- Consider category exclusivity opportunities
- Evaluate distinguished positioning possibilities
- *Example opportunity:* Being the only paving contractor at commercial property management events

Creating an annual community event strategy ensures proactive selection rather than reactive response to opportunities.

High-Value Event Types for Paving Contractors

These event categories typically deliver the strongest results for paving companies:

Home and Garden Shows

- Target audience: Homeowners actively planning property improvements
- Value opportunity: Direct interaction with qualified residential prospects
- Participation approach: Interactive displays, video demonstrations, before/after photos, consultations
- Cost range: $1,000-$5,000
- Measurement: Leads, estimate requests, conversions

Commercial Real Estate Events

- Target audience: Property managers, facility directors, commercial owners
- Value opportunity: Access to decision-makers for larger commercial projects
- Participation approach: Focus on maintenance planning, ROI calculators, case studies, assessments
- Cost range: $1,500-$7,500
- Measurement: Commercial leads, proposal requests, project values

Community Festivals and Fairs

- Target audience: General local population within service area
- Value opportunity: Brand awareness and community goodwill
- Participation approach: Equipment displays, interactive activities, branded giveaways, community messaging

- Cost range: $500-$3,000
- Measurement: Impressions, brand surveys, website traffic correlation

Neighborhood Block Parties

- Target audience: Concentrated homeowners in specific neighborhoods
- Value opportunity: Clustered project potential within efficient service areas
- Participation approach: Neighborhood offers, local project examples, referral incentives, community improvement messaging
- Cost range: $250-$1,000
- Measurement: Leads by neighborhood, conversion rates, cluster efficiency

Educational Seminars and Workshops

- Target audience: Property owners seeking information and solutions
- Value opportunity: Position as expert while identifying qualified prospects
- Participation approach: Present valuable content, address problems, provide resources, offer assessments
- Cost range: $500-$2,000
- Measurement: Engagement, follow-up meetings, conversions

For each selected event, develop specific goals, messaging, and follow-up processes rather than general "brand awareness" objectives.

Effective Sponsorship Strategies

Community sponsorships can deliver significant value when strategically selected and leveraged:

Strategic Selection Process

- Develop annual sponsorship budget with ROI expectations
- Create evaluation criteria aligned with business objectives
- Proactively research opportunities rather than reactively responding
- Negotiate custom packages beyond standard offerings
- *Example approach:* Allocate sponsorship budget quarterly with specific lead generation and relationship development goals

Activation Maximization

- Fully utilize all benefits included in sponsorship packages
- Create additional activation opportunities beyond standard inclusions
- Develop integration with other marketing channels
- Train staff to maximize relationship development during events
- *Example activation:* Rather than just having your logo on materials, negotiate a "property maintenance tip" branded content piece in event communications

High-Value Sponsorship Types

- Youth Sports Teams and Facilities: Long-term community presence with parent demographics matching residential target audience
- Business Award Programs: Direct connection with commercial property decision-makers
- Educational Initiatives: Position as community-invested expert
- Public Space Improvements: Direct demonstration of your work quality
- Charitable Construction Projects: Showcase capabilities while building goodwill
- *Example high-value opportunity:* Sponsoring parking lot maintenance for community facilities demonstrates your work while supporting worthy causes

Measurement Systems

- Establish clear metrics before committing to sponsorships
- Create tracking mechanisms for lead source identification
- Survey new customers about sponsorship awareness
- Calculate lifetime value of sponsorship-sourced customers
- *Example metrics:* Track leads, conversions, average project value, and customer retention rates from each sponsored event or organization

Long-Term Relationship Development

- Focus on multi-year partnerships with increasing value
- Build relationships with organization leadership beyond events
- Create year-round engagement rather than event-specific visibility
- Develop progressive involvement leading to leadership opportunities
- *Example approach:* Three-year sponsorship commitment with annual evaluation and adjustment rather than one-off participations

One successful paving contractor focused their entire community marketing budget on youth sports facilities, providing discounted services and financial support for local athletic complexes. This strategy generated significant residential business from parents while solving the perennial challenge of portfolio examples for prospective commercial clients.

Maximizing Event Participation ROI

Effective execution transforms event participation from an expense to an investment:

Pre-Event Promotion

- Announce participation through all marketing channels
- Invite existing customers and prospects through personalized com-

munications

- Schedule specific appointment times with high-value prospects
- Create event-specific landing pages with pre-registration opportunities
- *Example tactic:* Send personalized invitations to your top 25 prospects with specific times to meet during the event

On-Site Engagement Optimization

- Create interactive rather than passive displays
- Train staff on engagement questions and qualification techniques
- Develop compelling demonstration or education components
- Implement systematic lead capture with permission-based follow-up
- *Example approach:* Rather than static displays, create a "pavement health check" interactive assessment that educates while capturing contact information

Effective Booth Design

- Focus on problem-solution messaging rather than company features
- Use professional-quality visuals and demonstrations
- Incorporate technology for engagement and information capture
- Ensure adequate space for meaningful conversation
- *Example design:* Before/after video display with sample materials visitors can touch, paired with digital assessment tool collecting contact information

Strategic Staff Selection

- Choose representatives based on communication skills rather than seniority
- Include technical experts paired with relationship developers
- Ensure adequate staffing for peak periods

- Train all staff on qualification questions and next steps
- *Example staffing:* Pair estimators who can provide technical answers with customer service personnel skilled at relationship building

Systematic Follow-Up Process

- Categorize leads by quality and timing during the event
- Implement immediate follow-up for hot prospects (same day)
- Develop multi-step nurture process for longer-term opportunities
- Track conversion through each stage of the follow-up process
- *Example system:* High-interest leads receive same-day personal calls, while information-gathering prospects enter an educational email sequence with periodic personal check-ins

The most successful contractors view event participation as the beginning of their marketing process rather than a stand-alone activity. They allocate as much attention to follow-up as they do to the event itself.

Building Relationships With Complementary Businesses

Beyond formalized networking organizations, strategic relationships with complementary businesses create mutual growth opportunities. These partnerships extend your reach through existing trust relationships and provide access to customers you might not otherwise encounter.

Identifying Strategic Partners

The most valuable business relationships typically include:

Preceding Services

- Businesses customers engage before needing paving: Real estate agents, Home inspectors, General contractors, Landscapers, Architects

- Value proposition: You provide reliable solutions to their clients' needs, enhancing their service value

Following Services

- Businesses customers engage after paving projects: Landscapers, Line striping specialists, Concrete contractors, Drainage solution providers, Outdoor lighting installers
- Value proposition: You create project opportunities for their services through your completed work

Parallel Services

- Businesses serving same customers with different needs: Property management companies, Commercial cleaning services, Snow removal contractors, Roofing companies, HVAC contractors
- Value proposition: Shared customer base with non-competing services creates mutual referral opportunities

Supply Chain Partners

- Businesses in your supply network with customer visibility: Material suppliers, Equipment rental companies, Engineering firms, Soil testing companies
- Value proposition: Technical collaboration creates superior customer solutions

The ideal partner shares these characteristics:

- Serves similar customer demographics
- Maintains comparable quality standards
- Holds similar values and business philosophy

- Has complementary seasonal patterns
- Demonstrates relationship orientation rather than transaction focus

Relationship Development Process

Building productive business relationships requires systematic approach rather than chance encounters:

Research and Selection

- Identify potential partners meeting your strategic criteria
- Research reputation, work quality, and business stability
- Evaluate cultural fit and relationship potential
- Prioritize based on customer overlap and mutual benefit potential
- *Example research:* Create list of 10-15 top landscaping companies serving your market, then investigate their project portfolio, online reviews, and business longevity

Initial Connection

- Create value-focused approach rather than immediate request
- Offer meaningful introduction discussing mutual benefit potential
- Share specific examples of how customers could benefit from cooperation
- Suggest low-commitment initial collaboration
- *Example approach:* >"I've admired your landscaping work at several properties and believe our services could complement each other. Many of our clients ask for recommendations for quality landscaping after paving projects. Would you be open to discussing how we might collaborate?"

Relationship Cultivation

- Focus initially on building trust rather than transactions
- Share expertise and market insights of value to the partner
- Demonstrate commitment to mutual success
- Create regular communication rhythm
- *Example cultivation:* Quarterly coffee meetings to discuss market trends and potential collaboration opportunities

Formalization Options

- Develop appropriate structure based on relationship depth: Informal Referral Arrangement, Referral Fee Structure, Co-Marketing Agreement, Strategic Alliance, Joint Venture
- *Example formalization:* Start with simple referral arrangement, then progress to co-marketing opportunities as trust develops

Ongoing Management

- Maintain regular communication beyond transactions
- Track referrals and business generated in both directions
- Ensure timely follow-up on all referrals
- Address any service or quality issues immediately
- Continuously seek new collaboration opportunities
- *Example management:* Monthly referral report sharing outcomes and status of all referred projects

This systematic approach transforms random networking into strategic relationship development with measurable business impact.

Collaborative Marketing Initiatives

Beyond simple referrals, strategic partners can engage in collaborative marketing that benefits both businesses:

Content Collaboration

- Co-created educational materials addressing complementary aspects of property improvement
- Joint case studies showcasing collaborative projects
- Shared expertise articles for publications and websites
- Video series featuring both companies' roles in property enhancement
- *Example initiative:* Paving contractor and landscaper create "Complete Property Renovation Guide" showing how paving and landscaping work together

Event Partnerships

- Shared booth presence at industry events
- Co-hosted educational seminars for property owners
- Joint client appreciation events
- Collaborative demonstrations at home shows
- *Example partnership:* Paving contractor and concrete specialist host "Hardscape Design Workshop" for homeowners planning outdoor improvements

Cross-Promotion Systems

- Featured partner sections on respective websites
- Shared discount programs for mutual clients
- Inclusion in customer communications and newsletters
- Testimonial exchange for marketing materials
- *Example cross-promotion:* "Preferred Partner Network" discount where customers using multiple partner services receive cumulative discounts

Bundle Offerings

- Combined service packages with preferential pricing
- Coordinated project scheduling for efficiency
- Joint maintenance programs for commercial properties
- Unified warranty or guarantee programs
- *Example bundle:* "Complete Driveway Renovation Package" combining paving, landscaping, and lighting services with coordinated installation and unified warranty

Digital Cross-Promotion

- Reciprocal website links and featured partner pages
- Social media cross-promotion and sharing
- Guest blog posts on partner websites
- Joint email marketing to combined customer lists (with permission)
- *Example digital strategy:* Monthly featured partner spotlight in email newsletters and social media, highlighting recent collaborative projects

These collaborative initiatives create marketing impact beyond what either company could achieve independently while sharing costs and expanding reach.

Community Project Collaborations

Collaborative community improvement projects create multiple benefits beyond direct business development:

Charitable Infrastructure Projects

- Joint contribution to community facility improvements
- Collaboration on nonprofit organization needs
- Participation in community rebuilding efforts
- Support for schools and youth facilities

- *Example project:* Partnering with concrete contractor to renovate playground surfacing at local elementary school

Educational Initiatives

- Collaborative trades education programs
- Joint scholarship funding for construction education
- Shared apprenticeship or internship programs
- Community workshops on property maintenance
- *Example initiative:* Creating "Trades Career Day" with multiple contractors showcasing career opportunities to high school students

Environmental Improvements

- Stormwater management demonstration projects
- Sustainable materials education initiatives
- Green infrastructure collaborations
- Public park enhancements
- *Example collaboration:* Partnership with landscaper on permeable paving demonstration project at community garden

Emergency Response Coordination

- Disaster recovery preparation
- Post-storm cleanup collaboration
- Infrastructure restoration partnerships
- Community emergency planning participation
- *Example coordination:* Formal agreement with equipment providers and debris removal companies for coordinated storm response

These community-focused collaborations build relationships with partners while enhancing community visibility and goodwill. They demonstrate practical capabilities while contributing to causes that matter to your target audience.

Tracking Offline Relationship Marketing ROI

The relationship-based nature of networking and community marketing creates unique measurement challenges. While less directly trackable than digital channels, systematic approaches can quantify the impact of these investments:

Attribution Systems

Implement these tools and processes to track relationship marketing results:

Source Coding

- Create specific source codes for each networking organization and event
- Implement consistent usage in CRM and lead tracking systems
- Train all team members on proper attribution
- Regularly audit for attribution accuracy
- *Example system:* Unique source codes for each Chamber, association, and community event, with sub-codes for specific activities

Relationship Mapping

- Document connection pathways for each new lead and customer
- Identify multiple influence points in complex relationships
- Map relationship networks showing interconnections
- Track relationship development stages
- *Example approach:* Record all touchpoints from initial meeting through project completion, noting which relationships influenced each stage

Value Attribution

- Assign appropriate value to different relationship contributions: Direct referrals, Introductions, Information sharing, Collaborative projects
- Create weighted scoring system reflecting relationship impact
- *Example attribution:* Assign full value to direct referrals, partial value to introductions that later convert, and relationship-building value to ongoing interactions

Multi-Touch Recognition

- Acknowledge multiple influence sources for complex sales
- Create proportional attribution for shared influence
- Document relationship sequences leading to conversions
- Track influence patterns over time
- *Example approach:* Record and weight all networking connections that contributed to a project, rather than assigning full credit to the last touchpoint

Qualitative Assessment

- Supplement quantitative data with relationship quality evaluation
- Document strategic value beyond immediate transactions
- Assess long-term potential vs. current results
- Consider market positioning benefits
- *Example assessment:* Quarterly review of key relationships evaluating both current results and strategic potential

These systems transform subjective "networking feels valuable" assessments into measurable business impact analysis.

Key Performance Indicators for Relationship Marketing

Track these metrics to evaluate your networking and community marketing effectiveness:

Direct Metrics

- Network-Sourced Revenue
- Relationship Conversion Rate
- Average Network Project Value
- Network Customer Retention
- Referral Reciprocity
- *Example benchmark:* Track percentage of total revenue directly attributable to networking activities, with goal of 15-25% for established programs

Investment Metrics

- Relationship Acquisition Cost
- Cost Per Network Lead
- Network Marketing ROI
- Time Investment Analysis
- Membership Efficiency
- *Example analysis:* Calculate fully-loaded cost including membership fees, event costs, travel expenses, and time value, then compare to revenue generated

Activity Metrics

- Relationship Development Activity
- Follow-Up Completion Rate
- Network Growth Rate
- Network Engagement Level

- Leadership Progression
- *Example tracking:* Document all new relationships initiated at events, then track progression through defined relationship development stages

Influence Metrics

- Reputation Enhancement
- Competitive Positioning
- Community Visibility
- Media Mentions
- Partnership Quality
- *Example measurement:* Annual survey of market perception among property managers, comparing visibility and reputation between actively networking contractors and those without community presence

Strategic Value Metrics

- Market Intelligence Value
- Opportunity Access
- Competitive Insulation
- Crisis Management Support
- *Example assessment:* Document specific opportunities, information, or assistance that would have been unavailable without network connections

These metrics provide a comprehensive view of networking ROI beyond simple lead counting, acknowledging the multi-dimensional value of relationship marketing.

Case Study: Integrated Community Marketing Strategy

To illustrate the impact of a comprehensive networking and community involvement approach, consider the experience of Alliance Paving, a mid-sized contractor serving both residential and commercial clients in a competitive suburban market:

Initial Situation

- Limited community visibility despite 15 years in business
- Reliance on traditional advertising with declining results
- No formal networking or community involvement strategy
- Inconsistent reputation across market segments
- Increasing competition from larger regional firms

Strategic Approach Alliance Paving developed a comprehensive community presence strategy with these elements:

Focused Organizational Involvement

- Strategic selection of two primary organizations: Local Chamber of Commerce & State Asphalt Pavement Association
- Commitment to leadership involvement rather than passive membership
- Integration with sales and marketing strategy rather than separate "community" function

Systematic Relationship Development

- Identification of 25 high-potential strategic connections
- Development of multi-touch relationship cultivation plan
- Regular communication rhythm with key relationships
- Documentation of all interactions and opportunities

- Integration of relationship data into CRM system

Community Visibility Initiatives

- Strategic selection of three community priorities: Youth sports facility improvement, Municipal park enhancement, Trade education initiative
- Development of long-term commitment rather than one-time donations
- Integration of community projects into marketing content
- Employee involvement beyond financial support

Strategic Partnership Program

- Formal relationships with five complementary businesses: Landscaper, Concrete Contractor, Engineering Firm, Property Manager, Real Estate Brokerage
- Structured referral systems with tracking
- Regular joint marketing initiatives
- Quarterly partnership review meetings

Measurable Goal Setting

- Specific objectives for each networking investment
- Detailed tracking of all relationship-sourced opportunities
- Regular ROI analysis and program adjustment
- Integration of relationship metrics with overall marketing analytics

Results After 24 Months The impact of this systematic approach was significant:

- Network-sourced revenue increased from 8% to 32% of total revenue

- Average project size from network sources was 41% larger than other channels
- Leadership positions in key organizations led to municipal contract opportunities
- Strategic partnerships generated 47 qualified leads with 63% conversion rate
- Community visibility created preference advantage in competitive bid situations
- Employee engagement and retention improved through community involvement
- Overall marketing cost per acquisition decreased 28% despite increased networking investment

Most importantly, Alliance Paving transformed from "just another paving company" to a recognized community partner, creating a sustainable competitive advantage that competitors found difficult to replicate.

Implementation Checklist

Use this comprehensive checklist to implement an effective networking and community marketing program:

Strategic Planning

- Define networking and community involvement objectives
- Establish budget including both financial and time investments
- Identify target relationship categories and prioritization
- Create evaluation criteria for organizational involvement
- Develop measurement systems for relationship marketing
- Set initial goals and success metrics

Organization Selection and Involvement

- Research potential networking organizations
- Evaluate membership demographics against target customers
- Attend events as guest before committing to membership
- Meet with organization leadership to discuss opportunities
- Join 1-2 strategically selected organizations
- Identify and apply for appropriate committee involvement
- Develop leadership progression plan within key organizations

Relationship Development

- Create database of high-potential connections
- Develop systematic approach to relationship cultivation
- Establish follow-up protocols for new connections
- Implement relationship tracking in CRM system
- Define relationship stages and progression markers
- Create ongoing communication plan for key relationships
- Develop method for relationship valuation and prioritization

Community Involvement

- Identify community initiatives aligned with business values
- Evaluate sponsorship opportunities against strategic criteria
- Develop employee involvement opportunities
- Create integration between community involvement and marketing
- Establish measurement system for community investment
- Plan long-term community commitment strategy
- Develop public relations approach for community activities

Strategic Partnerships

- Identify potential complementary business partners
- Research and evaluate partnership candidates
- Develop partnership value proposition

- Create formal or informal agreement structures
- Implement cross-referral tracking system
- Design collaborative marketing initiatives
- Establish regular partnership review process

Measurement and Optimization

- Implement source coding for network-generated leads
- Create relationship attribution system in Revenue Commander
- Establish regular reporting schedule for relationship metrics
- Develop ongoing optimization process for networking activities
- Schedule quarterly review of all networking investments
- Calculate comprehensive ROI for relationship marketing
- Adjust resource allocation based on performance data

Conclusion: The Community Connection Advantage

In the increasingly digital world of marketing, personal relationships and community connections provide a powerful competitive advantage for paving contractors. While digital channels efficiently generate leads, relationship marketing builds the trust foundation that converts prospects into long-term customers.

The most successful paving companies recognize that networking and community involvement aren't separate from their marketing strategy but integral components that enhance all other channels. When customers encounter your company through multiple touchpoints—seeing your trucks in their neighborhood, meeting your team at community events, hearing recommendations from respected business connections, and then finding your professional online presence—the cumulative impact creates a compelling case for choosing your services.

The key to success lies in approaching networking strategically rather than haphazardly. By carefully selecting organizations, systematically developing relationships, thoughtfully engaging with community initiatives, and meticulously measuring results, you transform networking from a hit-or-miss activity into a reliable business development system.

As competition increases and digital marketing costs rise, your community connections and business relationships become increasingly valuable assets. Unlike paid advertising that stops producing results when you stop paying, the relationships you build create compounding returns over time, often developing into your most valuable and least expensive source of new business.

In the next part of our book, we'll explore how to integrate all these marketing channels—both online and offline—into a cohesive, synergistic system that maximizes your marketing investment and creates sustainable growth for your paving company.

IV

Part Four

Now we'll look at "integrated marketing systems," or, putting it all together. This part is meant to be broad, giving you ideas, targets, and "food-for-thought."

21

Introduction to Integrated Marketing Systems

The most successful paving companies don't view marketing channels as separate, independent activities but as interconnected components of a unified system. By strategically integrating online and offline marketing efforts, you create a synergistic effect where each channel enhances the effectiveness of the others.

In Part 4, we'll explore how to build these integrated systems, beginning with Revenue Commander—our comprehensive platform designed specifically for service businesses to manage, measure, and optimize their multi-channel marketing efforts. We'll then cover lead management and conversion processes, campaign integration and customer journey mapping, analytics and performance measurement, and strategies for scaling your marketing operations as your business grows.

Let's start by examining how Revenue Commander serves as the central hub of your integrated marketing system, connecting all your channels into a cohesive, data-driven growth engine for your paving business.

22

Revenue Commander: Your All-In-One Marketing Platform

As we've explored throughout this book, effective marketing for paving companies requires coordinating multiple channels—from SEO and PPC to direct mail and yard signs. Managing these separate channels without a central system creates numerous challenges.

Lead attribution becomes difficult when customers interact with multiple marketing touchpoints.

- Follow-up processes may be inconsistent when leads come from different sources.
- Marketing data remains siloed, making holistic performance analysis impossible.
- Valuable insights about customer behavior and preferences get lost.
- Staff must navigate multiple systems, wasting time and creating opportunities for error.

Revenue Commander solves these challenges by providing a comprehensive, integrated platform designed for service businesses like paving contractors. It centralizes all your marketing activities, lead management, and customer communications in one powerful system.

Platform Overview and Capabilities

Revenue Commander combines the functionality of multiple marketing tools into a single, unified platform. For paving companies, this means you can manage your entire marketing and sales process—from lead generation to project completion and beyond—without switching between different software systems.

Customer Relationship Management (CRM)

At the heart of Revenue Commander is a powerful CRM that tracks every interaction with leads and customers. You can maintain contact profiles with complete communication history, track lead sources and attribution, store project details and documentation, create custom fields for tracking job specifics like square footage and materials, implement automated lead scoring based on engagement and behaviors, and view activity timelines showing every touchpoint in the customer journey.

Marketing Channel Integration

Revenue Commander integrates with all major marketing channels. This includes website integration via tracking pixels and form captures, Google

Ads and Facebook Ads integration for performance tracking, email marketing with automation capabilities, SMS/text messaging for immediate response, Google Business Profile management, social media scheduling and monitoring, call tracking with recording and transcription, and direct mail campaign management.

Workflow Automation:

The platform's features let you create automated sequences that save time and ensure consistency. You can build lead nurturing campaigns based on prospect behavior, set up follow-up reminders for your team, implement appointment scheduling and confirmation sequences, create project updates and milestone communications, establish post-completion review requests and referral solicitation, and set maintenance reminders based on project completion dates.

Reporting and Analytics

Comprehensive dashboards provide clear visibility into marketing performance through robust reporting and analytics. You can see lead source attribution and ROI calculations, conversion metrics at each stage of the customer journey, team performance metrics for sales and operations, cost per lead and cost per acquisition by channel, revenue tracking and forecasting, and customer acquisition trends and seasonal patterns.

Sales Tools

The platform includes tools to streamline your sales process. These include estimate templates for different services, digital signature capabilities for contracts, payment processing for deposits and final invoices, appointment scheduling with calendar integration, sales pipeline visualization, and quote follow-up automation.

Client Portal

To enhance customer experience, Revenue Commander offers a branded client portal. This gives your customers access to project updates and timeline information, document sharing and approvals, secure messaging, payment processing, maintenance scheduling, and referral opportunities.

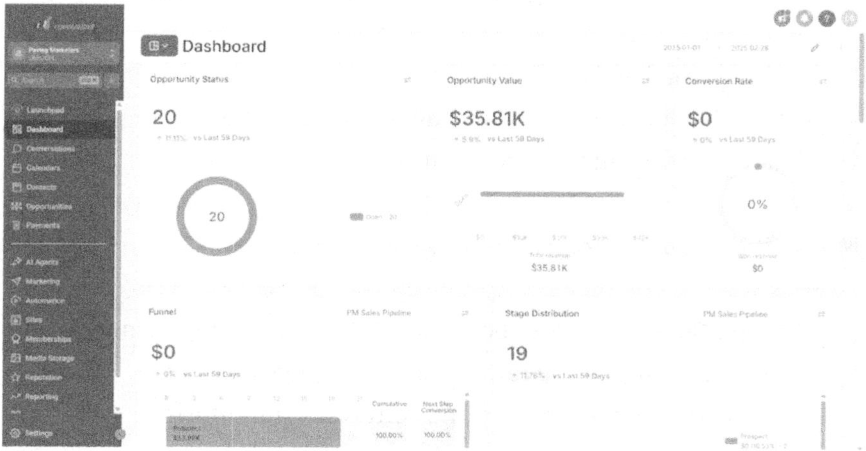

Setup and Onboarding

Implementing Revenue Commander follows a structured process designed to ensure successful adoption and immediate value for your paving business. The typical implementation follows several phases:

Discovery and Planning (Approx. 1 week):

- Review current marketing channels and processes
- Define key objectives and success metrics
- Identify team members and their roles in the system
- Map your current customer journey and identify improvement oppor-

tunities
- Prioritize initial implementation components

Core System Setup (Approx. 2-3 weeks):

- Configure company settings and user accounts
- Set up lead capture forms for website and landing pages
- Implement call tracking numbers for each marketing channel
- Import your existing customer database
- Connect email and calendar systems
- Establish your service catalog and pricing structures
- Create estimate and proposal templates

Marketing Channel Integration (Approx. 1-2 weeks):

- Connect Google Ads, Facebook, and other advertising accounts
- Set up email marketing templates and sequences
- Implement website tracking and conversion monitoring
- Configure SMS messaging capabilities
- Set up online review management
- Integrate offline marketing tracking mechanisms

Automation Development (Approx. 2-3 weeks):

- Build lead nurturing sequences
- Create task automation for your sales team
- Develop customer communication workflows
- Implement follow-up reminders and escalations
- Configure reporting dashboards for key metrics
- Set up team notification protocols

Training and Optimization (Approx. 2 weeks):

- Conduct role-specific training sessions
- Develop standard operating procedures
- Begin active campaign management
- Monitor system performance and user adoption
- Make refinements based on initial feedback
- Establish an ongoing optimization schedule

To maximize the value of Revenue Commander for your paving business, you should:

Define Clear User Roles:

- Admin (System configuration/oversight): Owner, Marketing Manager
- Sales (Lead/estimation management): Sales Team, Estimators
- Operations (Project coordination/communication): Project Managers
- Marketing (Campaign management/analysis): Marketing Staff

Standardize Naming Conventions:

- Lead Sources (e.g., Google_Organic, Facebook_Paid, Billboard_Main_St)
- Project Types (e.g., Residential_Driveway, Commercial_Parking_Lo t)
- Pipeline Stages (e.g., New_Lead, Estimate_Scheduled, Quote_Sent)
- Campaign Names (e.g., Spring2023_Residential)

Prioritize Data Fields:

- Required: Name, Contact Info, Lead Source, Property Type
- Important: Project Timeframe, Budget, Property Size
- Secondary: How Heard, Previous Paving History
- Custom: Specific Concerns, Material Preferences, Access Issues

Establish Processes for Data Entry:

- Define responsibility for creating new records
- Set standards for when/how information is updated
- Ensure data completeness
- Implement regular data cleaning

Ensure Successful Team Adoption:

- Provide **role-based training**: Executive overview, Lead management, Customer communication, Campaign management.
- Use a **progressive implementation**: Start with essentials, add advanced features later, create "quick wins."
- Provide **ongoing support**: Designate an internal power user, schedule check-ins, create knowledge base, offer refresher training.
- Implement **accountability systems**: Set usage expectations, monitor metrics, tie usage to reviews, foster friendly competition.

Remember that successful adoption takes time. Plan for a 60-90 day ramp-up period before expecting full utilization across your organization.

Integration with Existing Systems

Revenue Commander is designed to work with your existing business systems, creating a unified operational environment without disrupting established workflows. Common integration points include:

- **Accounting Software**: QuickBooks Online/Desktop, Xero, FreshBooks, Wave (Sync customer info, invoices, payments).
- **Field Service Management**: Schedule coordination, job dispatching, material tracking, crew assignment, job costing.
- **Email Platforms**: Gmail/Google Workspace, Microsoft 365/Outlook (Email sync, calendar integration, contact sync).
- **Telephony Systems**: VoIP integration, call recording/logging, voicemail transcription, call disposition tracking.

- **Payment Processing**: Credit card processing, ACH/bank transfers, automated payment reminders, payment plan management.
- **Website Platforms**: WordPress, Wix/Squarespace, Custom Websites via API (Form capture, conversion tracking, landing pages).

Moving your existing customer and prospect data into Revenue Commander requires careful planning:

- **Data Preparation**: Audit current data, standardize formats, de-duplicate records, fill critical gaps, categorize contacts.
- **Migration Process**: Export data, map fields, upload in batches, verify samples, activate automation after verification.
- **Post-Migration Validation**: Confirm record counts, test search, verify history, check relationships, run test reports.

Common migration challenges include inconsistent formats, missing information, duplicate records, complex relationships, and incompatible history records. For paving companies with extensive customer history, we typically recommend a phased approach—migrating active customers and current prospects first, then adding historical data over time as needed.

For specialized needs or proprietary systems, Revenue Commander offers **custom integration capabilities**:

- API Connectivity (REST API)
- Webhook Functionality
- Custom Field Mapping
- Secure Authentication

Third-party integration platforms extend connectivity options:

- Zapier

- Integromat/Make
- Tray.io
- Custom middleware development

When considering custom integrations, prioritize based on data volume, update frequency, operational impact, complexity, and cost-benefit analysis. For most paving companies, the standard integrations satisfy 90–95% of requirements without the need for custom development.

Lead Tracking and Nurturing

Effective lead management is critical for paving companies, where a single converted lead can be worth thousands of dollars. Revenue Commander provides comprehensive tools for capturing, tracking, and nurturing leads throughout their journey.

Centralized Lead Capture Revenue Commander centralizes lead capture from all marketing channels:

- **Digital Sources**: Website forms, landing pages, social media inquiries, email responses, live chat, online directories (Angi, HomeAdvisor), Google Business Profile messages.
- **Traditional Media**: Call tracking numbers, SMS responses, QR codes, dedicated landing pages, event/trade show collection.
- **Referral & Repeat**: Customer referral tracking, reactivation campaigns, partner referral programs, automated referral requests.

Each lead is automatically tagged with its source, allowing you to track performance by channel throughout the sales process.

Automated Lead Assignment Revenue Commander ensures every lead receives prompt attention:

- **Geographic Routing**: Assign by zip code or service area, route commercial/residential differently, match to specialists, balance distribution.
- **Time-Based Assignment**: Route based on availability, implement after-hours/weekend/holiday protocols, set up escalation for delays.
- **Project-Based Qualification**: Route by project size/value, assign by service type, direct property types to specialists, prioritize high-value opportunities.
- **Notification System**: Instant mobile/email/SMS alerts, dashboard alerts, escalation procedures.

These assignment rules ensure that every lead receives appropriate follow-up regardless of when or how they enter your system.

Automated Nurturing Sequences Not all leads are ready to buy immediately. Revenue Commander's automation tools help you stay connected:

- **Inquiry Response Sequence**: Immediate acknowledgment, educational content, social proof, consultation invitation, follow-up reminders.
- **Post-Estimate Nurturing**: Thank you, info on materials/process, FAQs, testimonials, time-limited incentives.
- **Seasonal Re-engagement**: Spring prep reminders, summer updates, fall maintenance, winter planning, early booking incentives.
- **Long-Term Prospect Nurturing**: Quarterly check-ins, educational content, project showcases, industry updates, special offers.

These automated sequences maintain consistent communication without requiring manual effort from your team, ensuring no opportunity falls through the cracks.

Lead Scoring and Prioritization Not all leads have equal potential. Revenue Commander's lead scoring helps you focus on the most promising opportunities:

- **Behavioral Scoring**: Email opens/clicks, website visits, form submissions, calls, quote requests, follow-up responses.
- **Demographic Scoring**: Property type/size, location, timeline, budget, decision-maker status, previous customer relationship.
- **Temporal Scoring**: Recency, frequency of engagement, seasonal relevance, urgency indicators, competitive quoting timeline.
- **Automated Prioritization**: Dynamic lists sorted by score, visual indicators, task prioritization, alert thresholds, performance reporting by score.

This scoring system ensures your team focuses their time on the opportunities most likely to convert, maximizing the return on your sales efforts.

Reporting and Analytics

Making data-driven decisions requires comprehensive visibility into your marketing and sales performance. Revenue Commander provides robust reporting capabilities designed for service businesses like paving contractors.

Real-Time Dashboards Revenue Commander offers dashboards for at-a-glance understanding:

- **Lead Generation Dashboard**: Leads by source/medium, volume trends, CPL by channel, geographic distribution, peak times, quality score distribution.
- **Sales Performance Dashboard**: Conversion rates by stage, estimate volume/value, close rates by source, average days to close, team performance, win/loss analysis.
- **Revenue Dashboard**: Projected vs. actual revenue, average project value, revenue by service type, payment tracking, outstanding bal-

ances, forecasting.

- **Marketing ROI Dashboard**: Campaign performance, ROAS by channel, CAC, LTV calculations, cost comparison, trend analysis.

These dashboards can be customized to focus on the specific metrics most important to your business goals.

Custom Reporting Create reports for specific business questions:

- **Components**: Data source selection, field selection, filter criteria, sorting/grouping, visualization choices, calculation capabilities.
- **Common Reports**: Neighborhood penetration, service popularity by area, seasonal comparison, referral source effectiveness, customer retention, estimate-to-job conversion by project type.
- **Scheduling/Distribution**: Automated delivery, PDF/CSV/Excel export, role-based access, interactive online access, mobile formats.
- **Visualization**: Line charts, bar/column charts, pie charts, maps, heat maps, scatter plots.

With these reporting capabilities, you can answer specific business questions and identify opportunities for growth and optimization.

Attribution and ROI Tracking Understanding which marketing efforts drive results is essential:

- **Multi-Touch Attribution Models**: First-touch, last-touch, linear, position-based, data-driven.
- **Cross-Channel Tracking**: Connects online/offline interactions, tracks journey across devices, identifies assisted conversions, measures path length, visualizes journey maps.
- **Conversion Point Analysis**: Website forms, calls, chat, email responses, text messages, in-person appointments.
- **ROI Calculation**: Channel-specific return, campaign profitability,

acquisition cost comparison, LTV attribution, seasonal ROI analysis.

This comprehensive attribution ensures you understand exactly which marketing investments are delivering results, allowing you to continuously optimize your budget allocation.

Market and Competitive Insights Revenue Commander helps track your market position:

- **Market Share Indicators**: Geographic penetration, service category dominance, share of voice, review comparison, search visibility.
- **Competitive Activity Monitoring**: Competitor ad messaging/offers, social engagement, review trends, service/pricing adjustments, new offerings.
- **Benchmarking**: Industry average comparison, performance vs. similar markets, seasonal patterns, growth rates, conversion metrics.
- **Opportunity Identification**: Underserved areas, service gaps, pricing opportunities, messaging differentiation, competitor weaknesses.

These insights help you identify strategic opportunities and threats, informing both marketing and broader business decisions.

Automating Marketing Workflows

Automation is one of Revenue Commander's most powerful capabilities, enabling your paving business to maintain consistent, personalized communication without manual effort.

Automated Lead Response Speed and quality of initial response impact conversion rates:

- **Instant Acknowledgment**: Automated email/text confirmation, voicemail response, chatbots, form confirmation pages.

- **Information Collection Automation**: Qualification questionnaires, property info requests, timeline inquiries, budget confirmation, service interest clarification.
- **Initial Information Delivery**: Service overview, case studies, educational content, FAQs, team intro.
- **Appointment Scheduling Automation**: Self-service links, calendar invitations, confirmation/reminders, rescheduling, prep info.

These automated responses ensure consistent information delivery while your team prepares for personal follow-up.

Customer Journey Automation Automate communications throughout the lifecycle:

- **Pre-Sale Journey**: Educational content, social proof, objection handling, competitive differentiation, decision timeline follow-ups.
- **Active Project Journey**: Project confirmation, prep instructions, milestone updates, weather communications, payment reminders.
- **Post-Completion Journey**: Satisfaction surveys, review requests, referral solicitation, maintenance recommendations, warranty info.
- **Long-Term Relationship Automation**: Seasonal reminders, service anniversaries, related service recommendations, customer appreciation, re-engagement campaigns.

These automated journeys maintain consistent communication, enhancing satisfaction and retention.

Internal Process Automation Automate internal workflows:

- **Sales Team Tasks**: Follow-up reminders, estimate prep deadlines, proposal follow-ups, check-in prompts, opportunity aging alerts.
- **Project Management Workflows**: Job scheduling reminders, material ordering tasks, permit deadlines, inspection scheduling, documenta-

tion requirements.
- **Customer Service Protocols**: Satisfaction check-ins, issue tracking, escalations, follow-up verification, warranty claim processing.
- **Team Collaboration**: Handoff notifications, status updates, customer communication alerts, document sharing prompts, info requests.

These automated processes ensure nothing falls through the cracks and maintain accountability.

Campaign Management Automation Streamline campaign execution across channels:

- **Email Campaigns**: Scheduled delivery, segmentation, personalization, engagement-based follow-up, A/B testing.
- **Social Media**: Content scheduling, cross-platform coordination, engagement monitoring, hashtag tracking, paid campaign management.
- **SMS/Text Campaigns**: Scheduled delivery, compliance, response handling, conversation threading, opt-out processing.
- **Direct Mail Coordination**: Digital integration, trigger-based sequences, cross-channel reinforcement, response tracking, follow-up coordination.
- **Review Management**: Automated solicitation, platform requests, positive review amplification, negative feedback interception, response workflows.

These campaign automations ensure consistent execution while adapting to customer responses.

Connecting Online and Offline Marketing Efforts

One of Revenue Commander's most valuable capabilities is bridging the gap between digital and traditional marketing channels.

Unified Customer Journey Tracking Connect touchpoints across all channels:

- **Digital-to-Offline**: Website visits to calls, email opens to appointments, social engagement to estimates, ad exposure to visits, retargeting after direct mail.
- **Offline-to-Digital**: Direct mail to website visits, radio/TV to search, billboard to brand search, trade show to online engagement, yard sign to website traffic.
- **Multi-Device Tracking**: Cross-device ID, mobile-to-desktop journey, call-to-website connection, text-to-email sequences, in-person to digital follow-up.
- **Unified Timeline View**: Comprehensive contact history, chronological touchpoints, interaction sequencing, engagement intensity, journey mapping.

This unified tracking creates a complete picture of how prospects interact with your business.

Integrated Campaign Execution Coordinate execution across all channels:

- **Unified Campaign Planning**: Central calendar, cross-channel message coordination, consistent branding, integrated offer management, coordinated timing.
- **Channel Sequencing**: Strategic ordering, reinforcement scheduling, optimal timing between touches, channel-specific message adaptation, integrated triggers.
- **Budget Allocation**: Performance-based distribution, cross-channel ROI comparison, dynamic adjustment, seasonal optimization, channel interaction value assessment.
- **Creative Asset Management**: Centralized library, format adaptation, version control, performance tracking by creative, effectiveness analytics.

This integrated approach ensures your marketing efforts work together.

Closed-Loop Reporting Connect marketing activities directly to business results:

- **Lead Source Attribution**: First/last touch, multi-touch models, online-to-offline, assisted conversions, source quality scoring.
- **Revenue Tracking**: Channel revenue contribution, campaign ROI, LTV by source, acquisition cost ratio, profit margin by channel.
- **Customer Quality Analysis**: Retention rates by source, project value by origin, referral generation by source, payment reliability, service type correlation.
- **Long-Term Impact**: Time-delayed conversion, seasonal patterns, channel effectiveness over time, cumulative ROI, investment depreciation models.

This closed-loop reporting ensures you understand which channels deliver the most valuable customers over time.

Offline Conversion Tracking Track traditionally difficult-to-measure offline conversions:

- **Call Tracking**: Channel-specific numbers, recording/transcription, quality scoring, keyword spotting, outcome classification.
- **Direct Mail Response**: Unique QR codes, PURLs, promo codes, call tracking numbers, text-to-respond keywords.
- **Traditional Media Measurement**: Dedicated landing pages, offer codes, time-correlation analysis, search lift measurement, brand search monitoring.
- **In-Person Interaction**: Digital check-in, mobile lead capture, QR codes, text-to-join, digital follow-up.

These methods transform traditionally unmeasurable activities into trackable lead sources.

Implementation Case Study: Northwest Paving

To illustrate how Revenue Commander transforms marketing operations for paving companies, let's examine Northwest Paving's implementation experience.

Company Profile: Mid-sized paving contractor (residential/commercial), 3-county area, 15 years in business, solid reputation, inconsistent lead flow, difficulty tracking effectiveness.

Challenges Before Revenue Commander: 5 disconnected software systems, unable to determine channel profitability, inconsistent lead follow-up, no systematic nurturing, difficulty scaling sales.

Phased Implementation Process:

- **Phase 1 (Discovery/Planning)**: Documented current tools, identified goals (lead tracking, conversion, communication), mapped current process, prioritized implementation.
- **Phase 2 (Core System Setup)**: Configured profile/services, created user accounts, implemented forms/call tracking, imported data, established templates.
- **Phase 3 (Marketing Integration)**: Connected Ads accounts, implemented offline tracking, set up email/SMS, integrated accounting, created landing pages.
- **Phase 4 (Automation)**: Built lead response/nurturing workflows, estimate follow-up, project updates, review requests, maintenance campaigns.
- **Phase 5 (Training/Optimization)**: Conducted role-specific training, developed SOPs, implemented weekly reviews, refined automations, established 90-day plan.

Results After Six Months:

- **Lead Management**: 34% increase in capture, response time down from 26 hrs to 37 mins, lead leakage reduced by 92%, qualification accuracy improved 43%.
- **Sales Performance**: Estimate conversion up from 23% to 38%, average project value increased 17%, sales cycle duration reduced by 9 days, sales capacity increased 35%.
- **Marketing Optimization**: Discovered Direct Mail had 2.3x higher ROI than thought, identified underperforming Google Ads ($1.3k/mo waste), found Facebook remarketing drove 27% conversions, correlated billboard exposure with 41% higher website conversion.
- **Customer Experience**: Satisfaction up from 4.2 to 4.8, Google reviews grew from 34 to 126, referral business increased 28%, repeat customer rate improved 18%.
- **Operational Efficiency**: Eliminated 3 software subscriptions, reduced admin time by 22 hrs/week, improved cash flow, enhanced scheduling efficiency.

Success Factors: Leadership commitment, phased approach, process refinement, consistent training, data-driven decisions.

This case study illustrates how Revenue Commander can transform not just marketing activities but entire business operations for paving companies willing to commit to implementation and ongoing optimization.

Conclusion: The Power of Integration

Revenue Commander provides paving companies with a comprehensive system to manage, measure, and optimize their entire marketing and sales operation. By centralizing all activities in one platform, you gain unprecedented visibility into what's working and what isn't, while automating routine tasks to enhance efficiency.

The most successful implementations share common characteristics:

- **Strategic Approach**: View implementation as a business transformation.
- **Complete Adoption**: Commit to using the platform for all customer interactions.
- **Continuous Improvement**: Leverage insights to refine marketing mix, messaging, and customer experience.
- **Team Engagement**: Ensure the entire team understands value and actively participates.
- **Patient Persistence**: Recognize that full implementation takes time (typically 3-6 months).

For paving companies ready to elevate their marketing effectiveness, Revenue Commander provides the infrastructure to compete at a higher level, regardless of company size. The system scales from solo operators to multi-location businesses, providing the tools to optimize marketing performance and drive sustainable growth.

In the next chapter, we'll explore how to maximize lead conversion once prospects are in your system—turning expensive marketing-generated leads into profitable paving projects through effective qualification, response, and follow-up processes.

23

Lead Management and Conversion

You've invested significant resources to generate leads for your paving business—now comes the crucial process of converting those leads into paying customers. Even the most effective marketing campaign will fail if your team can't efficiently convert inquiries into projects. In fact, poor lead management can waste up to 80% of your marketing budget, while an optimized conversion process can double or even triple your results without spending an additional dollar on marketing.

In this chapter, we'll explore how to implement a systematic approach to lead management and conversion that maximizes the return on your marketing investments. From initial contact to signed contract, we'll cover each step in the process and how to optimize it for paving contractors.

The Lead Qualification Process

Not all leads are created equal. Some are ready to purchase immediately, while others may be months away from making a decision or simply not qualified for your services. Implementing a structured qualification process helps your team focus on the most promising opportunities.

Initial Lead Assessment

When a new lead enters your system, the first step is to determine their basic fit and readiness to purchase. This initial qualification should happen quickly—ideally during the first conversation or interaction—and assess several key factors:

- **Project Requirements**: Ensure they align with your services. Mismatches can be obvious (concrete vs. asphalt) or subtle (specialized treatments outside core expertise).
- **Location Verification**: Confirm the property is within your profitable service area, considering travel time and logistics.
- **Budget Alignment**: Tactfully gauge expectations versus typical project ranges. Example: "Most residential driveways we install typically range from $X to $Y. Does that generally align with your expectations?"
- **Timeline Assessment**: Determine urgency (immediate need vs. future research). This affects prioritization and nurturing.
- **Decision-Making Authority**: Verify if you're speaking with the owner or authorized decision-maker (e.g., both spouses for residential, facility manager needing board approval for commercial).
- **Motivation**: Understand the 'why' behind the inquiry (problem-driven, maintenance, aesthetic upgrade). Different motivations require different sales approaches.

The Qualification Matrix

A structured qualification framework helps your team consistently evaluate leads. We recommend using a simple scoring system (1-5) in four categories:

Need Alignment (1-5)

- 1: No clear need / misalignment
- 3: Moderate alignment / customization needed
- 5: Perfect fit for core services

Financial Qualification (1-5)

- 1: Budget expectations far below realistic costs
- 3: Budget in lower range of typical projects
- 5: Budget aligned with premium services

Timeline Appropriateness (1-5)

- 1: Indefinite timeline / too far out
- 3: Planning for project within 3-6 months
- 5: Ready to proceed immediately

Decision Readiness (1-5)

- 1: Early research / comparing many contractors
- 3: Actively comparing final options
- 5: Ready to decide pending proposal

By totaling these scores, classify leads:

- **Hot Leads (16-20 points)**: Immediate need, budget, timeline, authority. Highest priority, same-day follow-up, experienced staff.
- **Warm Leads (10-15 points)**: Genuine interest, some gaps (timeline, budget). Require nurturing, good potential.
- **Cool Leads (4-9 points)**: Significant issues (location, budget, timeframe). Minimal resource investment unless situation changes.

This qualification system should be implemented in Revenue Commander to automatically score and categorize leads.

Qualification Questions for Paving Leads

Ask the right questions naturally during conversation:

- **Project Basics**: "Tell me about the project..." "Specific needs?" "Approximate square footage?" "New install or replacement/repair?"
- **Timeline**: "When were you hoping for completion?" "Specific deadline?" "Started getting estimates?" "How long considering project?"
- **Budget/Decision**: "Established budget range?" "Most important decision factors?" "Who else involved?" "Why contact us?"
- **Property/Logistics**: "Access challenges?" "Drainage issues?" "Previous paving work?" "HOA/permit requirements?"

Gather information while building rapport and demonstrating expertise.

Qualifying Commercial vs. Residential Leads

Adapt your approach based on lead type:

Residential Leads:

- **Decision**: More emotional, fewer stakeholders (homeowner/couple).
- **Budget**: Important, but often flexible for the right solution.
- **Timeline**: Seasonal, aesthetic concerns, urgent problems.
- **Sales Cycle**: Shorter (days to weeks).
- **Value**: Smaller scope ($ thousands to tens of thousands).
- **Focus**: Homeowner concerns, aesthetics, property value/enjoyment, personal trust.

Commercial Leads:

- **Decision**: Rational, process-driven, multiple stakeholders (property managers, boards).

- **Budget**: Usually pre-determined, inflexible, formal approval needed.
- **Timeline**: Tenant impact, business operations, fiscal year considerations.
- **Sales Cycle**: Longer (weeks to months, even a year).
- **Value**: Larger scope ($ hundreds of thousands).
- **Focus**: Credentials, insurance, professional processes, minimizing business disruption, ROI, fiscal calendar, procurement procedures.

Tailor the qualification process appropriately for each type.

Response Time Optimization

Speed of response dramatically impacts conversion:

- Leads contacted within **5 minutes** are **21x more likely to qualify** than after 30 minutes.
- After **1 hour**, odds decrease by over **10x**.
- **78%** of customers buy from the **first responder**.

Time sensitivity exists because inquiries often happen during moments of high interest (e.g., noticing damage). The first responder frames the conversation.

Creating an Immediate Response System

Requires technology and process optimization:

Response Time Standards:

- New Inquiries: < 5 mins (business hours), < 2 hrs (evenings/weekends).
- Follow-ups: < 4 business hours.

- Scheduling: Confirm within 2 hours.

Multi-Channel Notifications: Instant mobile/text/email alerts for new leads, escalation protocols.

Team Assignment & Backup: Primary responders, backup system, after-hours/weekend rotation, possible answering service.

Automated Initial Response: Auto-responders for forms, chatbots, text acknowledgments, custom voicemail greetings.

The Ideal First Contact

Set the tone for the relationship:

- **Establish Rapport/Credibility**: Thank prospect, introduce company/-experience, mention connections, demonstrate local knowledge.
- **Gather Qualification Info**: Ask targeted questions, listen for pain points, capture details, identify decision-makers.
- **Set Clear Next Steps**: Schedule site visit/estimate, outline info to be sent, establish follow-up timeframe, confirm best contact method.
- **Differentiate from Competitors**: Emphasize unique capabilities, mention similar local projects, highlight warranties, address common concerns proactively.

Managing Lead Flow During Peak Seasons

Handle heavy inquiry periods effectively:

- **Lead Prioritization**: Dynamic scoring, express qualification, prioritize referrals/repeat customers, geographic clustering.
- **Temporary Staffing**: Extend office hours, cross-train staff, hire seasonal support, engage part-time professionals.

- **Technology**: Scheduling software, automated workflows, self-service info access, chatbots.
- **Expectation Management**: Be transparent about lead times, create priority queues, develop waitlist protocols, consider surge pricing/seasonal rates.

Prompt acknowledgment, even with realistic expectations, is better than delayed response.

Estimate Delivery

A well-crafted estimate builds confidence, addresses concerns, and differentiates your company.

Components of an Effective Paving Estimate

Go beyond price; include:

- **Professional Presentation**: Branded template, customer/project info, consistent formatting, easy readability, digital delivery/e-signature option.
- **Detailed Project Specs**: Precise measurements, material depths, material type/grade, prep process, drainage details.
- **Clear Scope**: State inclusions/exclusions, transition handling, special considerations, cleanup/debris removal, property access plan.
- **Visual Elements**: Site plan/sketch, annotated before photos, similar project samples, diagrams for complex features.
- **Transparent Pricing**: Cost breakdown, payment terms/schedule, explanation of variables, deposit info, validity period.
- **Value Justification**: Material quality comparison, long-term benefits, warranty/guarantees, QC process, testimonials.
- **Next Steps/Timeline**: How to accept, estimated start timeline, project duration, customer prep needs, contact info.

Estimate Delivery Best Practices

How you deliver matters:

- **Timing**: Provide estimate timeframe upfront, deliver on time (or communicate delays), follow up within 24-48 hours. Estimates delivered promptly after site visits convert better.
- **Delivery Method**: In-person presentation for complex estimates, email for convenience, physical mail for larger projects, digital platforms with e-signature.
- **Presentation Approach**: Emphasize value (overview of needs, recommended solution, visuals, comparison to alternatives, long-term value framing) before price.
- **Anticipate Questions**: Explain warranty, material quality, timeline factors, insurance/licensing, payment process proactively.

Competitive Differentiation in Estimates

Clearly communicate why you're the best choice:

- **Quality Differentiators**: Detail material specs, base prep process, specialized equipment, crew experience, QC processes.
- **Value-Added Services**: Complimentary inspections, free sealcoating, extended warranties, documentation, referral incentives.
- **Risk Factors Addressed**: Prevention of common problems, seasonal considerations, access mitigation, permit handling, weather contingency.
- **Social Proof**: Specific testimonials, links to reviews, nearby project photos, notable projects, certifications/awards.

Aim to justify pricing through compelling value, reducing emphasis on price comparison.

Follow-Up After Estimate Delivery

Conversion often happens during follow-up:

- **Structured Sequence**: Initial call (24-48 hrs), follow-up email (3-4 days), second call (~1 week), "last chance" communication (~2 weeks).
- **Address Concerns**: Provide more info, offer references, discuss financing, suggest phased approaches, clarify estimate details.
- **Value Reinforcement**: Send case studies, educational content, more photos, offer tours of completed projects, introduce project manager.
- **Create Urgency (Appropriately)**: Mention schedule lead times, seasonal factors, material price trends, scheduling priority, modest incentives.
- **Maintain Consultative Approach**: Help prospect make informed decision, don't pressure.

Follow-Up Sequences

Systematic follow-up separates top performers.

Designing Effective Follow-Up Sequences

Maintain contact without annoyance, provide value, guide decision:

- **Timing/Frequency**: High frequency initially, tapering based on engagement (Hot: 2-3 days -> weekly; Warm: weekly -> bi-weekly; Cool: bi-weekly -> monthly).
- **Multi-Channel Approach**: Alternate phone, email, text based on preference. Use high-impact channels for key points, lower-impact for info sharing.
- **Value at Each Touchpoint**: Share educational materials, maintenance tips, case studies, seasonal info, testimonials.

- **Personalization**: Reference specific project details, acknowledge concerns, mention local info, adapt to communication style.

Automated vs. Personal Follow-Up

Balance automation and personal touch:

- **Automation Best For**: Pre-scheduled educational emails, text reminders, engagement alerts, ensuring timely follow-up during busy times.
- **Personal Contact Essential For**: Initial estimate follow-up, addressing questions/concerns, discussing pricing/contracts, responding to inquiries.
- **Hybrid Approaches**: Use automation for consistency/timing but personalize key elements, review automated messages before sending, use human approval triggers, create personalized workflows based on behavior.
- **Technology for Personalization**: Merge fields, segmentation, behavioral triggers, conditional content.

Goal: Follow-up that feels personal while maintaining efficiency.

Nurturing Long-Term Prospects

Keep top-of-mind until prospects are ready:

- **Structured Nurturing**: Calendar check-ins based on timeline, increase frequency near start date, set interval reminders (30/60/90 days), adjust based on engagement.
- **Content**: Seasonal relevance, industry updates, planning tools, company news, similar project testimonials.
- **Periodic Re-qualification**: Confirm timeline, scope, budget, decision-makers, property conditions.

- **Transition Strategies**: Increase contact frequency near timeframe, offer updated estimate, suggest fresh site visit, provide commitment incentives, create seasonal urgency.

Re-Engagement Campaigns

Revive stalled or delayed opportunities:

- **Reactivation Approach**: Wait ~30 days, send "checking in" email, try different channel, offer new value, move to quarterly check-ins if no response.
- **Value-Oriented Re-engagement**: Share new case studies, updated educational content, offer property reassessment, seasonal tips, introduce new services.
- **Incentives**: Time-limited discount, "second chance" promo, added value services, neighborhood discounts, seasonal specials.
- **Re-qualification**: Verify needs, decision-makers, contact info, timeline, budget, competing priorities.

Persistence and the right approach can revive many apparently lost opportunities. Data suggests 30-50% of sales go to vendors who follow up after the initial process seems ended.

Revenue Commander CRM Capabilities

A robust CRM is essential. Revenue Commander provides specialized functionality:

Lead Tracking and Management

- **Centralized Database**: Prospects/customers, contact details, property info, interaction history.
- **Automated Lead Capture**: Website forms, calls, emails, etc.

- **Activity Timeline**: Chronological touchpoints for each lead.
- **Lead Assignment**: Assign to team members, track accountability.
- **Custom Fields/Data Structures**: Tailor to paving specifics (sq ft, surface type, access). Custom qualification criteria. Property type categories.
- **Visual Pipeline Management**: Customizable stages, status indicators, automated advancement, stuck opportunity alerts.
- **Task Management**: Assign/track follow-ups, automated reminders, task lists, escalation protocols.

Communication Tracking and Templates

- **Integrated History**: Emails, calls, texts, notes in one place.
- **Call Recording/Transcription**: For phone interactions.
- **Email Sync**: Two-way sync with timeline.
- **Text Message Capture**: Document conversations.
- **Secure Document Sharing**: Estimates, contracts, etc.
- **Communication Templates**: Standardized emails, texts, call scripts. Automated personalization.
- **Activity Logging**: One-click call logging, mobile access, voice dictation, standardized outcome categories.
- **Scheduling/Calendar Integration**: Syncs with Google/Outlook, automated reminders, availability management, self-booking links.

Sales Process Automation

- **Lead Nurturing Workflows**: Multi-step sequences based on qualificat ion/status, triggered emails/texts, conditional paths based on engagement.
- **Proposal Generation/Management**: Customizable templates, e-signature, automated follow-up, status/version tracking, expiration reminders.
- **Task Automation**: Auto-create follow-up tasks, set milestone re-

minders, escalation protocols, assign tasks by role.
- **Activity Monitoring**: Track team performance, identify bottlenecks, highlight stage conversion rates, monitor response times, alert for stalled opportunities.

Analytics and Reporting

- **Performance Dashboards**: Real-time conversion rates, cycle duration, close rates, proposal acceptance.
- **Pipeline Analysis**: Weighted value, historical conversion forecasting, bottleneck identification, velocity tracking, comparison to previous periods.
- **Sales Team Analytics**: Compare rep performance, identify training needs, recognize top performers, analyze time allocation, establish benchmarks.
- **Custom Reporting**: Focus on specific periods/areas/project types, combine data sources, schedule automated delivery, export data, save templates.

These analytics transform sales into a data-driven, continuously improving operation.

Closing Techniques for Paving Projects

Effective closing helps customers make confident decisions.

Understanding Customer Decision Factors

Tailor your approach:

Residential:

- Budget/Financing

- Aesthetics/Curb Appeal
- Timing/Disruption
- Quality/Durability/Maintenance
- Trust/Reputation/Connection

Commercial:

- ROI/Durability/Maintenance Savings
- Liability/Safety/ADA Compliance
- Disruption Minimization
- Compliance/Specifications/Documentation
- Budget Cycle Timing

Consultative Closing Approaches

Help customers decide, don't pressure:

- **Options Close**: Present 2-3 choices (good, better, best). Focus conversation on best *option*, not yes/no. Highlight pros/cons. Guide toward best fit. Customer feels in control.
- **Summary Close**: Summarize needs and how solution addresses them. Review important benefits. Confirm proposal meets requirements. Present price in context of agreed value. Ask if benefits justify investment.
- **Assumptive Close**: Use forward-looking language ("when we start"). Discuss logistics/scheduling as next step. Address implementation details. Provide agreement as simple next step. Focus on execution.
- **Authorization Close**: Frame signature as authorization, not major commitment. Simplify paperwork/process (e-signature). Minimize perceived complexity. Present as confirming discussion.

Handling Common Objections

Prepare your team:

- **Price Objections ("Too high")**: Avoid immediate discounts. Reframe around value/TCO. Compare materials/methods. Explain long-term costs of cutting corners. Offer payment plans/financing. Present reduced scope option if appropriate.
- **Timing Concerns**: Offer flexible scheduling. Explain seasonal factors. Discuss benefits of securing schedule slot. Create urgency based on material trends. Offer off-season incentives.
- **Comparison Shopping ("Thinking about it")**: Acknowledge due diligence. Provide clear differentiators. Offer references. Create comparison worksheet (beyond price). Set specific follow-up timeframe.
- **Authority Limitations ("Need to discuss")**: Offer to join discussion. Provide materials for other decision-makers. Schedule meeting with all parties. Create summary document. Offer to present to committees/boards (commercial).
- **Specification Uncertainty**: Explain pros/cons clearly. Provide samples/demos. Share photo examples. Visit similar completed projects. Emphasize warranty/guarantees.

Creating Appropriate Urgency

Help prospects overcome inertia legitimately:

- **Seasonal Factors**: Educate on optimal conditions/timing. Explain weather impact. Share benefits of pre-booking. Be truthful about timelines.
- **Capacity Limitations**: Share actual lead times transparently. Explain scheduling process. Discuss quality standards limiting simultaneous projects. Describe benefits of pre-booking slot. Offer priority scheduling for prompt decisions.

- **Material Considerations**: Explain availability/delays. Discuss price trends (if relevant). Mention special opportunities. Explain ordering lead times. Share benefits of pre-ordering.
- **Special Offers**: Use genuine, time-limited promotions. Offer group/neighbor discounts. Create package pricing. Provide incentives for signing at estimate meeting. Ensure clear parameters/limitations.

The Follow-Up Contract Process

Make signing smooth:

- **Convenience**: E-signature options, bring printed contracts, multiple payment methods, simple deposit process, clear instructions.
- **Clear Contract**: Plain language, detailed specs matching estimate, clear payment/warranty/timeline/contingency terms, complete scope of work.
- **Post-Signing Communication**: Immediate thank you/confirmation, welcome package (timeline/expectations), introduce key team members, explain next steps.
- **Prevent Buyer's Remorse**: Reinforce value/benefits, share testimonials, provide prep updates, set realistic expectations, be available for questions.

Conversion Rate Benchmarks by Lead Source

Understanding typical rates helps set goals and identify improvements.

Industry Benchmarks for Paving Contractors

(% of leads becoming paying customers)

- **Website Form Submissions**: 15-25% (Avg). Factors: Response time, form complexity, landing page optimization. Top performers >30%.

- **Direct Phone Inquiries**: 20-35% (Avg). Factors: Call handling, technical answers, follow-up. Top performers >40%.
- **Google Business Profile**: 15-25% (Avg). Factors: Review quality, profile completeness, response speed. Best practices: Monitor messages, update photos, manage reviews.
- **Referrals**: 40-60% (Highest). Factors: Quality consistency, nurturing referrer relationships, expedited response. Top performers >70%.
- **Lead Service Providers (Angi, etc.)**: 5-15% (Lowest). Factors: Speed, pricing/differentiation, presentation, follow-up. Top performers >20%.
- **Social Media**: 10-20% (Avg). Factors: Engagement quality, content relevance, response systems. Best practices: Monitor DMs, rapid response, move conversations direct.
- **Direct Mail**: 15-25% (Avg). Factors: Mail piece quality, offer relevance, follow-up. Top performers >30%.
- **Traditional Ads (TV, Radio, etc.)**: 10-20% (Avg). Factors: Brand consistency, call handling, qualification. Best practices: Tracking numbers, specialized handling, tailored follow-up.
- **Trade Shows/Events**: 15-25% (Avg). Factors: Lead capture quality, post-event follow-up speed, contact accuracy. Best practices: Detailed notes, follow up <24 hrs, reference interaction.

Factors Affecting Source-Specific Conversion

- **Intent Level**: High (Referrals, Direct Inquiries) -> Medium (Search) -> Low (Social, Trad Ads).
- **Competition Level**: High (Lead Services) -> Medium (Organic Search) -> Low (Direct Inquiries, Referrals).
- **Relationship Temperature**: Warm (Referrals, Repeat) -> Cool (Cold Leads).
- **Information Quality**: High (Phone Calls) -> Medium (Forms) -> Low (Lead Services, Social).

Allocate resources and customize processes based on these factors.

Improving Conversion by Source

- **Website Forms**: Immediate automated + personal response (<5 mins), optimized forms, source-specific landing pages, lead scoring.
- **Phone Inquiries**: Trained staff, consistent protocol, schedule estimate on call, call recording, specialized follow-up.
- **GBP Leads**: Monitor/respond < minutes, updated profile, solicit/respond to reviews, Google Posts, track attribution.
- **Referrals**: Formal program/incentives, prioritize response, acknowledge relationship, update referrer, exceptional service.
- **Lead Services**: Ultra-rapid response (< mins), differentiation, rigorous qualification, competitor analysis, test premium placement.
- **Social Media**: Monitor DMs/comments, platform-specific templates, move conversations direct, remarketing, value content, track touchpoints.
- **Direct Mail**: Team alignment for response period, specialized handling, targeted follow-up based on offer, track by segment/offer/design, test CTAs.
- **Traditional Ads**: Tracking numbers, trained staff on promos, source-specific scripts, tailored follow-up, ensure response capacity.
- **Trade Shows/Events**: Follow up <24 hrs, categorize leads at event, event-specific offers, reference conversation, track event ROI.

Conclusion: The Conversion System

Successful companies implement systematic processes, not just rely on sales ability. Key elements include:

- Prompt response
- Thorough qualification
- Professional estimate delivery (value > price)

- Consistent follow-up
- Effective closing techniques
- Continuous measurement and optimization

This systematic approach typically improves conversion rates by 50-100%. For a company investing $10k/mo for 50 leads, improving conversion from 20% to 35% adds 7-8 projects monthly (potentially hundreds of thousands annually) without increasing marketing spend.

In the next chapter, we'll explore integrating these processes with campaigns for seamless customer journeys.

24

Campaign Integration and Customer Journey Mapping

Customers rarely interact with just one channel. Integrating campaigns and mapping the customer journey optimizes the path to purchase.

Creating Marketing Funnels for Different Services

Align marketing efforts with the unique consideration process for different offerings.

The Modern Marketing Funnel Model Less linear, prospects move between stages:

1. **Awareness**: Initial exposure (trucks, billboards, social, job sites). Metrics: Impressions, reach, brand recognition.
2. **Consideration**: Recognizing need, exploring options (search, reviews, website, recommendations). Metrics: Website visits, time on site, page views, content engagement.
3. **Intent**: Showing clear interest, narrowing options (estimate requests, calls, forms, pricing content). Metrics: Leads, estimate requests, calls, pricing engagement.

4. **Decision**: Conversion point (signing contract, deposit, scheduling). Metrics: Close rate, project value, time to close, sales by source.
5. **Retention/Advocacy**: Ongoing relationship (maintenance, referrals, reviews). Metrics: Repeat rate, referrals, reviews, LTV.

Service-Specific Funnel Characteristics

Residential Driveway Installation: Medium cycle (2-8 wks).
Awareness: Neighborhood visibility.
Consideration: Visuals crucial.
Decision: Aesthetics, function, curb appeal.
Trigger: Deterioration, home sale.
Funnel Focus: Before/after visuals, appearance/durability benefits, address disruption, target by neighborhood age/value, seasonal triggers.

Commercial Parking Lot Projects: Long cycle (3-12 mos).
Awareness: Reputation, relationships.
Consideration: Specs, liability.
Decision: Multiple stakeholders, formal process.
Trigger: Safety, tenant complaints, budget cycle.
Funnel Focus: Case studies, technical expertise, minimize disruption, liability/safety, align with fiscal year, target by business type/property mgmt.

Asphalt Repair/Maintenance: Short cycle (1-4 wks).
Awareness: Problem-driven.
Consideration: Convenience, quick resolution.
Decision: Timing, price.
Trigger: Damage, pooling, season change.
Funnel Focus: Quick response, prevent costly issues, weather triggers, target past projects, urgency for safety.

Sealcoating Services: Very short cycle (1-2 wks).

Awareness: Outreach to existing customers.

Consideration: Timing, convenience, prevention.

Decision: Largely price-driven.

Trigger: Maintenance routines, fading.

Funnel Focus: Value protection, efficiency, seasonal campaigns, target existing customers, bundle services.

Specialty Paving (Decorative, etc.): Longer cycle (2-6 mos).

Awareness: Showcases, high-end visibility.

Consideration: Aesthetics, unique performance.

Decision: Appearance vs. function.

Trigger: Major upgrades, specific requirements.

Funnel Focus: Unique advantages, distinctive projects, premium materials, target high-end areas, connect with architects/designers.

Building Integrated Service Funnels

- **Identify Entry Points**: Residential (visibility, search), Commercial (networking, reputation), Repair (need search, past customer), Specialty (design pubs, property marketing).
- **Develop Stage-Appropriate Content**: Awareness (problem ID, brand intro), Consideration (education, expertise), Intent (evaluation, value prop), Decision (reduce anxiety, build confidence), Retention (relationship, advocacy).
- **Align Channel Selection**: Awareness (billboards, wraps, social), Consideration (blog, videos, guides), Intent (PPC, direct mail offers, retargeting), Decision (estimates, testimonials, guarantees), Retention (email, reminders, referral programs).
- **Implement Measurement**: Track progression: Awareness (visibility), Consideration (engagement), Intent (leads), Decision (conversions), Retention (repeat/referrals/reviews).
- **Continuously Optimize**: Address drop-offs, test messaging, adjust channel allocation, refine targeting, implement automation.

Touchpoint Optimization

Every interaction shapes perception. Optimize for better experience and conversion.

Mapping Current Customer Touchpoints Audit all potential interactions:

- **Pre-Contact**: Trucks/equipment, yard signs, billboards, website visits, social content/ads, online reviews, direct mail/print ads, recommendations.
- **Initial Contact**: Phone calls, web forms, email inquiries, chat, text messages, walk-ins, social media messages.
- **Sales Process**: Estimate scheduling/confirmation, estimate visit/pro fessionalism, estimate document/presentation, follow-up comms, contract signing, deposit handling, pre-project comms.
- **Project Execution**: Pre-work comms, crew arrival/inspection, crew appearance/professionalism, progress updates/issue resolution, site cleanliness, final walkthrough/inspection, final payment.
- **Post-Project**: Thank you/satisfaction check, warranty info, follow-up inspection offers, maintenance reminders, referral requests, review requests, seasonal check-ins.

Document current experience, responsibilities, systems, and metrics for each.

Evaluation and Prioritization

- **Impact Assessment**: Influence on perception, impact on purchase, visibility/frequency, emotional impact, source of feedback.
- **Gap Analysis**: Compare current vs. expected experience, survey customers, review competitors, identify inconsistencies, look for friction points.
- **Prioritization Framework**: Consider performance gap, potential im-

pact, cost/complexity, resources, dependencies, strategic alignment.
- **Low-Hanging Fruit**: Simple process changes, quick tech solutions, clear ownership, measurable results <90 days.

Optimization Strategies for Key Touchpoints

- **Website Inquiry Handling**: Immediate automated + personal response (<10 mins), standardized templates + personalization, track response times, escalation process.
- **Phone Call Experience**: Standard greeting/script, consistent info collection, call recording, clear hold/transfer protocols, after-hours handling.
- **Estimate Appointments**: Detailed confirmation (estimator bio/photo), clear process/duration explanation, branded vehicle/professional attire, standardized evaluation, tech for measurement, clear next steps.
- **Estimate Documents**: Professional templates, visuals, detailed scope, highlight value/guarantees, testimonials, digital delivery/e-signature.
- **Pre-Project Communication**: Automated confirmation sequence, detailed prep instructions, single point of contact, reminders, weather contingency plan, build excitement.
- **Project Execution**: Crew intros, regular progress updates, clear comms protocols, site cleanliness standards, formal walkthrough, satisfaction confirmation.
- **Post-Project Follow-up**: Thank you (<24 hrs), 30-day inspection offer, warranty info, review request sequence, referral program intro, maintenance schedule.

Document optimizations as SOPs with ownership, metrics, and standards.

Technology and Tools for Touchpoint Management

- **Revenue Commander Capabilities**:
- **Automated Communication Workflows**: Multi-step sequences, conditional paths, personalization, time-delays, monitoring.
- **Appointment Management**: Online scheduling, calendar sync, automated confirmations/reminders, prep instructions.
- **Document Automation**: Templates (estimates, contracts), e-signature, automated customization, engagement tracking, A/B testing.
- **Customer Portal**: Project details/timeline access, document sharing, messaging, payments, scheduling.
- **Team Accountability**: Task management, notification systems, completion tracking, quality scoring, performance dashboards.

Measuring Cross-Channel Performance

Go beyond last-touch attribution.

Attribution Modeling Approaches

- **Last-Touch**: Simplest, credits final interaction. Overvalues bottom-funnel. Ignores assisting channels. Okay for short cycles.
- **First-Touch**: Credits initial interaction. Highlights awareness channels. Ignores subsequent influence. Overvalues broad awareness.
- **Linear**: Distributes credit equally. Acknowledges all channels. Fails to weight influence. Requires better tracking. More balanced.
- **Position-Based (U-shaped)**: Weights first/last touches heavily, distributes rest. Recognizes awareness/conversion importance. Acknowledges middle touches. More complex. Good compromise.
- **Time-Decay**: More credit to recent touchpoints. Recognizes stronger recent influence. Good for longer cycles. Requires sophisticated tracking. May undervalue early touches.

- **Data-Driven**: Algorithmic, determines credit based on actual impact. Most accurate. Requires significant data/resources. Adapts to behavior.

Recommendation: Start with position-based, evolve to data-driven.

Implementing Cross-Channel Tracking

- **Digital Tracking**: Google Analytics/eCommerce, conversion tracking, UTM parameters, Google Tag Manager, cross-domain tracking.
- **Online-to-Offline**: Call tracking (DNI), unique offline numbers, dedicated landing pages, promo codes, QR codes.
- **Customer Journey Reconstruction**: Cookie tracking, logged-in experiences, device matching, CRM integration, unique customer IDs.
- **First-Party Data Collection**: "How did you hear?" question, post-conversion surveys, customer interviews, feedback requests, sales team documentation.
- **Privacy Compliance**: Clear policies, cookie consent, opt-out options, data security, stay current on regulations.

Key Cross-Channel Metrics

- **CAC by Channel Combination**: Efficiency of different pathways.
- **Assisted Conversion Analysis**: How channels work together. Value of supporting channels.
- **Multi-Touch Conversion Rate**: Success across different journey patterns. Most effective touchpoint combinations.
- **Path Length & Time to Conversion**: Sales cycle dynamics. Average touchpoints/timeframe. Acceleration opportunities.
- **Cross-Channel Engagement Depth**: Research level before conversion. Correlation between engagement/conversion. Critical thresholds.
- **Return on Marketing Investment (ROMI)**: Overall effectiveness. Revenue vs. total investment. Profit margin inclusion.

Visualizing the Customer Journey

- **Journey Mapping Visualizations**: Flowcharts of common paths, entry points, drop-offs. Segment comparisons.
- **Attribution Dashboards**: Channel contribution (first/last touch), touchpoint mapping, high-performing combos, trend tracking.
- **Funnel Visualization**: Volume/conversion between stages, drop-off points, segment comparisons, optimization tracking.
- **Channel Interaction Matrices**: Heat maps of combo effectiveness, synergistic channels, channel conflicts, optimal sequencing.
- **Custom Reports**: Tailored for stakeholders (exec summaries, channel manager details, sales dashboards, ops reports). Automated delivery.

25

Analytics and Performance Management

Robust analytics transform data into insights.

Key Performance Indicators for Paving Marketers

Metrics by business function:

Executive-Level KPIs

- **Return on Marketing Investment (ROMI)**: Revenue per marketing dollar. ROMI = [(Revenue - Cost) / Cost] * 100%. (Ex: $5k cost, $25k revenue = 400% ROI).
- **Customer Acquisition Cost (CAC)**: Total marketing/sales cost per new customer. CAC = Total Cost / New Customers. (Ex: Paving: $200-$800).
- **Customer Lifetime Value (CLV)**: Total expected revenue per customer (initial + repeat + maintenance + referrals). Basic CLV = Avg Annual Revenue * Avg Lifespan. Healthy LTV:CAC = 3:1+.
- **Market Share Growth**: Share of total projects in service area over time. Trend matters.
- **Brand Awareness**: Unaided recall, share of voice, brand mentions.

Marketing Team KPIs

- **Lead Generation Metrics**: Total leads by source, CPL by channel, lead quality scores, MoM growth, lead-to-opportunity rate.
- **Channel Performance Metrics**: Channel conversion rates, traffic/engagement by source, campaign ROI, CPC/CPM/CPV, audience growth.
- **Content Effectiveness Metrics**: Engagement rates, time on page, download/view counts, content lead contribution, social sharing.
- **Website Performance Metrics**: Traffic/sources, bounce rate, form completion rates, page speed, mobile vs. desktop engagement.
- **Local Visibility Metrics**: Maps ranking, local impression share, "near me" visibility, directory completeness, citation consistency.

Sales Team KPIs

- **Lead Quality Metrics**: Lead-to-appointment rate, show rate, response time, scoring accuracy, source quality ranking.
- **Sales Performance Metrics**: Quote-to-close ratio, avg deal size, sales cycle length, margin %, upsell/cross-sell rate.
- **Customer Relationship Metrics**: Satisfaction scores, referral rate, repeat business %, NPS, retention rate.

Setting Up Revenue Commander Dashboards

Customize dashboards for different stakeholders:

Executive Dashboard

- **Business Impact Summary**: MTD/YTD revenue from marketing, ROMI trend, new customer count/CAC, market share indicators, YoY growth.
- **Channel Mix Performance**: Revenue attribution, budget vs. performance, ROI combos, emerging opportunities, allocation recommen-

dations.

- **Customer Acquisition Trends**: CAC trends, LTV by source, LTV:CAC ratio, new vs. repeat revenue, referral metrics.
- **Forecasting Elements**: Pipeline projection, seasonal comparison, market opportunity, growth trajectory, budget scenario modeling.

Marketing Operations Dashboard

- **Campaign Performance Tracking**: Status, performance vs. targets, creative comparison, A/B test results, budget pacing.
- **Lead Generation Analytics**: Real-time lead count/source, quality distribution, CPL benchmarks, volume trends, geo heat maps.
- **Content Effectiveness Metrics**: Top content, conversion paths, gap analysis, download tracking, optimization recommendations.
- **Competitive Intelligence**: Share of voice, position monitoring, keyword comparison, review sentiment analysis, market positioning.

Sales Dashboard

- **Lead Management View**: New leads, aging reports, appointment status, scoring/prioritization, follow-up task tracking.
- **Sales Opportunity Pipeline**: Active opportunities by stage, close dates/values, weighted value, stalled alerts, win/loss analysis.
- **Customer Relationship Metrics**: Recent feedback, review generation, referral performance, maintenance renewal opps, upsell/cross-sell suggestions.
- **Performance Comparison**: Individual vs. team metrics, close rate comparison, response time compliance, quote volume/value, commission projections.

Call Tracking Implementation

Essential for accurate attribution.

Call Tracking Technology Integration

- **Dynamic Number Insertion (DNI)**: Different numbers based on website source, visitor-specific tracking, session persistence, GA integration, call recording.
- **Offline Channel Tracking**: Dedicated numbers for billboards, print, vehicles, direct mail, radio/TV.
- **Conversation Intelligence**: Auto transcription, keyword spotting, sentiment analysis, question detection, conversion prediction.
- **Integration Capabilities**: CRM sync, marketing automation connection, lead scoring, sales enablement, BI tools.

Call Quality Scoring Evaluate call quality:

- **Quality Scoring Criteria**: Duration thresholds, qualifying questions asked, timeline/budget discussed, appointment scheduled.
- **Automated Qualification**: IVR, conversational analysis, speech patterns, intent classification, lead scoring integration.
- **Agent Performance Measurement**: Script compliance, response time, info gathering, objection handling, appointment setting success.
- **Training Integration**: Identify common objections, create targeted training, personalized coaching, script improvements, share best practices.

Call-Based Attribution Models

- **Last-Click**: Credits last touch before call. Simple, good for immediate response. Limited view.
- **First-Click**: Credits initial touch. Values awareness channels. Ignores

subsequent influence.

- **Multi-Touch**: Distributes credit (Position-based, Linear, Time-decay). More accurate, requires better tracking.
- **AI-Enhanced**: Dynamic allocation based on patterns. Most accurate, requires data volume.

Data-Driven Decision Making

Use analytics to improve decisions.

Automated Insights and Alerts

- Performance anomaly detection
- Trend deviation alerts
- Goal progress tracking
- Competitive movement alerts
- Budget pacing notifications

Transforms data into actionable intelligence.

Scenario Modeling and Forecasting

- "What-if" budget allocation analysis
- Seasonal performance forecasting
- Pipeline value projection
- Market opportunity sizing
- Competitor response modeling

Moves management from reactive to proactive.

Continuous Optimization Framework

- A/B testing management

- Multivariate testing capabilities
- Performance benchmarking
- Optimization prioritization
- ROI projections for initiatives

Applies scientific method for steady improvement.

Cost Per Lead Benchmarks by Channel

Typical ranges for paving companies:

- **Google Organic Search**: $25-75 (Avg $35). Cost-effective long term. High conversion.
- **Google Map Listings**: $30-80 (Avg similar to Organic). Highest conversion.
- **Google Ads**: $45-120 (Avg $72). Immediate results, precise targeting.
- **Facebook Ads**: $40-90 (Avg $58). Lower intent, good for nurturing. Visual.
- **Direct Mail**: $50-125 (Avg $68). Higher quality leads often.
- **Yard Signs/Vehicle Branding**: $10-40 (Lowest). Passive, constant visibility. Harder to track.
- **Referral Programs**: $10-50 (Very low). Highest conversion.

Goal: Most *profitable* acquisition strategy, not necessarily lowest CPL.

26

Scaling Your Marketing Operations

As your company grows, marketing needs evolve. Revenue Commander scales with you.

Building Your Marketing Team

Structure depends on size/growth/sophistication:

Team Structures for Different Growth Stages

- **Early-Stage (<$1M)**: Solo Marketer (Owner, Office Mgr, Coordinator). Generalist + freelancers/agency. RC helps automate/guide.
- **Mid-Sized ($1-5M)**: Core Team (2-3 staff: Mgr, Digital Specialist, Comms Coordinator). + specialized agencies/freelancers. RC supports roles/coordination.
- **Growth-Stage ($5M+)**: Specialized Team (4+ staff: Director, Digital Mgr, Trad Mgr, Content Creator, Analyst). RC enhances with analytics /collaboration/campaign mgmt.
- **Multi-Location**: Centralized Team (Brand, Strategy, Resources) + Local Coordinators. RC supports location reporting, brand management, coordinated execution.

Key Roles and Responsibilities

- **Marketing Director/Manager**: Strategic leadership, budget, coordination, vendor relations, ROI accountability. RC Support: Dashboards, budget tracking, forecasting.
- **Digital Marketing Specialist**: Online presence/campaigns (Website, SEM, Social, Email, Directories). RC Support: Channel mgmt, reporting, optimization recs.
- **Customer Experience Coordinator**: Existing customer value (Reviews, Comms, Referrals, Data Mgmt, Loyalty). RC Support: Journey tracking, automation, relationship scoring.
- **Marketing Analyst/Data Specialist**: Measurement/optimization (Tracking systems, performance analysis, reporting, research). RC Support: Centralized analytics, auto-reporting, data viz.
- **Creative Production (In-house or Outsource)**: Graphic design, content creation (writing, photo, video), web dev, print production. RC Support: Project mgmt, asset libraries, creative performance tracking.

Training and Skill Development

- **Platform-Specific Training**: RC onboarding, role-specific modules, advanced certification, refreshers, custom workflow training. (Online courses, webinars, coaching, docs).
- **Marketing Skills Development**: Digital fundamentals, analytics, journey mapping, content marketing, local marketing strategies. (RC provides guidance, alerts, benchmarks).
- **Industry-Specific Knowledge**: Paving terminology, seasonality, customer education needs, competitive landscape, regulations. (Industry associations, mentoring, field experience).
- **Leadership Development**: Project/budget mgmt, team coordination, strategic planning, executive comms. (Helps translate metrics to business impact).

Outsourcing vs. In-House

Most use hybrid approach. RC supports collaboration.

Agency Partnership Models

- **Full-Service**: Comprehensive management (strategy, creative, execution, analysis). Good for limited internal expertise. Monthly retainer ($2.5k-10k+).
- **Channel Specialists**: Deep expertise (SEO, PPC, Social, Direct Mail). Good with strong internal coordination. Channel retainers ($1k-3k/mo) or performance-based.
- **Project-Based Creative**: Specific deliverables (Website, Video, Graphics). Good with internal management needing production. Project-based pricing.
- **Fractional CMO**: Part-time executive leadership. Strategic guidance without full-time cost. Good for needing direction but not full-time exec. Monthly retainer ($2k-5k).

RC supports via collaboration features, access controls, accountability tracking.

Vendor Selection Criteria

- **Industry Experience**: Paving/home services. Case studies/references.
- **Technical Capabilities**: Expertise in relevant channels/platforms.
- **Cultural Alignment**: Understands values, communication style, goals. Feels like extension of team.
- **Size Appropriateness**: Match service level needs (not too big/small).
- **Communication/Reporting**: Frequency, methods, depth, accountability. Transparent updates.
- **Contract Terms**: Cancellation, IP ownership, performance guarantees, pricing. Avoid long-term lock-in initially.

In-House Capability Development

- **Core In-House Competencies**: Strategy, Brand Standards, Customer Data Mgmt, Campaign Coordination, Performance Tracking.
- **Supporting Tech**: CRM (RC), CMS, Design Tools, Analytics, Project Mgmt.
- **Knowledge Transfer**: Documentation repository, vendor training, shadowing, skill-sharing, transition plans.
- **Build/Buy/Partner Decisions**: Build (strategic, high-frequency, proprietary), Buy (specialized, intermittent, evolving), Partner (scale, specialized equipment). Revisit regularly.

RC supports via training, guidance, scalable workflows.

Training and Process Documentation

Consistent, documented processes are essential.

Standard Operating Procedures (SOPs)

- **Lead Handling**: Capture to handoff, response times, templates, qualification criteria, CRM entry, handoff protocols. (RC automates/documents).
- **Campaign Execution**: Planning/approval workflows, channel checklists, tracking setup, QA processes, optimization schedules. (RC provides templates).
- **Performance Reporting**: Metrics definition, frequencies/formats, data sources/calcs, visualizations, distribution lists. (RC automates/documents).
- **Vendor Management**: Selection criteria, briefing templates, review protocols, performance evaluation, payment workflows. (RC tracks deliverables/performance).

Knowledge Management Systems

- **Central Documentation Repository**: Campaign briefs, creative assets, reports, brand guidelines, research, specs, personas, journey maps. (RC integrates).
- **Asset Management**: Version control, naming conventions, permissions, archiving, searchable taxonomies. (RC connects assets to campaigns).
- **Tribal Knowledge Capture**: Debriefings, "lessons learned," marketing FAQ, process videos, onboarding materials. (RC annotation helps).
- **Cross-Training Programs**: Skill matrices, shadowing, peer teaching, backup procedures, knowledge-sharing sessions. (RC training supports).

Workflow Automation

- **Marketing Approvals**: Routing, version tracking, status dashboards, escalations, sign-off documentation. (RC tools support).
- **Customer Communication Sequences**: Welcome, nurture, post-service, anniversary/maintenance, re-engagement. (RC automation manages).
- **Report Generation/Distribution**: Scheduled generation, customized formats, exception alerts, progressive disclosure, automated distribution. (RC handles).
- **Task Management Automation**: Recurring tasks, auto-assignment, dependencies, status tracking, escalations. (RC features support).

Budgeting for Growth

Strategic allocation is essential.

Budget Planning Methodologies

- **Percentage of Revenue**: Sustainable, scalable. (Paving: 5-10% established, 10-15% new/growth). RC tracks vs. targets.
- **Customer Acquisition Cost**: Based on growth goals. Budget = Target Customers * Avg CAC. Connects spend to objectives. RC tracks CAC.
- **Competitive Matching**: Based on competitor spend. Prevents being outmarketed. Good in competitive markets. RC tracks competitive visibility.
- **Zero-Based Budgeting**: Justify all expenses from objectives. Prevents inertia, eliminates waste. Good for restructuring. RC ROI tracking supports.
- **Hybrid Models**: Combine approaches (e.g., % base + project budgets). Flexible. RC supports complex models.

Allocation Across Channels

- **Channel Efficiency**: Allocate based on performance (ROI, CAC). Increase high performers, maintain testing budget. RC attribution supports.
- **Customer Journey Alignment**: Distribute across awareness, consideration, decision, retention based on funnel dynamics. Address bottlenecks. Ensure balance. RC journey mapping helps.
- **Seasonal Adjustment**: Vary spending based on demand. Increase peak, reduce slow. Build awareness before peaks. Focus retention/referrals during slow times. RC seasonal analysis supports.
- **Geographic Prioritization**: Allocate based on profit potential/com petition. Higher spend in high-potential areas. Defensive spend in established territories. Test budgets for expansion. RC geographic analysis helps.
- **Service Line Weighting**: Allocate based on profitability/growth potential. Higher spend on better margin/LTV services. Balance core vs. new offerings. Consider CAC by service. RC service tracking supports.

ROI Projection and Tracking

- **Campaign-Level ROI**: Track costs/leads/customers/revenue per campaign. Compare projected vs. actual. RC automates.
- **Customer Lifetime Value Models**: Connect marketing to long-term value. Include repeat/maintenance/referrals. Retention curves by source. Prevents undervaluing loyal customer channels. RC tracking supports.
- **Attribution Modeling**: Multi-touch analysis. Compare models. Recognize initiating/closing/assisting channels. Avoid last-touch over-optimization. RC models support.
- **Predictive Modeling**: Analyze historical patterns. Project performance based on scenarios. Incorporate seasonal/competitive factors. Create confidence intervals. Improves planning accuracy. RC forecasting supports.
- **Regular Review & Adjustment**: Annual planning, quarterly reviews, monthly checks. Contingency plans. Disciplined refinement. RC reporting supports.

Conclusion & Next Steps

Effective marketing requires integrating strategy, execution, and optimization. Revenue Commander provides the central hub.

Marketing Audit Checklist

Assess current state before implementing RC:

Digital Presence

- Website: Conversion effective? Mobile/fast? Quality photos/testimonials? Clear CTAs? Service/location pages? Contact info? SEO optimized? Lead tracking?
- Search Visibility: Map Pack ranking? Organic ranking? GBP complete/optimized? Directory consistency? Backlink strategy? NAP

consistency?
- Online Reputation: Google rating/quantity? Responding to reviews? Review request process? Reviews featured on site?
- Social Media: Profiles complete/branded? Regular relevant content? Project showcases? Engaging/responding? Frequency/quality competitive?
- Digital Advertising: Running Google Ads? Conversion tracking? Geo targeting? Tested social ads? Ad/landing page alignment?

Traditional Marketing

- Print Collateral: Professional cards/brochures/forms? Consistent branding? Project photos? UVP clear? Current contact info?
- Signage/Vehicles: Using job signs? Vehicles branded professionally? Equipment branded? Current contact info? Graphics quality/maintenance?
- Direct Marketing: Tested direct mail? Using door hangers? Tracking response? Compelling offers? Consistent messaging?
- Broadcast/Outdoor: Evaluated radio? Considered TV/billboard? Sponsoring events/orgs? Broadcast message alignment? Tracking response?
- Referral Marketing: Structured program? Asking systematically? Incentives? Nurturing past customers? Partner relationships?

Strategic Elements

- Target Market: Ideal segments defined? Profitable services known? Geo sweet spot? Decision factors understood? Messages tailored?
- Competitive Positioning: Differentiators identified/meaningful? Communicated clearly? Monitoring competitors? Distinct niche?
- Marketing Systems: CRM/lead mgmt? Tracking ROI? Defined follow-up process? Marketing calendar? Defined budget?
- Team Capabilities: Responsibility assigned? Skills/training adequate?

Quality vendors/agencies? Sales/marketing alignment? Ops communication?

Prioritize based on audit results.

Getting Started with Revenue Commander

Proven process for implementation:

- **Phase 1: Foundation Building (Wks 1-4)**: System config, connect data sources, import history, user accounts, initial training. (Centralized visibility).
- **Phase 2: Channel Integration (Wks 5-8)**: Implement digital tracking, call tracking, offline tracking, campaign tagging. Train team. (Unified performance view).
- **Phase 3: Automation Deployment (Wks 9-12)**: Lead nurturing, reporting automation, task mgmt, campaign templates. Train team. (Efficiency/consistency).
- **Phase 4: Advanced Analytics (Wks 13-16)**: Multi-touch attribution, journey mapping, predictive analytics, custom dashboards. Train advanced users. (Strategic insights).
- **Phase 5: Optimization & Growth (Ongoing)**: Performance reviews, A/B testing, segment refinement, capability expansion, skill development. (Continuous value).

Success Factors: Executive sponsorship, internal champions, realistic timeline, comprehensive training, celebrate early wins.

Staying Updated on Marketing Trends

Maintain current knowledge:

- **Paving Marketers Resources**: Newsletter, webinars, forecast, Facebook group, assessment tool.

- **Professional Development**: Industry conferences (NPE, WoA), marketing certifications, online learning, associations (CMA).
- **Technology Monitoring**: Martech news, Google/social platform updates, emerging channels, measurement capabilities. (RC updates incorporate).
- **Customer Behavior Tracking**: Search/evaluation changes, communication preferences, decision factors, service expectations. (RC analytics help).
- **Competitive Intelligence**: Track messages/positioning, new entrants, pricing shifts, new offerings, geo focus changes. (RC tracking helps).

The journey to marketing excellence is ongoing. Revenue Commander provides the system to implement strategies, deliver leads, maximize value, and drive growth.

V

Part Five

Now we will talk about implementation and resources available to help you.

27

Marketing Calendar and Implementation Plan

Planning your marketing efforts throughout the year is essential for paving companies facing seasonal fluctuations in demand, weather constraints, and customer buying cycles. A well-structured marketing calendar helps you anticipate opportunities, allocate resources efficiently, and maintain consistent lead generation even during traditionally slower periods.

Seasonal Marketing Considerations for Paving Companies

The paving industry is inherently seasonal in most regions, with customer needs and purchasing behavior shifting throughout the year. Understanding these patterns allows you to adjust your marketing emphasis, messaging, and budget allocation accordingly.

Spring (March-May) Spring represents a critical marketing period for paving companies as weather improves and property owners notice winter damage.

Customer Mindset:

- Property owners notice winter damage as snow melts and temperatures rise
- Homeowners begin outdoor improvement planning
- Commercial property managers implement repairs from allocated yearly budgets
- Real estate transactions increase, prompting property improvements

Key Marketing Themes:

- "Repair Winter Damage" messaging resonates strongly
- "Beat the Rush" creates urgency to book before peak season
- "Protect Your Investment" highlights preventative maintenance
- "Increase Curb Appeal" connects with home sellers

Optimal Channel Emphasis:

- Google Ads and Local Services Ads should receive maximum budget as search volume increases
- Direct mail campaigns targeting neighborhoods with visible winter damage
- Door-to-door canvassing becomes effective as weather improves
- Email campaigns to previous customers highlighting seasonal maintenance needs

According to our research, March typically sees a 40-60% increase in paving-related searches compared to winter months. This makes it the ideal time to increase digital marketing budgets to capture this surge in interest. However, many paving contractors make the mistake of waiting until they're already busy in late spring to ramp up marketing efforts, missing this early opportunity to fill their schedules.

Summer (June-August) Summer represents peak season for most paving companies, with ideal weather conditions and maximum customer demand.

Customer Mindset:

- Homeowners actively implementing outdoor projects
- Commercial clients scheduling work during lower traffic periods (weekends/holidays)
- Maximum weather-related urgency to complete projects
- New construction completions requiring final paving

Key Marketing Themes:

- "Limited Availability" creates scarcity and urgency
- "Neighborhood Discounts" incentivize clustered jobs
- "Complete Your Outdoor Transformation" connects paving to broader property improvements
- "Heat-Related Damage Protection" highlights maintenance benefits

Optimal Channel Emphasis:

- Job site signage and truck branding maximize impact during high-visibility working season
- Referral programs capitalize on active projects generating neighbor interest
- Social media featuring current project photos and videos
- Strategic radio or billboard advertising to build brand during peak visibility period

Our data shows that summer response rates to marketing increase by 25-35% compared to spring, but competition also intensifies. The most successful contractors maintain strong marketing through summer rather than reducing it because "they're busy enough." This approach generates excess leads that can be scheduled into fall, creating momentum beyond the peak season.

Fall (September-November) Fall offers a strong secondary peak as property owners prepare for winter and complete postponed projects.

Customer Mindset:

- "Last chance" mentality before winter weather arrives
- Commercial budget utilization before year-end
- Preparation for winter conditions
- Value-focused decisions as holiday expenses approach

Key Marketing Themes:

- "Protect Before Winter" creates seasonal urgency
- "Use It or Lose It" targets commercial budget holders
- "Fall Discount Pricing" appeals to value-conscious customers
- "Weather-Proof Your Property" highlights preventative benefits

Optimal Channel Emphasis:

- Email marketing to unconverted summer leads with special offers
- Direct mail with seasonal preparation messaging
- Commercial-focused LinkedIn campaigns targeting year-end budgets
- Google Ads adjustments to capture "before winter" search terms

According to industry data, September and October represent the second-highest lead generation months for paving companies. Contractors who maintain strong marketing presence during this period often secure enough work to extend their season and strengthen their winter cash flow position.

Winter (December-February) While traditionally slower for actual paving work in many regions, winter offers unique marketing opportunities to build your pipeline for spring.

Customer Mindset:

- Planning mode for spring projects
- Budget allocation for coming year
- Indoor time increases online research
- Year-end financial planning and tax considerations

Key Marketing Themes:

- "Early Bird Pricing" for spring scheduling
- "Winter Planning, Spring Paving" educational content
- "Lock in Current Pricing" creates urgency against potential increases
- "Tax Advantages" for commercial property improvements

Optimal Channel Emphasis:

- Content marketing and SEO to capture increased research activity
- Email nurturing campaigns to maintain relationship with prospects
- Social media highlighting previous year's transformations
- Direct mail focused on planning and early scheduling incentives

Our research indicates that companies who maintain marketing presence during winter experience 35-45% faster spring startup and secure higher-quality projects than those who go dormant. While reducing certain marketing investments is appropriate, maintaining visibility during these planning months positions you as proactive and professional compared to competitors who disappear.

Research Findings on Optimal Timing for Marketing Efforts

Beyond general seasonal patterns, our research has identified specific timing considerations for different marketing channels that significantly impact their effectiveness for paving companies.

Digital Marketing Timing Considerations

Google Ads & Paid Search:

- Highest conversion periods occur Wednesday-Thursday and Sunday evenings
- Cost per click typically increases 15-25% during peak season (June-August)
- Weather-related bid adjustments (increasing bids during periods after rainfall) show 30% higher conversion rates
- Seasonal search term variations require quarterly keyword updates (e.g., "winter damage repair" in spring shifts to "new driveway installation" in summer)

Social Media:

- Facebook engagement for home improvement content peaks on Thursday evenings and Sunday afternoons
- Project showcase posts perform 40% better when posted within 3 days of completion
- Before/after content generates 3.2x more engagement than other post types
- Video content showing actual paving work generates 2.8x more shares than static images

Email Marketing:

- Tuesday and Wednesday mornings show highest open rates (24-28%) for residential customers
- Thursday late morning generates best response for commercial property managers
- Maintenance reminder emails sent 12-14 months after project completion convert at 22% for residential clients
- Seasonal preparation emails perform best 4-6 weeks before typical weather changes

Traditional Marketing Timing Considerations

Direct Mail:

- Spring campaigns perform best when delivered 2-3 weeks prior to consistently warm weather
- Neighborhood-targeted mailings generate 40% higher response within 2 weeks of visible paving work in the area
- Multiple-touch campaigns (2-3 mailers) spaced 14 days apart show 34% higher cumulative response than single mailings
- Monday and Tuesday mail delivery produces highest response rates for both residential and commercial targets

Door-to-Door Canvassing:

- Response rates double when conducted while crews are working in the neighborhood
- Saturday morning (9am-noon) generates highest contact rates for residential properties
- Post-work canvassing (4-7pm) shows 25% higher conversion than mid-day efforts
- Temperature significantly impacts success—optimal range is 65-80°F with minimal rain probability

Radio Advertising:

- Morning drive (6-9am) delivers best response for commercial messaging
- Evening drive (4-7pm) performs better for residential-focused ads
- Weather-triggered ads (running during/after rain events) show 45% higher recall
- Response increases when ads run 5+ times weekly versus intermittent scheduling

Billboard & Outdoor:

- Locations within 3 miles of active projects show 37% higher attribution
- Maximum effectiveness requires 8-12 weeks minimum presence in one location
- Digital billboards updating content based on time of day (work commute vs. weekend) increase response by 28%
- Messages that change seasonally (quarterly) maintain attention better than static content

12-Month Marketing Calendar Template

Based on our research and experience with hundreds of paving companies, we've developed this strategic marketing calendar template that you can adapt to your specific geographic region, service mix, and business goals.

January

Primary Focus: Planning and early booking for spring projects

- **Key Activities:**
- Annual marketing plan development and budget allocation

- Website updates with new project photos and current year dates
- Email campaign to previous customers offering early-bird spring booking discounts
- Content creation focusing on "Winter Damage Warning Signs" and "Planning Your Spring Paving Project"
- Begin SEO improvements to rank for spring search terms
- Commercial prospect outreach for yearly maintenance contracts
- **Budget Allocation:**
- Digital (SEO, content, email): 70-80%
- Traditional (direct mail planning, early-bird offers): 20-30%

February

Primary Focus: Building spring project pipeline and educational content

- **Key Activities:**
- Launch early-bird direct mail campaign for spring projects
- Develop spring radio or local TV ad concepts (if applicable to your market)
- Begin remarketing campaigns targeting previous website visitors
- Create and schedule social media content for next 90 days
- Update Google Business Profile with seasonal offers and winter damage content
- Prepare door hangers and job site signage for upcoming season
- **Budget Allocation:**
- Digital (SEO, remarketing, paid search): 60-70%
- Traditional (direct mail, production of materials): 30-40%

March

Primary Focus: Accelerating lead generation as weather improves

- **Key Activities:**

- Increase Google Ads budget by 30-50% targeting spring-specific search terms
- Launch first phase of spring direct mail campaign to targeted neighborhoods
- Begin radio advertising if part of your media mix
- Implement email campaigns to all previous customers and leads from prior year
- Attend local home shows or community events if available
- Begin door-to-door canvassing in prime neighborhoods as weather permits
- **Budget Allocation:**
- Digital (paid search, social, email): 50-60%
- Traditional (direct mail, radio, events): 40-50%

April

Primary Focus: Maximum lead generation to fill schedule

- **Key Activities:**
- Peak Google Ads and Local Services Ads investment
- Second phase of direct mail with urgency messaging
- Aggressive job site signage at all projects
- Vehicle branding inspection and refreshing if needed
- Before/after content creation from early season projects
- Commercial property manager outreach campaign
- Social media advertising with spring project showcases
- **Budget Allocation:**
- Digital (paid search, social): 50-60%
- Traditional (direct mail, signage, outreach): 40-50%

May

Primary Focus: Maintaining momentum and referral generation

- **Key Activities:**
- Continue aggressive digital advertising
- Begin neighborhood-cluster marketing around current projects
- Implement customer referral program for active projects
- Local news outreach for potential feature stories
- Review and optimize ad performance based on early season results
- Begin collecting testimonials and reviews from completed projects
- **Budget Allocation:**
- Digital (paid search, social): 40-50%
- Traditional (neighborhood marketing, referral program): 50-60%

June

Primary Focus: Neighborhood domination and schedule extension

- **Key Activities:**
- Door-to-door canvassing in active project neighborhoods
- Targeted social media ads to neighborhoods with current projects
- Implement weather-triggered ad adjustments during rainy periods
- Launch "Neighbor Discount" program to cluster jobs efficiently
- Begin collecting video testimonials for future marketing
- Adjust messaging to focus on aesthetic benefits and property value
- **Budget Allocation:**
- Digital (paid search, social): 40-50%
- Traditional (neighborhood marketing, door-to-door): 50-60%

July

Primary Focus: Commercial projects and scheduling optimization

- **Key Activities:**
- Increased focus on commercial property marketing
- LinkedIn campaigns targeting facility and property managers

- Direct outreach to property management companies
- Implement weekend scheduling options for residential projects
- Adjust Google Ads to emphasize specific services with available capacity
- Social media content highlighting commercial project capabilities
- **Budget Allocation:**
- Digital (paid search, LinkedIn, social): 50-60%
- Traditional (direct outreach, signage): 40-50%

August

Primary Focus: Fall schedule filling and commercial project pipeline

- **Key Activities:**
- Begin fall marketing campaign preparation
- Email campaign to unconverted spring leads with new offers
- Commercial project case study development
- School and church property outreach before academic year
- Review YTD marketing performance and adjust fall strategy
- Begin "end of summer" limited availability messaging
- **Budget Allocation:**
- Digital (email, paid search, case studies): 50-60%
- Traditional (commercial outreach, direct mail): 40-50%

September

Primary Focus: Fall project booking and winter preparation messaging

- **Key Activities:**
- Launch fall direct mail campaign with winter preparation messaging
- Adjust Google Ads for fall-specific keywords and messaging
- Implement "before winter" email campaign to all prospects
- Commercial "use it or lose it" budget campaign for year-end planning

- Begin collecting and organizing content for winter marketing
- Social media featuring fall project transformations
- **Budget Allocation:**
- Digital (paid search, email): 40-50%
- Traditional (direct mail, commercial outreach): 50-60%

October

Primary Focus: Creating urgency before winter and commercial year-end projects

- **Key Activities:**
- Final push direct mail with "last chance before winter" messaging
- Increased Google Ads with weather-related urgency
- Commercial property "tax advantage" campaign for year-end budgets
- Begin early-bird discount development for next spring
- Content creation focusing on winter preparation and damage prevention
- Website updates highlighting winter maintenance information
- **Budget Allocation:**
- Digital (paid search, commercial email campaigns): 40-50%
- Traditional (direct mail, commercial outreach): 50-60%

November

Primary Focus: Commercial projects and early spring booking

- **Key Activities:**
- Launch early spring booking campaign with incentives
- Commercial project completion push before winter
- Begin winter content marketing strategy implementation
- Reduce paid search budget as searches decline
- Thanksgiving email campaign to thank customers

- Planning and budgeting for next year's marketing
- **Budget Allocation:**
- Digital (content, email, reduced paid search): 60-70%
- Traditional (direct mail for early booking): 30-40%

December

Primary Focus: Planning, relationship maintenance, and early spring booking

- **Key Activities:**
- Year-end review of marketing performance
- Holiday greeting cards/emails to customers and prospects
- Commercial client planning meetings for next year's projects
- Winter content marketing execution
- Spring marketing material development
- Database cleaning and organization for next year
- **Budget Allocation:**
- Digital (content, email, planning): 70-80%
- Traditional (greeting cards, planning materials): 20-30%

Implementation Checklists

Successful marketing implementation requires systematic processes and clear accountability. Use these checklists to ensure thorough execution of your marketing plan.

Quarterly Planning Checklist Complete this process at the beginning of each quarter to maintain strategic focus:

- Review previous quarter performance metrics for all marketing channels
- Analyze cost per lead and conversion rates by channel

- Update customer acquisition cost and lifetime value calculations
- Adjust budget allocations based on performance data
- Review upcoming seasonal opportunities and challenges
- Update key messaging and offers for the coming quarter
- Refresh creative materials (images, ads, emails) with recent projects
- Establish specific KPIs and targets for each marketing channel
- Assign responsibilities and deadlines for all marketing activities
- Schedule bi-weekly marketing review meetings for the quarter
- Share quarterly focus and goals with all customer-facing team members

Monthly Implementation Checklist Complete this process at the beginning of each month to ensure consistent execution:

- Review previous month's marketing metrics and lead generation
- Update tracking documents with latest performance data
- Make budget adjustments based on previous month results
- Refresh all Google Ads with seasonal messaging and offers
- Schedule social media content and email campaigns
- Plan direct mail drops and door-to-door canvassing routes
- Update website content with seasonal information
- Check Google Business Profile for new reviews and questions
- Review competitive activity and adjust strategy if needed
- Ensure all materials and supplies are available for planned activities
- Conduct team training on monthly focus and messaging

Weekly Action Checklist Complete this process each week to maintain marketing momentum:

- Review lead generation numbers across all channels
- Check Google Ads performance and make bid adjustments
- Update job site signage plan based on current projects
- Process and post new project photos to website and social media

- Request reviews from recently completed projects
- Respond to all social media comments and messages
- Check direct mail delivery status and response tracking
- Update canvassing maps based on new and completed projects
- Review upcoming weather forecast for marketing timing adjustments
- Hold brief marketing touchpoint meeting with key staff
- Update CRM with new leads and follow-up requirements

Channel Launch Checklist Complete this process when implementing a new marketing channel:

- Define specific goals and success metrics for the channel
- Establish baseline tracking mechanisms before launch
- Create channel-specific messaging and creative materials
- Set up proper attribution tracking in Revenue Commander
- Determine testing period length and evaluation criteria
- Allocate initial test budget with clear spending parameters
- Identify responsible team member for managing the channel
- Create reporting template for performance tracking
- Schedule specific review dates to evaluate performance
- Develop contingency plan if performance targets aren't met
- Document process for ongoing management if successful

Resource Allocation Guidance

Determining how to allocate limited marketing resources is one of the most challenging aspects of implementation. This framework will help you make strategic decisions based on your company's specific situation.

Budget Allocation by Growth Stage Your company's growth stage significantly impacts optimal marketing resource allocation:

Startup Phase (Under 2 years in business or entering new market)

- Digital foundation: 50-60% (website, SEO, Google Business Profile)
- Lead generation: 30-40% (Google Ads, direct mail to targeted areas)
- Brand building: 10-20% (vehicle branding, yard signs, logo development)

Growth Phase (Established with 2-5 years in market, actively expanding)

- Digital foundation: 30-40% (ongoing SEO, content development, reputation management)
- Lead generation: 40-50% (Google Ads, direct mail, canvassing, email marketing)
- Brand building: 20-30% (radio, community involvement, broader awareness)

Market Leadership Phase (Well-established 5+ years, focusing on dominance)

- Digital foundation: 20-30% (maintaining SEO leadership, advanced content)
- Lead generation: 30-40% (highly targeted campaigns, referral programs)
- Brand building: 30-50% (radio, TV, billboards, community leadership)

Budget Allocation by Service Mix Your service focus also impacts optimal resource allocation:

Primarily Residential

- Google Ads/Local Services Ads: 25-35%
- SEO and content marketing: 15-25%
- Direct mail and local print: 15-20%
- Social media marketing: 10-15%

- Job site signage and vehicle branding: 10-15%
- Radio advertising (if applicable): 0-15%
- Email marketing: 5-10%

Primarily Commercial

- Google Ads: 20-30%
- LinkedIn and targeted B2B marketing: 15-20%
- SEO and content marketing: 15-20%
- Direct outreach and relationship building: 15-20%
- Case study development: 5-10%
- Industry association involvement: 5-10%
- Email marketing: 5-10%

Balanced Mix

- Google Ads/Local Services Ads: 20-30%
- SEO and content marketing: 15-20%
- Direct mail and canvassing: 10-15%
- Social media marketing: 5-10%
- LinkedIn and B2B outreach: 5-10%
- Job site signage and vehicle branding: 10-15%
- Radio or broader awareness: 5-15%
- Email marketing: 5-10%

Budget Allocation by Seasonality In most regions, marketing investment should shift seasonally:

- **Spring (Mar-May)**: Increase budget (120-140% baseline). Emphasize Ads, Direct Mail, Door-to-Door.
- **Summer (Jun-Aug)**: Maintain peak budget (110-130% baseline). Shift toward Job Site Marketing, Referrals. Balance leads/brand.
- **Fall (Sep-Oct)**: Maintain strong budget (100-120% baseline). Reem-

phasize Ads, Direct Mail. Focus urgency/winter prep.
- **Winter (Nov-Feb)**: Reduce budget (60-80% baseline). Shift toward Content Marketing, Relationships, Early Booking.

Adjust based on your specific climate and demand patterns.

Prioritization Framework

Determine which activities to prioritize with limited resources.

The Impact-Effort Matrix Evaluate activities based on:

- **Impact:** Potential ROI, lead generation, strategic importance.
- **Effort:** Time, cost, complexity required.

This creates four categories:

Quick Wins (High Impact, Low Effort)

- Google Business Profile optimization
- Job site signage implementation
- Email campaigns to existing customers
- Review generation system
- Social media project showcases

Major Projects (High Impact, High Effort)

- Website redesign or significant upgrades
- Comprehensive SEO campaign
- Sophisticated Google Ads management
- Integrated direct mail campaign
- Vehicle fleet branding
- Radio advertising campaign

Fill-Ins (Low Impact, Low Effort)

- Social media maintenance posting
- Basic email newsletters
- Industry association listings
- Simple community sponsorships
- Holiday greeting cards

Thankless Tasks (Low Impact, High Effort)

- Broad untargeted advertising
- Complex social media contests
- High-effort activities with poor attribution
- Overly complex tracking systems

Implementation Priority Sequence The most effective sequence typically follows:

- **Fix Critical Gaps**: Address foundation issues (GBP, basic website, signage, lead tracking).
- **Optimize Existing Channels**: Improve current activities (website conversion, Ads targeting, mail response, creative, lead nurturing).
- **Add High-Impact New Channels**: Expand to complementary channels (LSA, strategic direct mail, canvassing, email nurturing).
- **Build Long-Term Assets**: Invest in appreciating assets (SEO, content, case studies, relationships, brand).
- **Test and Experiment**: Allocate resources to testing new approaches (platforms, geo targets, messaging, creative).

This framework ensures a solid foundation while enabling continuous improvement and expansion.

Seasonal Implementation Case Study: Northeast Paving

To illustrate these principles, let's examine how Northeast Paving, a mid-sized contractor in the northeastern United States, implements their seasonal marketing plan.

Company Profile

- 8 years in business
- $2.2 million annual revenue
- 60% residential, 40% commercial
- Strong seasonal fluctuations due to harsh winters
- $180,000 annual marketing budget (8.2% of revenue)

Spring Implementation (March-May)

Strategic Focus: Capturing winter damage repair opportunities and filling summer schedule

- **Key Activities Implemented:**
- Digital Surge: Increased Google Ads budget by 50% in March, focusing on "winter damage repair" and "driveway cracks" keywords. Added specific landing pages for these services.
- Direct Mail Campaign: Sent 10,000 oversized postcards to targeted neighborhoods showing winter damage examples and offering early scheduling incentives. Staggered in three waves (March 15, April 1, April 15).
- Weather-Triggered Ads: Implemented automated system increasing bids by 30% during and immediately after rainfall when damage visibility increases.
- Commercial Outreach: Personal calls to previous commercial clients discussing winter damage assessment and maintenance planning.
- **Resource Allocation:**

- Google Ads: $12,000 monthly (40% increase from winter)
- Direct Mail: $12,500 total for spring campaign
- Commercial outreach: 15 hours weekly of sales time
- Content development: $2,500 for winter damage assessment guides
- **Results:**
- 146 direct response leads from mail campaign (1.46% response rate)
- 112 Google Ads leads at $89 average cost per lead
- 28 commercial project bookings for summer execution
- Schedule filled through August by end of May
- 22% increase in average project size vs. previous year

Summer Implementation (June-August)

Strategic Focus: Maximizing operational efficiency and leveraging active projects for marketing

- **Key Activities Implemented:**
- Neighborhood Domination: Implemented systematic door-to-door canvassing within 2-block radius of active projects, offering "neighborhood discounts" for adjacent properties.
- Referral Program: Launched structured referral incentive ($200 gift card for referring customers) with branded leave-behind cards at all project completions.
- Job Site Marketing: Upgraded to larger 4'x4' job site signs with QR codes linking to project galleries and before/after photos.
- Social Content Creation: Established process for crews to capture standardized before/during/after photos of all projects for social media content.
- **Resource Allocation:**
- Google Ads: $9,000 monthly (reduced slightly as organic lead flow increased)
- Door-to-door canvassing: 25 hours weekly of dedicated staff time

- Referral program incentives: $4,200 budget for summer
- Enhanced job site signage: $3,800 one-time investment
- **Results:**
- 37 new projects from neighborhood canvassing
- 22 referral program leads (16 converted to jobs)
- Reduced travel time between jobs by 28% through geographic clustering
- Increased profit margins by 4.2% due to operational efficiencies
- Generated 64 Google reviews through systematic request process

Fall Implementation (September-November)

Strategic Focus: Creating urgency before winter while building spring pipeline

- **Key Activities Implemented:**
- "Before Winter" Campaign: Launched integrated campaign across Google Ads, direct mail, and email emphasizing limited time before weather prevents paving work.
- Commercial Budget Push: Created targeted campaign for commercial property managers around "use it or lose it" budget considerations and tax advantages of completing work before year-end.
- Spring Booking Incentives: Began promoting early-bird pricing and priority scheduling for spring projects booked before December 31.
- Content Pivot: Shifted content focus toward winter preparation topics and preventative maintenance information.
- **Resource Allocation:**
- Google Ads: $10,000 monthly with weather-trigger adjustments
- Direct mail: $8,500 for "Before Winter" campaign
- Commercial outreach: Increased to 25 hours weekly
- Email marketing: $1,500 for campaign development
- **Results:**

- Extended paving season two weeks longer than previous year
- Secured 14 commercial projects for execution before winter
- Pre-booked 42 residential projects for early spring
- Collected 50% deposits on spring bookings, improving winter cash flow
- Generated 18 maintenance contracts for spring services

Winter Implementation (December-February)

Strategic Focus: Planning, relationship maintenance, and early spring booking

- **Key Activities Implemented:**
- Content Marketing: Increased production of educational content about paving planning, material options, and design considerations during reduced operational period.
- Customer Appreciation: Sent holiday cards and small branded gifts to previous customers with spring maintenance reminders.
- Spring Campaign Development: Created complete spring campaign materials, sales tools, and scheduling systems during slower operational period.
- Team Training: Conducted comprehensive sales and customer service training during reduced work period.
- **Resource Allocation:**
- Google Ads: Reduced to $5,000 monthly maintenance level
- Content creation: Increased to $3,500 monthly
- CRM and database management: 20 hours weekly
- Marketing planning and development: 15 hours weekly
- **Results:**
- Maintained steady lead flow despite seasonal reduction
- Pre-booked 30% of spring capacity before March
- Improved team capabilities through systematic training

- Developed 24 new content pieces for year-round use
- Refined systems for more efficient spring launch

This case study shows how a systematic, seasonally-adjusted approach delivers consistent results while adapting to natural business cycles. Northeast Paving maintained steady growth despite significant seasonal constraints by thoughtfully allocating resources and adjusting strategies throughout the year.

Conclusion

Effective marketing implementation requires understanding seasonal patterns, systematically allocating resources, and maintaining discipline through structured planning processes. The marketing calendar and implementation frameworks provided serve as your roadmap for transforming marketing strategy into consistent, profitable results.

Remember these key principles:

- **Respect Seasonality**: Align activities/investments with demand cycles/weather.
- **Maintain Consistency**: Keep branding, messaging, experience consistent across touchpoints.
- **Measure Meticulously**: Use Revenue Commander to track, analyze, and refine.
- **Build Systems**: Develop repeatable processes and checklists.
- **Think Holistically**: View channels as integrated, not isolated.

By following this structured approach, you transform marketing into a systematic business development process delivering predictable results regardless of seasonal fluctuations or market conditions.

In the next chapter, we'll examine real-world case studies of paving companies that have successfully implemented these principles.

28

Case Studies and Success Stories

There's no more powerful way to understand effective marketing strategies than by examining real-world examples of companies that have successfully implemented them. In this chapter, we'll explore detailed case studies of paving contractors who have transformed their businesses through strategic marketing investments. Each case study provides concrete examples of challenges, solutions, implementation details, and measurable results. By studying these success stories, you'll gain practical insights that can be applied to your own business, regardless of size, market, or current marketing sophistication.

Note that the company names and details are anonymized.

Residential Paving Company Growth Examples

Case Study 1: Precision Paving – From Startup to Market Leader

- **Company Profile:** Suburban Atlanta, GA; New business (owner/operator + 3 crew); Target: Residential driveways, small commercial.
- **Initial Challenges:** No customer base, limited budget, established competitors. Marketing: Basic signs, simple Wix site, sporadic social posts (~6 leads/mo). Needed systematic lead gen.

Strategic Approach (Phased):

- **Phase 1 (Months 1-3): Foundation Building.** Professional WordPress site ($4.8k, service/project pages, mobile optimized); GBP optimization (full profile, photos); Basic marketing materials (logo, cards, signs, uniforms, truck magnets).
- **Phase 2 (Months 4-6): Lead Generation Engine.** Google Ads ($1.5k/mo, geo-targeted, service ad groups, landing pages, call tracking); Neighborhood Targeting (premium signs, door hangers w/ discount/tracking); Review Generation (systematic requests, goal 8+/mo, website showcase).
- **Phase 3 (Months 7-12): Expansion & Optimization.** SEO Dev (local SEO, content, backlinks, GBP posts); Direct Mail Test (targeted neighborhoods, oversized B/A postcards, offer); Social Media Showcase (systematic B/A posts, boosted posts, customer spotlights).
- **Phase 4 (Year 2): Scaling & Systems.** Marketing Automation (nurturing, review requests, maintenance reminders); Fleet Branding ($3.2k truck graphics); Referral Program ($100 incentive, cards, tracking).

Results (24 Months):

Leads 6/mo -> 65+/mo
Revenue +580% ($240k -> $1.63M)
Team 4 -> 15
Google Reviews 87 (4.8*)
Repeat Business 28% (Yr 2)
Marketing ROI 4.6:1
CPL $78 -> $38

- **Key Success Factors:** Systematic Phased Approach, Measurement/A djustment, Geographical Focus (15-mile radius), Quality Emphasis, Reputation Management.
- **Owner Quote:** *"Marketing with a system... starting with a solid foundation and building methodically."*

Case Study 2: Evergreen Asphalt – Revitalizing a Stagnant Business

- **Company Profile:** Portland, OR metro; 12-year-old business, flat growth (5 yrs); Target: Primarily residential; Existing base aging.
- **Initial Challenges:** Declining referrals (-35% over 3 yrs), outdated marketing (old 1-page site, no social), revenue plateau ($850k/yr). Needed modernization while keeping reputation.

Strategic Approach:

- **Phase 1 (Months 1-4): Digital Transformation.** Digital Audit; Claim/Optimize GBP; Respond to old reviews; Update directories; Website Redevelopment ($7.5k, service pages, portfolio, lead tracking, content); Customer Database Activation (digitize records, CRM, segmentation, re-engagement campaign).
- **Phase 2 (Months 5-8): Local Visibility.** Local SEO (geo-keywords, citations, landing pages, regional content); Google Ads ($2.2k/mo, geo-campaigns, dayparting, extensions); Community Integration (Chamber membership, event sponsorship, partner relationships).
- **Phase 3 (Months 9-12): Differentiation.** Eco-Friendly Positioning ("Sustainable Asphalt Solutions", content, certifications); Visual Brand Enhancement (logo refresh, truck wraps ($5.6k), signs, uniforms); Customer Experience Redesign (digital quotes, visualization tools, care packages, follow-up).
- **Phase 4 (Year 2): Scaling.** Review Generation System (automated requests, incentives); Content Marketing Program (blog, guides, videos, newsletter); Targeted Expansion Campaign (3 underserved neighborhoods, direct mail, landing pages, neighbor discount).

Results (24 Months):

Revenue +127% ($850k -> $1.93M)

Leads 12-15/mo -> 70+/mo

Reviews 32 -> 186 (4.9*)
Website Visitors +820%
Conversion Rate 2.1% -> 7.8%
CAC $312 -> $178
Repeat/Referral 47% -> 62%

- **Key Success Factors:** Respecting Heritage + Evolving, Eco-Friendly Differentiation, Database Activation, Community Integration, Customer Experience Focus.
- **Owner Quote:** *"Marketing stuck in the 1990s... preserving quality while modernizing communication... making reputation visible to new customers."*

Commercial Contractor Marketing Cases

Case Study 3: Superior Paving Solutions – Transitioning from Residential to Commercial

- **Company Profile:** Phoenix, AZ metro; Established residential co. seeking commercial growth; Target: Commercial properties, HOAs.
- **Initial Challenges:** Limited commercial portfolio, low brand recognition (property mgrs), existing marketing homeowner-focused, strong competition. Needed repositioning.

Strategic Approach:

- **Phase 1 (Months 1-3): Market Research & Foundation.** Commercial Market Analysis (interviews, competitor analysis, segmentation); Portfolio Dev Strategy (smaller initial projects, special pricing, professional photos); Commercial Brand Positioning (messaging: durability/minimal disruption, "Commercial Division", UVP).
- **Phase 2 (Months 4-6): Commercial Platform Dev.** Website Segmentation (commercial section, specialized content, landing pages,

forms); Commercial Sales Tools (presentation pkg, proposal templates, educational content, ROI calculator); Lead Gen Infrastructure (property mgmt database, commercial CRM tracking, nurture campaigns).

- **Phase 3 (Months 7-12): Multi-Channel Commercial Outreach.** LinkedIn Campaign ($1.8k/mo sponsored content, target property/facility mgrs); Direct Mail Sequence (high-end brochure, 3-touch to top 200 targets); Industry Association Integration (BOMA, CAI membership, event sponsorship).
- **Phase 4 (Year 2): Commercial Growth Acceleration.** Commercial Google Ads (separate campaign, specialized ad groups); Case Study Marketing (detailed studies by property type, video testimonials); Referral Network Dev (property mgr incentives, GC relationships, complementary svcs).

Results (24 Months):

Commercial Revenue 12% -> 68% of total
Avg Project Size $8.4k -> $37.6k
Added 42 property mgmt clients
Secured 3 multi-year maint. contracts
15-20 qual. commercial leads/mo
Overall Revenue $1.2M -> $3.8M
Profit Margin 18% -> 26%.

- **Key Success Factors:** Segment-Specific Approach, Educational Positioning (Consultative Expert), Relationship Marketing (Associations), Portfolio Building Strategy (Initial Discounts), Balanced Transition (Maintained Residential).
- **CEO Quote:** *"Commercial clients buy differently... mitigate risk, max long-term value... shift messaging from 'beautiful driveways' to 'pavement asset management'."*

Case Study 4: Capital Paving – Dominating the Municipal Market

- **Company Profile:** Midwest metro (pop 1.2M); Mid-sized commercial, minimal gov't work; Target: Municipal contracts, schools, gov't facilities.
- **Initial Challenges:** Complex bids, entrenched competitors, certification requirements, no relationships. Needed systematic entry strategy.

Strategic Approach (3-Year Plan):

- **Phase 1 (Months 1-6): Qualification Dev.** Certification Acquisition (MBE, bonding, safety); Team Enhancement (hire municipal estimator, consultant, train PMs); Procedural Dev (bid tracking, compliant proposals, documentation systems).
- **Phase 2 (Months 7-18): Market Entry.** Relationship Dev (identify contacts, attend council mtgs, join gov't contractor assns); Strategic Subcontracting (partner w/ primes, build portfolio/references); Small Contract Focus (simplified bids, emergency repair, maint. contracts, ADA).
- **Phase 3 (Months 19-36): Prime Contractor Positioning.** Capabilities Marketing (gov't brochure, past performance docs, case studies, website section); Bid Strategy Dev (analyze winning bids, differentiate, value-adds, bid/no-bid process); Strategic Alliances (complementary svcs, suppliers, subs, JVs).
- **Phase 4 (Year 3+): Market Leadership.** Specialized Expertise Dev (ADA, environmental, equipment); Proactive Consulting (workshops, assessments, planning tools); Performance Optimization (project tracking, satisfaction measurement, dashboard).

Results (36 Months):

Municipal Revenue 5% -> 47%

Avg Contract Value $67k -> $310k

Win Rate (Municipal) 8% -> 36%
Total Revenue $3.2M -> $9.7M
17 municipal entity relationships
5 multi-year maint. contracts
Maintained 23% gross margin.

- **Key Success Factors:** Patience/Persistence (3-yr plan), Certification Investment (Foundation), Strategic Stepping Stones (Sub -> Small Prime -> Large Prime), Educational Approach (Resource, not just bidder), Specialization Strategy (ADA Compliance).
- **CEO Quote:** *"Hardest—and best—decision... municipal work isn't just lowest bid—it's lowest risk. Marketing had to focus on reliability, documentation, flawless execution."*

Revenue Commander Implementation Stories

Case Study 5: Asphalt Kings – Transforming Data into Decisions

- **Company Profile:** Milwaukee, WI metro; Established family biz, disjointed marketing; Target: Mixed residential/commercial.
- **Initial Challenges:** Disconnected channels, no tracking/ROI visibility, inconsistent lead nurturing, high lost lead rate (~40%), couldn't scale sales. Needed unified system & data.

Strategic Approach (Revenue Commander Implementation):

- **Phase 1 (Months 1-2): Tracking Implementation.** Unified Tracking (unique numbers, form tracking, UTMs, GA integration, RC pixel); Channel Integration (Ads accounts, offline tracking codes, QR codes); Team Training (attribution importance, "how heard" scripts, lead capture protocols).
- **Phase 2 (Months 3-4): Lead Mgmt Optimization.** Lead Response System (auto-notify, response time tracking, scripts, auto-response);

Follow-up Sequence Dev (cadence by source/quality, email drips, text options, reminders); Lead Nurturing System (segmentation, long-term content, reactivation, relationship comms).

- **Phase 3 (Months 5-6): Performance Analysis.** Reporting Dashboards (exec, channel, cost, conversion); ROI Analysis Framework (connect sales to source, profitability by channel, LTV calcs); Budget Optimization System (data-driven allocation, thresholds, testing protocols, forecasting).
- **Phase 4 (Months 7-12): Continuous Improvement.** Lead Quality Scoring (auto-scoring, differentiated follow-up); Customer Journey Mapping (path analysis, bottleneck ID, touchpoint optimization); Predictive Analytics (seasonal/lead flow forecasts, weather triggers).

Results (12 Months):

ROI Unknown -> 310%
CPL $115 -> $68
Conversion Rate 22% -> 34%
Response Time 26 hrs -> 38 mins
Budget Reallocated (35% more leads, same spend)
Revenue +54% ($2.4M -> $3.7M)
Lost Leads <8%
LTV +29% ($4.8k -> $6.2k).

- **Key Success Factors:** Data-Driven Decisions, Unified Customer View, Process Standardization, Continuous Optimization, Team Accountability.
- **Owner Quotes:** *"Flying blind... couldn't connect dollars to sales... now see exactly what's profitable." // "Discovered 'cheapest' leads were most expensive factoring conversions/value." // "Losing nearly half our leads... system ensures prompt, appropriate follow-up."*

Case Study 6: Metro Pavement – Scaling Through Systems

- **Company Profile:** Tampa Bay, FL; Fast-growing ($4.2M), hit ops ceiling; Target: Commercial (40% maint contracts).
- **Initial Challenges:** Growth limits, inconsistent marketing results, reactive mgmt, disconnected systems, data silos, feast/famine cycles. Needed systems for predictable scaling.

Strategic Approach (Revenue Commander as Operating System):

- **Phase 1 (Months 1-3): System Unification.** Tech Integration (CRM, Accounting, Calendar, Marketing Channels -> RC); Lead Flow Restructuring (scoring, routing, capacity-aware distribution, auto-qualification); Team Reorganization (specialized roles, KPIs, SLAs, training).
- **Phase 2 (Months 4-6): Marketing Systematization.** Channel Performance Audit; Granular Tracking; Attribution Modeling; ROI Framework; Benchmarking; Customer Journey Mapping; Touchpoint Optimization; Seasonal Strategy Dev.
- **Phase 3 (Months 7-9): Growth Capacity Building.** Lead Nurturing Automation; Resource Forecasting (Lead flow, crew capacity, materials); Scheduling Optimization; Performance Optimization Loop (Weekly reviews, hypothesis testing, A/B tests, incremental targets).
- **Phase 4 (Months 10-12): Strategic Acceleration.** Customer Value Maximization (Cross/upsell auto, maint contract conversion, referral auto); Geographic Expansion System (Territory testing, market entry playbook, benchmarks); Scalable Mgmt Dashboard (Exec KPIs, forecasting, efficiency metrics, team viz).

Results (12 Months):

Revenue +86% ($4.2M -> $7.8M)
Profit Margin 19% -> 24%
CAC -32%
Lead Handling Capacity +190% (120 -> 350+/mo)
Conversion Rate 18% -> 29%

LTV +47%
Maint Contracts 42 -> 118
Team 28 -> 47.

- **Key Success Factors:** Systems-First Approach, Capacity-Aware Marketing, Predictive Planning, Specialized Roles, Metrics-Driven Management.
- **CEO Quote:** *"Hit a ceiling where more money created chaos... RC provided complete operating system... shifted from reactive to strategic, systems-based... predictability and control over growth."*

Before/After Marketing Metrics with Real Data

Specific metric improvements illustrate the tangible impact:

Website Performance Transformation (Northern Asphalt Solutions, Minneapolis) - *12-month measurement*

- Visitors: +344%
- Organic Traffic: +499%
- Bounce Rate: -49.7%
- Session Duration: +225%
- Conversion Rate: +467% (1.2% -> 6.8%)
- Load Speed: -71%
- Avg Search Position: #6.8 -> #2.3

Google Ads Performance Transformation (Premier Paving, Sacramento) - *90-day comparison, Budget $3.5k/mo*

- Clicks: +66%
- CPC: -40% ($8.49 -> $5.12)
- Conversions: +241% (17 -> 58)
- CPL: -71% ($206 -> $60)

- Conversion Rate: +107% (4.1% -> 8.5%)
- Quality Score: 4.8 -> 8.1

Social Media Marketing Transformation (Quality Asphalt, Austin) - 6-*month comparison, Budget $1.2k/mo paid social*

- Followers: +965%
- Engagement Rate: +488%
- Monthly Reach: +1,497%
- Website Clicks: +1,405%
- Leads: +800% (3/mo -> 27/mo)
- CPL: -89% ($400 -> $44)

Direct Mail Campaign Transformation (Driveway Experts, Charlotte) - *Spring campaign YoY, 10k mailpieces*

- Response Rate: +300% (0.7% -> 2.8%)
- Leads: +300% (70 -> 280)
- CPL: -69% ($83 -> $26)
- Conversion Rate: +59% (22% -> 35%)
- New Customers: +553% (15 -> 98)
- CAC: -81% ($387 -> $73)

Email Marketing Performance Transformation (Elite Paving & Sealcoating, Denver) - 6-*month comparison, Database 2.7k*

- Open Rate: +166% (12.3% -> 32.7%)
- CTR: +443% (1.4% -> 7.6%)
- Leads Generated: +245% (11/mo -> 38/mo)
- List Growth: Negative -> +4.2%/mo
- Revenue Attributed: +408% ($8.4k/mo -> $42.7k/mo)

Review Generation Transformation (Superior Asphalt, Nashville) - *12-month comparison*

- Google Reviews: 23 -> 148
- Avg Rating: 4.2* -> 4.8*
- Acquisition Rate: +635% (1.7/mo -> 12.5/mo)
- Negative Review %: 17.4% -> 3.4%
- Response Rate: 26% -> 100%
- Impact: Consistent top 3 map pack, +34% website conversion

Lead Handling Transformation (Cornerstone Paving, Tampa) - *90-day comparison*

- Response Time: 26.4 hrs -> 14 mins
- Lost Leads: 31% -> 3%
- Contact Attempts: 1.7 -> 4.2
- Qualification Rate: 47% -> 86%
- Quote Rate (Qual Leads): 62% -> 93%
- Conversion Rate (Quote -> Job): 24% -> 42%

These examples show the potential across different marketing areas when systematic improvements are made.

Key Lessons from Case Studies and Metrics

1. **Systematic Approach Outperforms Ad Hoc**: Consistent processes yield compounding benefits.
2. **Integration Creates Multiplier Effects**: Channels working together are more powerful than isolated tactics.
3. **Data-Driven Decisions Eliminate Waste**: Tracking identifies profitable activities and eliminates inefficient spend.
4. **Consistency Builds Momentum**: Sustained effort is more important than short-term brilliance.

5. **Process Optimization Drives Incremental Gains**: Continuous refinement across multiple areas leads to dramatic overall improvement.
6. **Specialization Creates Competitive Advantage**: Focusing on niches or specific value propositions reduces price competition.
7. **System-Based Growth Is Sustainable**: Processes enable scaling predictability and resilience.

Conclusion

Exceptional marketing results come from disciplined implementation, meticulous measurement, and continuous optimization. The transformation from reactive tactics to systematic processes is key. These case studies show that dramatic improvements are achievable for paving companies of all sizes. By applying these principles, you can achieve similar transformative results.

In the next chapter, we'll explore how to calculate and optimize marketing ROI, with specific tools and frameworks.

29

Marketing ROI Calculator and Budget Planning

Effective marketing is ultimately an investment decision. Like any investment, it requires careful analysis of costs, potential returns, and resource allocation to maximize results. This chapter provides practical tools and frameworks to calculate marketing ROI, develop evidence-based budgets, and optimize resource allocation across marketing channels. By applying these calculations and planning methodologies, you'll transform marketing from a cost center with uncertain returns into a predictable revenue-generating system with measurable performance.

Research-Based Cost Benchmarks by Channel

Understanding industry cost benchmarks provides an essential foundation for budget planning and performance evaluation. Based on our research across hundreds of paving companies, here are current cost benchmarks for key marketing channels:

Digital Marketing Benchmarks

- **Google Ads/Pay-Per-Click** Based on aggregated data from paving contractors across North America:

Metric	Range	Average	Notes
Cost Per Click (CPC)	$3.50-$12.00	$6.80	Higher in competitive metros

Metric	**Range**	**Average**	**Notes**
Conversion Rate	3%-15%	7.2%	Higher with optimized landing pages
Cost Per Lead (CPL)	$40-$120	$72	Significant variance by region
Lead-to-Sale Conversion	20%-40%	28%	Higher for specific services
Customer Acquisition Cost	$145-$450	$257	Varies by project type
Key factors affecting costs: Geographic competition level, Seasonality, Campaign optimization level, Landing page quality, Ad quality and relevance.			

- **Search Engine Optimization (SEO)** SEO costs typically reflect ongoing investment rather than direct per-lead costs:

Metric	Range	Average	Notes
Monthly Investment	$500-$3,000	$1,400	Varies by company size and goals
Implementation Timeline	3-9 months	5 months	Until significant results visible
Organic Traffic Growth	40%-400%	140%	First-year improvement
Cost Per Organic Lead	$15-$60	$35	Calculated over 12+ months
SEO ROI (Year 1)	100%-500%	280%	Typically improves in years 2-3
Key factors affecting performance: Website technical foundation, Competitive landscape, Content development resources, Local citation quality, Review quantity and quality.			

- **Social Media Marketing** Social media costs for paving companies:

Metric	**Range**	**Average**	**Notes**
Facebook/Insta CPC	$1.25-$4.50	$2.80	Lower than search, but lower intent
Social Media CPL	$35-$90	$58	Higher for targeted campaigns
Organic Posting ROI	Minimal-Moderate	Low	Without paid amplification
Engagement Rate	0.5%-5%	1.8%	Higher with visual content
Conversion Rate	2%-10%	4.7%	For landing page visitors
Key factors affecting performance: Visual quality, Video content, Targeting precision, Ad relevance score, Page authority and engagement history.			

- **Email Marketing** Email marketing metrics for paving companies:

Metric	Range	Average	Notes
Cost Per Email	$0.01-$0.15	$0.05	Including platform and creation
Open Rate	15%-40%	24%	Higher for segmented campaigns
Click-Through Rate	2%-12%	5.3%	Higher with clear CTAs
Cost Per Lead	$12-$45	$28	Among lowest of all channels
Revenue Per Email	$0.25-$3.00	$0.85	When properly segmented
Key factors affecting performance: List quality and segmentation, Sending frequency, Mobile optimization, Personalization level, Content relevance.			

Traditional Marketing Benchmarks

- **Direct Mail** Direct mail performance metrics:

Metric	Range	Average	Notes
Cost Per Piece	$0.45-$0.95	$0.65	Higher for larger/premium formats
Response Rate	0.5%-3.5%	1.8%	Higher with targeted lists
Cost Per Lead	$35-$120	$68	Comparable to digital channels
Lead-to-Sale Conversion	20%-35%	28%	Often higher quality leads
ROI	15%-300%	120%	Higher with multi-touch campaigns
Key factors affecting performance: List quality and targeting, Mailpiece size and quality, Offer strength, Timing, Multi-touch approach.			

- **Radio Advertising** Radio performance benchmarks:

Metric	Range	Average	Notes
Cost Per 30-Second Spot	$35-$300	$120	Varies widely by market and station
Weekly Frequency Needed	12-21 spots	15 spots	For effective brand recognition
Cost Per Thousand (CPM)	$5-$20	$12	Efficient for reach
Cost Per Lead	$80-$200	$125	Harder to attribute precisely
Brand Recall Increase	15%-40%	25%	After 4-week campaign
Key factors affecting performance: Station audience alignment, Time slot selection, Creative quality, Frequency and consistency, Call tracking implementation.			

- **Billboard/Outdoor Advertising** Outdoor advertising benchmarks:

Metric	Range	Average	Notes
Monthly Cost (Static)	$1,000-$5,000	$2,400	Location dependent
Monthly Cost (Digital)	$1,200-$8,000	$3,500	For rotation in display cycle
Cost Per Thousand (CPM)	$3-$8	$5.50	Based on traffic counts
Typical Minimum Term	1-6 months	3 months	Longer terms offer discounts
Direct Response Rate	Very Low	Low	Better for brand building
Key factors affecting performance: Location and visibility, Creative impact, Placement context, Duration, Integration with other channels.			

- **Vehicle Branding** Vehicle branding metrics:

Metric	Range	Average	Notes
Full Wrap Cost	$2,000-$4,000	$2,800	Per vehicle, one-time cost

Metric	Range	Average	Notes
Partial Wrap/Graphics	$800-$2,000	$1,300	Per vehicle, one-time cost
Daily Impressions	15,000-70,000	30,000	In urban environments
Cost Per Thousand (CPM)	$0.30-$0.70	$0.48	Lowest of all channels
Lifespan	3-7 years	5 years	With proper maintenance
Key factors affecting performance: Quality of design and installation, Vehicle routes and visibility, Design simplicity, Integration with job site presence, Maintenance.			

- **Job Site Signage** Job site sign performance:

Metric	Range	Average	Notes
Cost Per Sign	$50-$200	$120	Depends on size and quality

Metric	Range	Average	Notes
Impressions Per Day	50-500+	200+	Location dependent
Response Rate	0.1%-2%	0.5%	Higher in targeted neighborhoods
Cost Per Lead	$15-$60	$35	Among most cost-effective methods
Lifespan	2-10 jobs	5 jobs	With proper maintenance
Key factors affecting performance: Sign size and quality, Placement location, Job quality context, Neighborhood demographic match, Duration.			

Expected Conversion Rates

Understanding realistic conversion benchmarks helps set appropriate expectations and identify opportunities for improvement. Based on our research, here are typical conversion rates for paving companies at each stage of the marketing funnel:

Top of Funnel Conversion Rates

- **Website Traffic to Lead Conversion**

Channel	Conversion Range	Average	Notes
Organic Search	2%-8%	4.3%	Higher for specific service searches
Google Ads Traffic	3%-15%	7.2%	With optimized landing pages
Social Media Traffic	1%-6%	2.8%	Lower intent than search traffic
Referral Traffic	4%-12%	7.6%	Higher trust factor
Direct Traffic	5%-15%	8.5%	Often returning visitors
Email Traffic	8%-20%	12.4%	Highest intent of all sources

- **Social Media Engagement to Website Visit**

Platform	Click-Through Range	Average	Notes
Facebook	0.5%-5%	1.6%	Higher for targeted ads
Instagram	0.2%-3%	0.9%	Better for awareness than clicks

Platform	Click-Through Range	Average	Notes
LinkedIn	0.2%-2.5%	0.8%	Higher for B2B targeting
YouTube	0.3%-3%	1.1%	Higher from how-to content

- **Email Marketing Conversion Funnel**

Metric	Range	Average	Notes
Open Rate	15%-40%	24%	Higher with compelling subject lines
Click-Through Rate	2%-12%	5.3%	From opened emails
Website Conversion	8%-20%	12.4%	From email click-throughs
Overall Funnel	0.2%-1%	0.6%	From send to final conversion

Middle of Funnel Conversion Rates

- **Lead to Appointment/Estimate**

Lead Source	Conversion Range	Average	Notes
Contact Form	40%-75%	58%	Higher with quick response
Phone Inquiry	50%-80%	65%	Direct conversations convert better
Email Lead	30%-60%	45%	Requires prompt follow-up
Social Media Lead	25%-50%	35%	Often earlier in buying process
Referral Lead	60%-90%	75%	Highest quality lead source
Purchased Lead	15%-40%	25%	Lower quality, shared with competitors

- **Estimate Request to Estimate Completion**

Factor	Completion Range	Average	Notes
Response Time (Same Day)	70%-90%	80%	Quick response critical
Response Time (2-3 Days)	40%-70%	55%	Significant drop-off

Factor	Completion Range	Average	Notes
Response Time (4+ Days)	15%-40%	25%	Many leads lost
Overall Average	50%-75%	65%	Across all response times

Bottom of Funnel Conversion Rates

- **Estimate to Project Booking**

Project Type	Conversion Range	Average	Notes
Residential Driveway	25%-45%	32%	Higher with clear value prop
Commercial Parking Lot	15%-30%	22%	Longer sales cycle, more competition
Sealcoat/Maintenance	30%-60%	42%	Lower price point, easier decision
Repair Work	40%-70%	55%	Urgency drives higher conversion
Overall Average	25%-45%	34%	Across all project types

- **Estimate Follow-up Impact**

Follow-up Approach	Conversion Lift	Notes
No Follow-up	Baseline	Many companies stop after estimate
Single Follow-up	+25%-40%	Simple call or email
Systematic Multi-Touch	+50%-80%	Planned sequence of touches
Value-Added Follow-up	+40%-60%	Educational content provided
Combined Approach	+70%-120%	Systematic + value-added

These conversion benchmarks provide context for evaluating your own performance at each stage of the marketing funnel. Significant deviation from these ranges suggests either a competitive advantage to be leveraged or an opportunity for improvement.

ROI Calculation Tools

Calculating true marketing ROI requires tracking both costs and results throughout the entire marketing and sales process. Here are practical frameworks and calculations for measuring marketing performance:

Basic ROI Formula ROI = (Revenue Generated - Marketing Cost) ÷ Marketing Cost × 100% Ex: $5k cost, $25k revenue -> ROI = ($20k / $5k) * 100% = 400% This means that for every dollar invested in marketing, you generated four dollars in return (400% ROI).

Channel-Specific ROI Calculator For more precise measurement, calculate ROI by individual marketing channel: Channel ROI = (Channel Revenue - Channel Cost) ÷ Channel Cost × 100% This requires: Tracking lead source for all inquiries, Connecting final sales back to original lead source, Maintaining accurate channel cost data. For example:

Channel	Investment	Revenue	ROI Calculation	ROI
Google Ads	$3,000	$42,000	($42,000-$3,000)÷$3,000×100%	1,300%
Facebook Ads	$1,500	$12,000	($12,000-$1,500)÷$1,500×100%	700%
Direct Mail	$4,000	$28,000	($28,000-$4,000)÷$4,000×100%	600%
Radio	$6,000	$22,000	($22,000-$6,000)÷$6,000×100%	267%

Customer Acquisition Cost (CAC) Understanding your cost to acquire a new customer is crucial for budget planning: CAC = Total Marketing Cost ÷ Number of New Customers Acquired For example, if you spent $10,000 on marketing and acquired 25 new customers: CAC = $10,000 ÷ 25 = $400 per new customer For channel-specific CAC: Channel CAC = Channel Marketing Cost ÷ Number of Customers from Channel This calculation helps compare efficiency across channels.

Lifetime Value to CAC Ratio (LTV:CAC) This critical metric compares the lifetime value of customers to the cost of acquiring them: LTV:CAC Ratio = Customer Lifetime Value ÷ Customer Acquisition Cost For paving companies, customer lifetime value should include: Initial project revenue, Future maintenance revenue, Additional project revenue, Referral value (average referred business per customer). For example, if your average customer has a lifetime value of $6,800 and costs $400 to acquire: LTV:CAC Ratio = $6,800 ÷ $400 = 17:1 Most successful paving companies maintain a ratio of at least 3:1, with top performers achieving 10:1 or higher.

Cost Per Lead (CPL) This metric helps evaluate marketing efficiency before sales conversion: CPL = Marketing Cost ÷ Number of Leads Generated For example, if your Google Ads campaign costs $3,000 and generates 45 leads: CPL = $3,000 ÷ 45 = $66.67 per lead Channel Comparison Example:

Channel	Monthly Cost	Leads Generated	CPL Calculation	CPL
Google Ads	$3,000	45	$3,000 ÷ 45	$66.67
Facebook	$1,500	32	$1,500 ÷ 32	$46.88
Direct Mail	$4,000	52	$4,000 ÷ 52	$76.92
SEO	$1,500	38	$1,500 ÷ 38	$39.47

Return on Ad Spend (ROAS) This simplified metric focuses on direct return from advertising investment: ROAS = Revenue Generated ÷ Advertising Cost For example, if you spend $2,000 on Google Ads that generates $16,000 in revenue: ROAS = $16,000 ÷ $2,000 = 8 (or 800%) This means you generated $8 for every $1 spent on advertising.

Conversion Rate Optimization (CRO) Impact CRO focuses on improving the percentage of visitors who become leads, and leads who become customers. Here's how to calculate the value of CRO improvements: Value of 1% Conversion Improvement = Monthly Visitors × 1% × Average Sale Value For example, if your website gets 2,000 monthly visitors and your average project is worth $4,000: Value of 1% Conversion Improvement = 2,000 × 1% × $4,000 = $80,000 annually This demonstrates why even small conversion improvements can dramatically impact revenue.

Budget Allocation Examples

Determining how to allocate your marketing budget requires balancing multiple factors: business goals, competitive landscape, historical performance, and seasonal considerations. Here are example allocations for different paving company profiles:

Example 1: New Residential Paving Co (Year 1) Total Annual Marketing Budget: $45,000 (9% of projected $500,000 revenue)

Channel	Allocation	Amount	Rationale
Website Dev	20%	$9,000	One-time foundation investment

Channel	Allocation	Amount	Rationale
Google Ads	30%	$13,500	Quick lead generation
GMB/Local SEO	15%	$6,750	Critical local visibility
Facebook/Instagram	10%	$4,500	Awareness & showcase work
Job Signs/Vehicle Graphics	15%	$6,750	Maximize job visibility
Basic Materials	5%	$2,250	Professional presentation
Miscellaneous/Testing	5%	$2,250	Flexibility

Quarterly Breakdown: Q1:15%, Q2:35%, Q3:35%, Q4:15% *Key Strategy*: Establish foundation, generate immediate leads. Heavy Google Ads initially.

Example 2: Established Residential Co (5+ Years) Total Annual Marketing Budget: $132,000 (6% of $2.2 million revenue)

Channel	Allocation	Amount	Rationale
Google Ads	25%	$33,000	Consistent lead gen
SEO & Content Marketing	20%	$26,400	Sustainable organic growth

Channel	Allocation	Amount	Rationale
Direct Mail Campaigns	15%	$19,800	Targeted neighborhood marketing
Facebook/Instagram Ads	10%	$13,200	Visual showcase & targeting
Email Marketing	5%	$6,600	Retention & referrals
Local Radio	10%	$13,200	Brand awareness
Job Site Marketing	5%	$6,600	Signs, neighborhood marketing
Vehicle Branding	5%	$6,600	Fleet visibility
Miscellaneous/Testing	5%	$6,600	Channel experimentation

Quarterly Breakdown: Q1:15%, Q2:35%, Q3:30%, Q4:20% *Key Strategy*: Balanced digital/traditional approach. Focus on measurable performance and multiple touchpoints.

Example 3: Commercial-Focused Paving Co Total Annual Marketing Budget: $240,000 (4% of $6 million revenue)

Channel	Allocation	Amount	Rationale
SEO & Content Marketing	20%	$48,000	Educational content for decision-makers

Channel	Allocation	Amount	Rationale
Google Ads	15%	$36,000	Targeted commercial keywords
LinkedIn Marketing	15%	$36,000	Reach facility/property managers
Direct Outreach Program	15%	$36,000	Relationship building
Case Study Development	10%	$24,000	Showcase successful projects
Industry Assoc. Marketing	5%	$12,000	Networking & referrals
Email Nurture Campaigns	5%	$12,000	Long-term prospect nurturing
Retargeting Campaigns	5%	$12,000	Stay visible to researchers
Print Advertising (Trade)	5%	$12,000	Industry visibility
Miscellaneous/Testing	5%	$12,000	New opportunity exploration

Quarterly Breakdown: More consistent year-round. Slightly higher (30%) in Q1 for budget planning cycle. *Key Strategy*: Emphasis on relationships, credibility, education. Position as trusted advisor. Reach decision-makers throughout long cycle.

Example 4: Mixed Residential & Commercial (Growth Phase) Total Annual Marketing Budget: $180,000 (7.2% of $2.5 million revenue)

Channel	Allocation	Amount	Rationale
Google Ads	25%	$45,000	Primary lead gen
SEO & Content	15%	$27,000	Long-term authority
Direct Mail (Residential)	10%	$18,000	Targeted neighborhoods
LinkedIn (Commercial)	10%	$18,000	B2B targeting
Facebook/Instagram	10%	$18,000	Visual portfolio
Local Radio	10%	$18,000	Brand awareness
Email Marketing	5%	$9,000	Nurturing & retention
CRM & Marketing Automation	5%	$9,000	Systems for scaling
Job Site & Vehicle Marketing	5%	$9,000	On-location visibility
Miscellaneous/Testing	5%	$9,000	Channel experimentation

Quarterly Breakdown: Q1:20% (Commercial focus), Q2:30% (Resi focus), Q3:30% (Peak both), Q4:20% (Commercial focus returns). *Key Strategy*: Balanced with segment-specific tactics. Residential heavier in season, Commercial more consistent.

Budget Planning Framework

Structure your budget planning:

Step 1: Establish Revenue Goals

- Overall Target, Marketing-Driven Portion, Segment Goals.
- Ex: $3M overall, 70% marketing-driven -> $2.1M target.

Step 2: Calculate Required Lead Volume

- Required Customers = Target Revenue / Avg Project Value
- Required Leads = Required Customers / Lead-to-Customer Conversion Rate
- Ex: $2.1M target / $5.8k avg value = 362 customers. 362 / 30% conversion = 1,207 leads needed.

Step 3: Determine Overall Budget Range

- Startup (10-15%), Growth (7-10%), Established (5-8%), Market Leader (3-6%) of target revenue.
- Ex: Growth phase, $2.1M target -> $147k (7%) - $210k (10%) range. Use Mid: $178.5k.

Step 4: Calculate Target Acquisition Cost

- Max Sustainable CAC = LTV / Target LTV:CAC Ratio (Healthy ratio 3:1 to 5:1).
- Ex: LTV $8.4k, Target Ratio 4:1 -> Max CAC = $2.1k.

Step 5: Validate Budget Against Acquisition Cost

- Planned CAC = Budget / Required Customers
- Compare Planned CAC vs. Max Sustainable CAC.
- Ex: $178.5k budget / 362 customers = $493 Planned CAC. ($493 < $2.1k Max -> Budget sustainable).

Step 6: Allocate Budget by Channel

- Distribute based on History, Journey Mapping, Competition, Capacity, Seasonality.
- Ex: (See Allocation Table Example 4 above for $178.5k budget).

Step 7: Create Seasonal Adjustment Plan

- Develop monthly allocations based on seasonal factors.
- Ex: (See Seasonal Allocation Table Example above).

Step 8: Establish Testing Budget

- Allocate 5-10% for testing new channels/approaches.
- Define test structure, success metrics, graduation criteria.
- Ex: $178.5k budget -> $8.9k testing budget (5%). Test duration 60-90 days. Success: CAC within 25% of established channels.

Step 9: Implement Measurement Plan

- Channel tracking (numbers, URLs, codes), Lead Source Capture, Revenue Attribution, Reporting Cadence, Dashboards.

Step 10: Create Budget Adjustment Triggers

- Establish conditions for mid-year adjustments (Performance thresholds, Warning indicators, Competitive changes, Seasonal factors, Cash flow).
- Ex: Increase channel budget 20% if CAC below target 60 days. Reduce 15% if conversion drops 25% for 30 days.

Conclusion

Effective budget planning transforms marketing into a reliable revenue system. Use frameworks, calculations, and benchmarks to develop data-driven budgets maximizing return.

Key principles: Clear Goals, Balanced Channels, Consistent Measurement, Seasonal Adjustment, Systematic Testing, Regular Review.

Successful companies view marketing as an investment system requiring careful allocation, measurement, and optimization. Use these ROI and budget planning frameworks to create a marketing operation delivering predictable, measurable results.

In the next chapter, we'll explore resources and tools to support your marketing implementation, including vendor directories, software recommendations, and industry associations that can enhance your marketing effectiveness.

30

Resource Directory

Throughout this book, we've covered comprehensive strategies and tactics for marketing your paving company effectively. Implementing these strategies often requires specialized tools, vendors, and resources. This chapter provides a curated directory of resources to help you execute your marketing plan successfully.

Vendors and Service Providers

Digital Marketing Agencies

While many paving companies handle some marketing in-house, partnering with specialized agencies can provide expertise and save time. Here are categories of agencies to consider and what to look for in each:

Full-Service Marketing Agencies These agencies handle all aspects of marketing from strategy to execution. When evaluating a full-service agency, look for:

- Previous experience with home services or specifically paving companies
- Case studies showing measurable results for similar businesses

- Comprehensive service offerings that align with your priorities
- Transparent reporting and communication practices
- Client references you can contact

Specialized Service Providers Rather than working with a single agency, you might choose specialists for different marketing functions:

SEO Specialists:

- Look for providers who understand local SEO specifically
- Ask for examples of Map Pack rankings they've achieved for clients
- Verify they use white-hat techniques that comply with Google's guidelines
- Request case studies specific to service businesses

PPC Management:

- Experience managing local service ads and Google Ads for contractors
- Understanding of geographic targeting and local intent keywords
- Track record of achieving reasonable cost-per-lead metrics
- Experience with call tracking and lead attribution

Web Design/Development:

- Portfolio of contractor or home service websites
- Mobile-first design approach
- Experience with conversion optimization
- Understanding of local SEO requirements
- Ability to integrate with your CRM and other tools

Content Creation:

- Writers familiar with construction terminology

- Photographers experienced in before/after project documentation
- Video professionals who understand how to showcase paving work
- Graphic designers who can create consistent branded materials

Production Vendors

These vendors help create physical marketing materials:

Print Providers

- Local print shops (for fast turnaround on yard signs, door hangers)
- Online printers like Vistaprint, Printplace, or GotPrint (for business cards, brochures)
- Large format printers for truck wraps and signage (FastSigns, SignaPrint)

Signage Vendors

- Vehicle wrap specialists (look for 3M certified installers)
- Billboard companies (Lamar, Clear Channel, Outfront Media, plus local providers)
- Yard sign manufacturers (BuildASign, Signs.com)

Direct Mail Services

- Full-service mail houses that handle design, printing, and mailing
- EDDM (Every Door Direct Mail) specialists
- List providers like InfoUSA, Experian, or Exact Data

Promotional Product Suppliers

- Branded items for customers and events
- Look for suppliers who can provide small minimum orders

- Consider useful items relevant to your services (tape measures, levels, etc.)

Media Partners

Established relationships with media representatives can provide better rates and placement:

Broadcast Media

- Local radio station representatives
- Cable TV advertising departments
- Streaming audio platforms (Pandora, Spotify)
- Podcast networks with local targeting

Print Media

- Community newspaper advertising departments
- Local magazine representatives
- Industry publication advertising contacts
- Cooperative mailer representatives (Valpak, Money Mailer)

Digital Media Networks

- Programmatic advertising platforms
- Geofencing providers
- OTT/CTV (Connected TV) advertising networks
- Local news website advertising representatives

Software Tools

The right software can streamline your marketing operations and improve results. Here are essential tools by category:

Customer Relationship Management (CRM)

A central system for tracking leads and customers is essential. Options include:

- **Revenue Commander**: Our integrated solution specifically designed for paving contractors
- **JobNimbus**: Popular with contractors, includes project management features
- **MarketSharp**: Designed for home improvement contractors
- **Salesforce**: Enterprise-level CRM with extensive customization options
- **HubSpot CRM**: User-friendly option with free starter tier
- **Zoho CRM**: Affordable solution with good customization capabilities

When selecting a CRM, consider:

- Integration with your estimating/quoting software
- Mobile access for field teams
- Ease of data entry for staff
- Lead tracking and source attribution
- Reporting capabilities
- Email marketing integration

Email Marketing Platforms

For nurturing leads and staying connected with customers:

- Mailchimp: User-friendly with templates and automation features
- Constant Contact: Easy to use with good support
- ActiveCampaign: Advanced automation capabilities
- Klaviyo: Powerful segmentation and personalization
- ConvertKit: Simple but effective system

Social Media Management

Tools to efficiently manage your social presence:

- Hootsuite: Manage multiple platforms, schedule posts
- Buffer: Simple scheduling and analytics
- Sprout Social: Comprehensive management and reporting
- Later: Visual planning tools for Instagram and other platforms
- Facebook Business Suite: Native management of Facebook and Instagram

Review Management

Monitoring and generating online reviews:

- GatherUp: Review generation and monitoring across platforms
- BirdEye: Comprehensive reputation management
- Podium: Text-based review requests with high conversion rates
- NiceJob: Automated reputation management for contractors
- Grade.us: Review management and marketing platform

SEO and Analytics

Tools for monitoring and improving search performance:

- Google Analytics: Essential free website analytics
- Google Search Console: Monitor search performance and issues
- Ahrefs: Comprehensive SEO research and monitoring
- SEMrush: Competitive research and keyword tracking
- Moz Local: Local listing management and tracking
- BrightLocal: Local SEO-specific tools and reporting

Call Tracking

Measuring phone leads from marketing channels:

- CallRail: Popular call tracking with conversation intelligence
- CallTrackingMetrics: Enterprise-level call analytics
- Invoca: Advanced call attribution and analytics
- DialogTech: AI-powered call analytics
- WhatConverts: Call tracking and lead management

Estimating and Project Management

While not strictly marketing tools, these integrate with your marketing systems:

- PavementPro: Estimating software for paving contractors
- HCSS HeavyBid: Estimating for infrastructure and heavy construction
- Buildertrend: Project management for contractors
- CoConstruct: Client communication and project management
- ProContractor: Complete construction management software

Design Resources

Professional design elevates your marketing materials and brand image:

Stock Photography

- Shutterstock: Extensive library of professional images
- Adobe Stock: High-quality images integrated with Adobe tools
- iStock: Getty Images' more affordable option
- Unsplash: Free high-quality stock photos
- Pexels: Free stock photos and videos

Consider investing in professional project photography rather than relying solely on stock images. Before/after photos of your actual work are far more effective than generic stock photos.

Graphic Design Tools

- Adobe Creative Suite: Professional-grade design software (Photoshop, Illustrator, InDesign)
- Canva: User-friendly design tool with templates for non-designers
- Affinity Designer/Photo: Professional alternatives to Adobe products
- PicMonkey: Simple photo editing and graphic design
- Snappa: Easy graphic creation for social media and ads

Design Services

- Fiverr: Affordable freelance designers for one-off projects
- Upwork: Freelance marketplace for finding designers
- 99designs: Design contests for logos and branding
- Design Pickle: Subscription-based graphic design service
- Penji: Unlimited graphic design service

Website Templates and Themes

If you're building your own website, consider these sources:

- ThemeForest: Marketplace for WordPress themes including contractor templates
- StudioPress: Premium WordPress themes with good support
- Divi: Versatile WordPress theme with visual builder
- Wix Templates: Ready-made contractor website templates
- Squarespace Templates: Professional designs for service businesses

Video Creation Tools

- Camtasia: Screen recording and video editing
- Adobe Premiere Rush: Simplified video editing for marketing content
- Lumen5: Text-to-video creation platform
- iMovie: Free video editing for Mac users
- Filmora: User-friendly video editing software

Industry Associations

Industry associations provide resources, networking, and credibility for paving contractors:

National Associations

- National Asphalt Pavement Association (NAPA): Industry standards, technical resources, and networking
- Asphalt Institute: Technical expertise and educational resources
- National Center for Asphalt Technology (NCAT): Research and educational resources
- American Public Works Association (APWA): Resources for contractors working with public agencies

- Associated General Contractors of America (AGC): Broader construction industry association

State Associations

Most states have asphalt pavement associations that provide local:

- Technical resources specific to regional conditions
- Regulatory updates and compliance assistance
- Educational events and certification programs
- Networking with other contractors
- Local government relations

Examples include:

- Asphalt Pavement Association of Indiana
- California Asphalt Pavement Association
- Florida Asphalt Contractors Association

Visit the NAPA website for a directory of state affiliates.

Local Business Organizations

These organizations can provide marketing opportunities and business connections:

- Chamber of Commerce: Local business networking and community visibility
- Business Improvement Districts: Connections to commercial property owners
- Builder and Contractor Associations: Networking with general contractors
- Local Chapters of BOMA (Building Owners and Managers Association):

Access to commercial property decision-makers
- Real Estate Investor Associations: Connections to property investors who often need paving

Marketing Templates

These templates will help you implement marketing strategies more efficiently:

Customer Communication Templates

- New Customer Welcome Email: Sent after project completion to establish ongoing relationship
- Seasonal Maintenance Reminder: Scheduled emails for service reminders
- Review Request Templates: Email and text message templates for requesting Google and other reviews
- Referral Request Email: Template for asking satisfied customers for referrals
- Project Anniversary Follow-up: Check-in email for 1-year, 2-year anniversaries of project completion

Marketing Planning Templates

- Annual Marketing Calendar: Month-by-month planning template for marketing activities
- Campaign Planning Worksheet: Template for organizing multi-channel marketing campaigns
- Budget Allocation Spreadsheet: Formula-based tool for distributing marketing budgets
- Competitor Analysis Framework: Template for analyzing competitor marketing strategies
- Target Market Profile: Worksheet for defining ideal customer seg-

ments

Performance Tracking Templates

- Marketing KPI Dashboard: Spreadsheet for tracking key marketing metrics
- Lead Source Analysis: Template for comparing lead sources and conversion rates
- ROI Calculator: Formula-based calculator for marketing return on investment
- Customer Acquisition Cost Worksheet: Template for calculating true cost of acquiring customers
- Lifetime Value Calculator: Tool for estimating customer lifetime value by segment

Content Planning Templates

- Content Calendar: Planning template for blog, social, and email content
- Social Media Post Templates: Frameworks for different types of social content
- Blog Post Outlines: Structures for common blog topics in the paving industry
- Email Newsletter Templates: Layouts for regular customer communications
- Case Study Format: Template for creating compelling project case studies

Resources from Paving Marketers

As part of our commitment to your success, Paving Marketers offers several free and premium resources:

Free Resources

- Paving Marketing Blog: Regular updates on marketing strategies for paving contractors
- Monthly Marketing Webinars: Educational sessions on specific marketing topics
- Paving Marketers Podcast: Interviews with successful paving company owners
- Facebook Group: Community of paving contractors sharing marketing ideas
- Marketing Assessment Tool: Self-evaluation of your current marketing efforts

Premium Resources

- Revenue Commander Platform: Complete marketing management system
- Marketing Implementation Services: Done-for-you marketing execution
- Custom Website Development: Paving-specific website design and development
- Marketing Strategy Consulting: Personalized marketing planning and guidance

31

Conclusion and Next Steps

Throughout this book, we've covered comprehensive strategies for marketing your paving company effectively. From digital foundations like your website and SEO to traditional channels like direct mail and billboards, you now have a complete toolkit for growing your business through strategic marketing.

Key Takeaways

Before we discuss next steps, let's review some of the most important concepts from this book:

- **Integrated Marketing Works Best**: The most successful paving companies use multiple marketing channels that work together. Each channel reinforces the others, creating multiple touchpoints with potential customers.
- **Digital Foundation Is Essential**: Your website, Google Business Profile, and online reputation form the foundation of all marketing efforts. Even traditional marketing channels like radio or billboards ultimately drive people to check you out online.
- **Consistent Branding Matters**: Across all channels, maintain consistent visual identity, messaging, and positioning to build recognition

and trust.

- **Measurement Drives Improvement**: Track the results of all marketing efforts to understand what's working and continuously improve your return on investment.
- **Marketing Is an Investment**: Approach marketing as an investment that builds equity in your brand, not just a short-term expense. The returns compound over time.
- **Visual Proof Is Powerful**: In the paving business, before/after photos and project showcases are your most persuasive marketing assets. Invest in quality photography and documentation.
- **Word-of-Mouth Can Be Amplified**: While referrals may happen naturally, systematic programs to encourage and reward them significantly increase their impact.
- **Seasonality Requires Planning**: Align your marketing calendar with seasonal patterns in the paving business for maximum effectiveness.
- **Targeting Beats Volume**: Reaching the right prospects with relevant messages outperforms broad, generic marketing every time.
- **Marketing Is Never "Done"**: Successful marketing requires ongoing attention, measurement, and refinement as markets, tools, and customer preferences evolve.

Marketing Audit Checklist

To determine where to focus your efforts first, conduct a comprehensive audit of your current marketing. This checklist will help identify your strengths and opportunities for improvement:

Digital Presence Audit

Website Evaluation:

- Does your website clearly communicate your services and service area?
- Is it mobile-friendly and fast-loading?

- Does it feature high-quality project photos and testimonials?
- Are there clear calls-to-action on every page?
- Does it include content for each of your core services?
- Is your contact information prominent and accurate?
- Is it optimized for search engines?
- Does it integrate lead tracking?

Search Visibility:

- Do you appear in the Google Map Pack for your primary services and locations?
- What is your organic ranking for key search terms?
- Is your Google Business Profile complete and optimized?
- Are you listed on other relevant directories with consistent information?
- Do you have a strategy for building relevant backlinks?
- Is your NAP (Name, Address, Phone) consistent across the web?

Online Reputation:

- What is your rating on Google Reviews?
- How many Google reviews do you have compared to competitors?
- Are you responding to all reviews, both positive and negative?
- Do you have a systematic process for requesting reviews?
- Are reviews featured prominently on your website?

Social Media Presence:

- Are your social profiles complete and branded consistently?
- Are you regularly posting relevant content?
- Do you showcase project photos and videos?
- Are you engaging with followers and responding to comments?
- Are your posting frequency and content quality competitive?

Digital Advertising:

- Are you running Google Ads campaigns targeting relevant keywords?
- Do you have conversion tracking properly implemented?
- Are you using appropriate geographic targeting?
- Have you tested Facebook or other social advertising?
- Are your ads and landing pages aligned for maximum conversion?

Traditional Marketing Audit

Print Collateral:

- Do you have professional business cards, brochures, and estimate forms?
- Is your branding consistent across all printed materials?
- Do your print materials include compelling project photos?
- Are your unique selling propositions clearly communicated?
- Do all materials include current contact information and website?

Signage and Vehicles:

- Do you use job site signs consistently?
- Are your vehicles professionally branded?
- Is your equipment identified with company branding?
- Do your signs and vehicle graphics include current contact information?
- Are graphics high-quality and well-maintained?

Direct Marketing:

- Have you tested direct mail to targeted neighborhoods?
- Do you have a process for door-to-door marketing around job sites?

- Are you tracking response from direct marketing efforts?
- Do your direct marketing materials include compelling offers?
- Are messages and visuals consistent with other marketing channels?

Broadcast and Outdoor:

- Have you evaluated the potential of radio advertising in your market?
- For larger companies: Have you considered television or billboard advertising?
- Do you sponsor any local events or organizations?
- Are broadcast messages aligned with your digital marketing?
- Do you have systems to track response from these channels?

Referral Marketing:

- Do you have a structured referral program?
- Are you systematically asking clients for referrals?
- Do you offer incentives for successful referrals?
- Are you maintaining relationships with past customers?
- Do you have partnerships with complementary businesses?

Strategic Elements Audit

Target Market Definition:

- Have you clearly defined your ideal customer segments?
- Do you know which services are most profitable?
- Have you identified your geographic sweet spot?
- Do you understand what factors most influence hiring decisions?
- Are your marketing messages tailored to different customer segments?

Competitive Positioning:

- Have you identified your key differentiators?
- Are these differences meaningful to customers?
- Do your marketing materials clearly communicate these differences?
- Are you monitoring competitor marketing activities?
- Have you positioned your company in a distinct market niche?

Marketing Systems:

- Do you have a CRM or lead management system?
- Are you tracking marketing ROI by channel?
- Do you have a defined follow-up process for leads?
- Is there a marketing calendar guiding your activities?
- Do you have a defined marketing budget?

Team Capabilities:

- Is marketing responsibility clearly assigned?
- Does your team have the necessary skills and training?
- Do you have relationships with quality vendors and agencies?
- Are salespeople aligned with marketing messages?
- Is there regular communication between marketing and operations?

After completing this audit, prioritize the areas where improvement would have the greatest impact on your business. Focus on addressing fundamental gaps before moving to more advanced strategies.

Getting Started with Revenue Commander

Throughout this book, we've referenced Revenue Commander as a comprehensive platform for managing your paving company's marketing. Here's how to get started:

What Is Revenue Commander?

Revenue Commander is our proprietary marketing system designed specifically for paving contractors. It integrates:

- **Lead Management**: Track leads from all sources in one centralized dashboard
- **Marketing Analytics**: Measure performance across digital and traditional channels
- **Reputation Management**: Generate and monitor online reviews
- **Email Marketing**: Nurture leads and maintain customer relationships
- **Website Integration**: Connect your website for seamless data flow
- **Call Tracking**: Attribute phone leads to specific marketing sources
- **Task Management**: Assign and track marketing-related tasks
- **Reporting**: Generate insights about your marketing performance

Implementation Steps

If you're interested in implementing Revenue Commander for your paving company, follow these steps:

1. Discovery and Needs Assessment The first step is a comprehensive assessment of your current marketing operations and goals. This includes:

- Review of existing systems and processes
- Identification of key performance indicators
- Definition of reporting requirements
- Assessment of team capabilities and training needs
- Clarification of growth objectives

2. System Configuration Based on your specific needs, you can configure Revenue Commander to align with your operations:

- Setting up lead tracking parameters
- Connecting your website and digital channels
- Establishing call tracking numbers
- Creating custom reports
- Building email templates and sequences
- Defining user roles and permissions

3. Data Migration and Integration If you're currently using other systems, you should transfer your data:

- Import customer and prospect records
- Connect with your existing CRM if applicable
- Integrate with your estimating or project management software
- Set up connections with Google Analytics and other platforms
- Ensure consistent data structure across systems

Working with Paving Marketers

While this book provides the knowledge to implement marketing strategies yourself, many paving companies choose to partner with specialists who can execute these strategies more efficiently. Here's how working with Paving Marketers can accelerate your results:

Our Approach

What makes Paving Marketers different from general marketing agencies:

Industry Specialization We work exclusively with paving contractors, giving us unmatched insight into:

- Industry-specific marketing challenges
- Seasonal patterns affecting the paving business
- Customer decision factors for paving services

- Competitive dynamics in local paving markets
- Most effective messaging for different paving services

Results-Based Approach Our services are designed around measurable outcomes:

- Clear KPIs established at the outset
- Transparent reporting on all activities and results
- Continuous optimization based on performance data
- Flexible adjustments to address market changes
- Focus on lead quality, not just quantity

Comprehensive Solutions We offer end-to-end marketing implementation:

- Strategic planning and positioning
- Website design and development
- Search engine optimization
- Paid advertising management
- Content creation and distribution
- Reputation management
- Traditional marketing coordination
- Performance tracking and reporting

Next Steps to Explore a Partnership

If you're interested in exploring how Paving Marketers can help accelerate your growth:

1. **Initial Consultation**: Schedule a no-obligation discussion about your business goals and marketing challenges.
2. **Needs Assessment**: We'll conduct a thorough review of your current marketing and competitive position.

3. **Strategy Presentation**: Based on our assessment, we'll present a customized marketing strategy and implementation plan.
4. **Proposal and Agreement**: You'll receive a clear proposal outlining services, expectations, and investment.
5. **Onboarding and Launch**: Our structured onboarding process ensures a smooth transition and quick implementation.

To schedule your initial consultation, visit www.pavingmarketers.com/apply-now or call 888-355-2952.

Staying Updated on Marketing Trends

The marketing landscape continually evolves with new platforms, technologies, and consumer behaviors. To ensure your paving company stays competitive, implement these practices for staying current:

Ongoing Education Resources

Reliable sources for marketing updates relevant to paving contractors:

Industry-Specific Resources

- Paving Marketers Blog and Newsletter
- NAPA Marketing Resources
- Contractor-focused publications like Pavement Maintenance & Reconstruction
- Industry association webinars and events

General Marketing Resources

- Search Engine Land (for SEO and PPC updates)
- Social Media Examiner
- Content Marketing Institute

- Local Search Forum
- Marketing Profs

Technology Updates

- Google Ads Blog
- Google Search Central Blog
- Facebook Business Blog
- Marketing Technology News
- Email marketing platform blogs (Mailchimp, Constant Contact, etc.)

Continuous Improvement Process

Implement a structured approach to marketing improvement:

Regular Performance Reviews Schedule monthly and quarterly reviews of your marketing performance:

- Monthly: Review key metrics, adjust tactical elements
- Quarterly: Deeper analysis, strategy refinement, budget adjustments
- Annually: Comprehensive planning, major strategy revisions

Competitive Monitoring Stay aware of competitor activities:

- Set up Google Alerts for competitor names
- Follow competitors on social media
- Mystery shop their services periodically
- Note changes to their advertising, messaging, and services
- Identify gaps and opportunities in their approach

Customer Feedback Integration Systematically gather and apply customer insights:

- Post-project surveys to understand decision factors
- Lost proposal follow-up to identify improvement areas
- Review monitoring for sentiment trends
- Sales team feedback on prospect questions and concerns
- Direct customer interviews about marketing effectiveness

Testing and Experimentation Dedicate resources to controlled marketing experiments:

- A/B testing of website elements
- Split testing of ad creative and copy
- Pilot programs for new marketing channels
- Limited geographic tests of new approaches
- Small-scale trials before full implementation

Industry Networking Connect with peers and experts for knowledge sharing:

- Attend industry conferences and trade shows
- Participate in marketing-focused webinars
- Join contractor networking groups
- Engage in online forums for contractors
- Consider joining peer groups or mastermind organizations

Final Thoughts

Marketing success doesn't happen overnight. It requires consistent effort, intelligent strategy, and ongoing refinement. The paving companies that achieve sustainable growth approach marketing as a systematic business process rather than a series of disconnected tactics.

Remember these principles as you implement your marketing plan:

- **Start with Strategy**: Begin with clear goals and positioning before jumping to tactics.
- **Build Foundations First**: Ensure your website, Google Business Profile, and core digital presence are solid before expanding to additional channels.
- **Measure Relentlessly**: If you can't measure it, you can't improve it. Track everything.
- **Be Patient and Persistent**: Marketing results compound over time. Consistency beats sporadic brilliance.
- **Adapt, Don't Abandon**: When something isn't working, refine your approach rather than giving up entirely.
- **Invest in Relationships**: The customer journey doesn't end with the sale. Nurture relationships for referrals and repeat business.
- **Focus on Differentiation**: In a competitive market, clear differentiation is essential for premium positioning.
- **Integrate All Channels**: Ensure your marketing works as a coordinated system rather than isolated pieces.
- **Balance Innovation and Reliability**: Test new approaches while maintaining proven channels that consistently deliver results.

Plan for Growth:

Ensure your marketing infrastructure can scale with your business ambitions.

Whatever path you choose—implementing these strategies yourself, working with Paving Marketers, or some combination—the comprehensive approach outlined in this book provides the roadmap for marketing success.

We hope this resource serves as a valuable guide as you build a marketing system that drives sustainable growth for your paving company. Remember that marketing is not just about generating leads today—it's about building a valuable brand asset that will continue to deliver returns for years to come.

Thank you for investing your time in Marketing for Paving Companies. We wish you tremendous success in your marketing endeavors and welcome your feedback on how this book has helped your business.

Chris Sloane
Founder, Paving Marketers

Made in the USA
Monee, IL
04 November 2026

67384883R00341